AN
OUTSIDER
INSIDE No 10

AN OUTSIDER
INSIDE No 10
PROTECTING THE PRIME MINISTERS, 1974–79

JOHN WARWICKER
FOREWORD BY LORD IMBERT

The
History
Press

For Ann

Cover illustrations

Front: Harold Wilson and author leaving No 10 for the House of Commons. (Author's collection/ *South Wales Evening Post*); b*ack left:* The famous front door of No 10 Downing Street. (Author's collection/Ann Warwicker); *back right:* James Callaghan and US President Jimmy Carter on a visit to the north-east of England. (Author's collection)

First published 2015

The History Press
The Mill, Brimscombe Port
Stroud, Gloucestershire, GL5 2QG
www.thehistorypress.co.uk

© John Warwicker, 2015

The right of John Warwicker to be identified as the Author
of this work has been asserted in accordance with the
Copyright, Designs and Patents Act 1988.

British Library Cataloguing in Publication Data.
A catalogue record for this book is available from the British Library.

ISBN 978 0 7509 5916 2

Typesetting and origination by The History Press
Printed in Great Britain

CONTENTS

FOREWORD

by Lord Imbert

Few of we ordinary mortals know what is happening behind the sturdy and well-guarded doors of No 10 Downing Street or who the people are who have official or even informal influence on the players who inhabit this residence: the prime minister and others who have the power to change our lives, indeed, to change the country and the world.

But one fly-on-the-wall who watched, listened and saw the human nuances and touches which had an otherwise unseen influence on those major players was John Warwicker, the Metropolitan Police Special Branch detective superintendent who, for almost six years, from Harold Wilson's second administration to Margaret Thatcher, was in a unique position to see behind the curtains and record the domestic and day-to-day incidents which shaped the lives of these powerful figures who in their turn shaped the daily lives of millions of we ordinary folk.

This is a most interesting, intimate, amusing and readable insight into those apparently everyday matters which – put together as John Warwicker has done so candidly – shows that behind the invisible and metaphorical iron facade of No 10 Downing Street are human faces. Who else would have sheltered under an upturned boat keeping the then prime minister and his wife from the worst of a Scilly Isles downpour or been with the same prime minister queuing for his breakfast sausages in the local Co-op.

John Warwicker, in the mould of a typical British Special Branch protection officer, gives away no state secrets, nor would we expect him to. But he gives us a most readable insight into the daily lives of those who run our country and also have the power to influence world events.

A splendidly informative and amusing peep behind the scenes of No 10.

Lord Imbert
The House of Lords

PREFACE

A ten-minute walk across St James's Park took me from New Scotland Yard, into Downing Street, and provided distinguished names to drop should I ever be persuaded to write about it.

The year was 1974, Harold Wilson was the prime minister and the public could still stand outside No 10 and point, gasp and giggle whenever they saw someone they recognised from television or the newspapers.

My mission was not a happy affair. I was about to be transferred from a posting as deputy head of the counter-terrorism squad of Scotland Yard's elite Special Branch and moved sideways into a downmarket, pinstriped backwater. The branch had reshuffled its four-man team of armed, close protection officers at No 10 and someone had suggested my name as a replacement for the No 2 slot. Having made waves inside Scotland Yard, perhaps it was an opportunity to transfer me into no-man's-land.

The decision now was in the hands of the prime minister, as he bustled in from the House of Commons. He was introduced by Detective Superintendent Arthur Smith, the experienced officer then in charge of his close protection. Mr Wilson asked a few, low-key questions to someone apparently hovering over my left ear. After a short hiatus I realised he was speaking to me, if not at me. It was my first lesson of life with this PM. He rarely looked you straight in the eye until he had decided – even with little to go on – that you were to be trusted. In an environment where leaks were endemic – mainly, it was said, from the PM himself – the ability to remain close-mouthed was important both for him and State Security. I was to discover the fallibility of some of his judgements as I became acquainted with his political cronies.

He nodded and marched off down the corridor leading to the Cabinet Room and I was enrolled into the No 10 network, under the unhappy impression that I was in for an uninspirational time.

Nearly six years later, and through the succeeding administration of James Callaghan and Margaret Thatcher's first year as well, I realised just how mistaken that foreboding had been.

ACKNOWLEDGEMENTS

The late Detective Superintendent Arthur Smith, Special Branch, kindly gave permission to display the images taken privately on the Scilly Isles and elsewhere when we were serving with Harold Wilson. Thanks to other, later colleagues at No 10 – Colin Colson, Peter Smither, Ian Brian and Ray Parker – for forming a close-knit, well co-ordinated team during sharp-end, often dangerous and always anxious years, and now for their valued co-operation and sure memories. Commander John Howley, former head of Special Branch, is thanked for authorising publication of this manuscript.

Morvyth and Charles Seeley of Rendham in Suffolk unhesitatingly devoted their time and literary expertise on my behalf. Their advice, experience and encouragement proved invaluable in areas of the publishing business not previously well known to me. Their help provided the means of avoiding many obstacles which might otherwise have proved seriously obstructive.

Raymond Carter provided reliable research into targeted episodes of modern political history, where the my failing faculties created log jams. His balanced assessments often provided useful background to otherwise trivial memories. Captain Barbara Culleton, TD, gave a great deal of her time to proofread the draft, often under difficult circumstances. Her attention to detail and fine knowledge of English usage made a major contribution to the reduction of my workload, which often seemed infinite. Barbara Howard also kindly surveyed the manuscript and offered valuable ideas for improvement and coherence. A number of grammar-usage guidelines were suggested by Margaret Aherne, together with kindly encouragement when inspiration was failing.

My wife, Ann, for whom this manuscript was written, died before completion. It is difficult to describe her contribution adequately. While she was still well enough to take an interest, her numerous acquired PC skills were in constant demand thanks, largely, to my own inability to master modern technological opportunities. Her aptitude in preparing and re-presenting elderly and often inadequate images was little short of remarkable, and greatly appreciated by me.

On the final lap, and with papers and records often in disarray, it was fortunate that I was able to meet June Hayes, on holiday from New Zealand. She certainly helped to maintain morale and to unravel the PC chaos into which I had steered myself. Once June had returned home, I leaned heavily upon Richard Harris, who offered talented and practical help with production and systems control of the final manuscript. This proved especially invaluable, as my remaining eyesight continued to fail after I had formally been registered severely sight disabled.

When writing a book, certain procedures - such as the creation of an index - cannot usually be completed until a final draft is agreed. Similarly, requests for the provision of a foreword cannot be solicited until the full content is available for inspection. At an appropriate time I was fortunate to rendezvous with Lord Imbert (at Lady Thatcher's funeral in St Paul's Cathedral). We had once worked in Special Branch at similar levels, and then he shot away climbing speedily from rank to rank, eventually to become Commissioner of London's Metropolitan Police – and much more. In spite of years combating ill health, Lord Imbert retained an active interest in the nation's affairs and the progress, or otherwise, of his former colleagues. When approached, he kindly agreed to provide the foreword for *An Outsider Inside No 10*. I am greatly honoured and thank both him and Lady Iris.

A number of individuals and institutions, knowingly or unknowingly, have provided the images included. A conscientious amount of trouble has been taken to establish origins and copyright commitment. However, there has been a considerable passage of time since they were created and, where credit is considered inadequate, apologies are willingly offered.

The difficult tasks of last proofreading and indexing largely fell upon the competent secretarial shoulders of Jill Sullivan, a friend of many years, whose timely entry into my life after almost a decade of residence in Ibiza could hardly have been more opportune. I am grateful for her patience and skills and also to those of the numerous individuals and Institutions who offered essential help with publication and the use of modern technology. These included, from The History Press, Commissioning Editor Mark Beynon and Editor Rebecca Newton. Peter Palmer was often called upon to lift me out of the IT minefield into which I had become marooned, and so was Paul Nugent and the charity Action for Blind People, which he represents, and the personnel of Blind Veterans, formerly St Dunstans, all co-operated with the utmost kindness and willingness.

INTRODUCTION

To work for a Prime Minister is a privilege only less than being Prime Minister himself. It compensates for the temporary destruction of one's private life; in return for total commitment it offers continuous excitement. To enjoy it to the full, it should never be out of one's mind that the job is, at best, temporary.

Joe Haines, The Politics of Power, p.9

Political leaders worldwide are obsessively insecure – even in stable western democracies such as our own – and haunted by the threat of losing their power base and an honourable place in history.

Within the United Kingdom their crisis may be within parliament or without. If within, there is not much the democratically committed Metropolitan Police Commissioner or his Special Branch can, nor should, do about it. But if a revolutionary tendency deploys unconstitutional violence, and appears to spearhead a breakdown of established order, the civil police could then be obliged to pre-empt or proscribe it by the use of Intelligence or counter violence. The departure of elected leaders, even legally, is potentially destabilising. When Harold Wilson resigned as prime minister in 1976, that ever-watchful extrapolation into the future, the Stock Exchange Index, sagged by nearly 10 per cent against the unlikely chance that a breakdown of organised government would follow.

The risks would be greater still if change at the top was accompanied by violence. The full-time task of improving the odds by protecting certain Cabinet Ministers (and, for broader reasons, foreign heads of state) traditionally fell upon Special Branch.

During inter-war years, Intelligence communities worked out gloomy worst-case scenarios, forecasting the possibility of disorder following an orchestrated, perhaps Bolshevik-inspired, revolution. With the Soviet uprising in 1917 as one example, the British Establishment was not exempt from these concerns. Indeed, the United Kingdom itself was sometimes on the brink during the 1920s and '30s.

In the event, little happened in the United Kingdom to disturb the status quo until the 1970s, but it was hardly a secret that government-funded counter vigilance was maintained both overtly and in various guises, to check upon extreme, politically motivated groups suspected of aiming at the overthrow of a lawfully elected government. It was here, again, that Special Branch – at least until its disbandment in the new millennium – worked pro-actively in concert with the government secret services, MI5 and MI6.

With the exception of members of the royal family, the prime minister was most vulnerable to assassination or abduction. Having the benefit of both a national Intelligence-gathering role and some small arms and Close Quarters Combat training for its teams of bodyguards, Special Branch was, on paper at least, well equipped to provide protection. Other politicians regarded as potential targets were the Foreign and Home Secretaries and the Secretary of State for Northern Ireland. For some reason never made clear, the Chancellor – who was certainly not universally adored – was not on the target list drawn up by risk assessors. Members of the royal family, not to be sullied by association with a politically oriented unit of the police service, were the exclusive preserve of Uniform Branch, although their appointed officers worked in plain clothes.

Although the traditional political right regarded the police service as an arm of the Conservative Party, and the far-out left of the Labour Party to view it with little better than sneering hostility, it is clear from history that not only were the appointed Special Branch protection officers able to forestall or prevent any major incidents against their various charges, but that they did so, in the main, with commendable impartiality. The fact is that where public officials were known to have close protection, terrorists preferred to look for softer targets.

It was not all good news for me, however. The problem was that our team was crucially underfunded, undertrained and under-resourced for weaponry and communications. Once I had been promoted to take charge, the fault lines showed just how disadvantaged we were against the escalating threat from terrorists, by overheated and over strident students and politically or racially motivated extremists.

Above all, the rules of engagement in the United Kingdom were rapidly being rewritten by the Provisional IRA. It all signaled a necessary end to protection by portly men in homburg hats and displays of bulging waistlines.

As long as danger to a prime minister was confined to the occasional, demented schizophrenic who had lost his pills, or an isolated hysteric with a grudge against the government of the day, our protection teams, if alert enough, could hitherto usually sort it on the spot. Both the Home Office and Scotland Yard were happy with low-profile cover – uncontroversial and inexpensive as it was. Even before the days when Islamic extremism was activated worldwide, it was clear to those of us in the firing line that Special Branch was not always ahead of new threats. Our experience with protection teams abroad confirmed their intense concerns, and to deal with them they developed impressive counter measures.

In General Orders for the Metropolitan Police, many hundreds of pages were devoted to the methodology of dealing with every imaginable contingency. Under the title 'Runaway Horses', for example, officers were still instructed to 'run in the same direction as the horse'. Just half a page dealt with close protection. It was clear enough that the academic, desk-bound authority which created General Orders, any breach of which was a disciplinary offence, had deliberately avoided committing themselves in the controversial and unpredictable field of armed protection. If it went wrong they were not going to be responsible.

So, if still alive, it was down to the protection officer. It may be argued that while this gave the officer unlimited scope to make up the rules as he went along, he had no cover when something went wrong and bodies were bleeding in the gutter. This gave the job a special glow of insecurity. Everything depended upon minimal threat. As terrorism escalated, this was clearly not good enough.

I was never to win the battle with the British authorities and for a while we remained the western security world's poor relations. But soon after James Callaghan replaced Harold Wilson as PM – and thanks to timely opportunism by my No 2, Detective (then) Chief Inspector Colin Colson – higher level official interest became focused on the problem too. The outcome supported our concerns; results were immediate and impressive.

Communications, transport, electronic defensive facilities, bullet and bomb proofing and administrative support quietly came our way. Plans were drawn up for new, more suitable limousines. The existing batch of Rovers were all well past sell by dates; rust was visible and interiors pockmarked with cigar and pipe ash. The elderly limos, whose underpaid drivers had only the most cursory evasive training and were not subject to our authority, were conscientiously maintained by Government Car Service, but increasingly fallible.

Home Office boffins had installed non-portable, overweight radio sets with which we could, if given time to find and dial the appropriate code for the district we were in, make contact with any police HQ in the UK. In theory at least, as long as we had a fully equipped limousine, or were in a train with a compatible radio set installed, the PM could be contacted in an emergency through this network. As far as I could see it was the only way for him to activate the four minutes technically allowed to set the nuclear deterrent into action. Perhaps there was no better than a fifty–fifty chance it would work harmoniously at critical times.

It was against this background that I entered into the Downing Street machine. For nearly six years I was able to assess many of its merits and demerits, and to be a small part of a fascinating institution – a small cog in a smooth wheel. My determination to remain politically impartial was respected. Smart footwork was often useful in an institution so intimate and personal that idiosyncrasies were impossible to hide, but it was never necessary to compromise standards, and only rarely to solicit favours. An understanding of operational imperatives was accepted by men and women whose careers would be entirely office bound. Support from the prime minister was always important, but, lest it might be forgotten, even more critical was full back up from resident civil servants, unencumbered as they were by the demands of a public image.

In return, I loyally kept most of this great experience to myself for more than thirty years. I hope that this volume does justice to all parties, but makes no apologies for opinions expressed as a result of my own experience, perception or even partial understanding. Some identities are omitted or disguised whenever the danger of causing offence becomes an important issue. I hope it will be clear to the reader that a policy of objectivity has been maintained, for I was rarely, if ever, the victim of personal animosity or malice during my term as an outsider inside Downing Street. The need for firmness in some areas seems to have been fully understood.

Three politically bruised, but physically unscathed prime ministers, survived during critical days and that was, it seems fair to claim, the bottom line!

ONE

Rule One? Keep belly full: bladder and bowels empty!

Detective Inspector Harry Gray, Veteran Protection Officer

Westminster and Whitehall are awash with history and it is no coincidence that Downing Street stands in their midst. With a wonderful heritage and some distinguished buildings, it seemed strange that, not unlike parts of otherwise glorious Greenwich, so much souvenir-shop tat and fast food was allowed to proliferate. In the 1970s, it was almost impossible to find somewhere decent and reasonably priced to eat in the locality and, without facilities within No 10 itself for anyone other than a select few, the rest of us lived on an unhealthy diet snatched from coffee and burger stalls. On really bad days, when there were no other pressures, the detectives might walk over to Scotland Yard. The canteen manageress there was trying to wean the troops away from the pies and trash diet which had dispatched so many healthy young policemen to the convalescent home at Brighton. Some never to return.

With republican sympathies, George Downing's family emigrated to America in the early 1600s, but, sensing that times they were a-changing, he returned to Britain during the Civil War and acquired Oliver Cromwell's blessing as his scoutmaster – or head of intelligence. Downing, with an opportunist's eye for a chance, noted the prospect of a great future for the Westminster area, in which the palaces of Westminster and Whitehall held the seats of monarchy and government and were situated directly alongside Britain's religious epicentre, Westminster Abbey. Perhaps he even saw a future for burger bars and tourists too but, in any event, Downing secured from the Commonwealth Parliament the right to redevelop Royal Cockpit Street with affordable housing. Those were the days when developments were already taking place, originals of which are now just names: Scotland Yard, the Royal Cockpit itself and Spring Gardens, for example.

Downing's plans suffered a credit crunch when the Stuarts were restored in 1666 and his rights declared void. Not a man to jeopardise his balance sheet, he successfully ingratiated himself with Charles II mainly, it is reported, by deploying the duplicitous self-interest not unexpected from an intelligence officer by changing sides and informing on his former parliamentary and republican comrades. This had two effects: they were executed and Charles II, instead of giving him an MBE, restored Downing's planning permission. Work on the construction of fifteen speculative quality town houses started in 1680 and was completed four years later. Downing failed to benefit; that was also the year he died. No doubt some surviving parliamentarians started to believe in God.

A few years earlier, Charles II had granted a site at the back of No 10, Royal Cockpit Street to his daughter (the Countess of Lichfield), her husband, his senior courtier and master of horse. A high-quality residence was built for them overlooking Horse Guards Parade. For nearly fifty years the residents of No 10 and Lichfield House talked to one another over the garden fence and probably grumbled about the difficulty of finding an honest plumber.

In 1732, the second of the Hanoverian kings, George II, offered the ownership of Lichfield House to his principal minister, Sir Robert Walpole. As Sir Robert was also First Lord of the Treasury, this very much smacked of bribery and corruption, which it probably was, and he sensibly declined the offer as a personal gift, but did accept it as a residence for the First Lord of the Treasury. Lichfield House was joined to No 10, Royal Cockpit Street, by a purpose-built corridor. At the same time, the composite unit was renamed Downing Street. It is still the gift of the First Lord of the Treasury, confirmed by a brass plaque outside No 10.

This brief history accounts for the disparity between the front of No 10 and the back. Speculative housing facing on to Downing Street is joined by a corridor leading to the posh quarters at the rear. These still overlook Horse Guards Parade. It was the posh part that the IRA targeted with home-made mortars in the 1990s, one day when the Cabinet was meeting under John Major. This assault really tested their individual fortitude. It is said that a few of them failed. Perhaps it was simply the problem of eyeball-to-eyeball contact with their party rivals while in a submissively crouching position under the Cabinet Room table as the IRA mortars exploded nearby.

⎯⎯⎯⎯⎯◦⎯⎯⎯⎯⎯

'Call me Tom,' said Lord Bridges, Foreign and Commonwealth Office (FCO) adviser to the prime minister and second-in-charge of Private Office. 'Everyone here is known by his first name. Welcome inside No 10.' He turned a page of the voluminous dossier on his desk and was obviously anxious to get back to business.

'Well. Thank you – er – Tom.'

Even junior NCOs in the Royal Marines had insisted on being addressed – preferably very loudly of course – as 'CORPORAL!' and I had not expected to be invited to call a lord of the realm by his first name. But Tom was right. That was the protocol in Downing Street. It had little to do with the prime minister and everything to do with the Principal Private Secretary (PPS), the focus of efficiency, dedication and morale in an often frenetic environment.

Arthur Smith had taken an early opportunity to introduce me to Private Office personnel – a PPS, five private secretaries, and appointments and duty clerks. Robert Armstrong (now Lord Armstrong of Ilminster, Secretary to the Cabinet from 1979) was overlord and he had responsibility for the efficiency and co-operative support which all the civil servant staff in No 10 were required to provide for the incumbent prime minister. He ensured, after an initial careful selection, that everyone worked to their maximum ability with a combination of energy and quiet efficiency. A mistake or two was permitted but not carelessness, laziness or disinterest. The back door to lesser offices was always open for staff who failed to match up. He was known to all as Robert, but no one was foolish enough to abuse this familiarity and mistake him for a soft touch.

The Treasury representative private secretary was Robin Butler, later to become PPS under Margaret Thatcher and then ennobled to spend a distinguished retirement as one of Whitehall's 'great and good'. And so it came to pass that here was the unique, elite Whitehall group of Oxbridge (Hons) – or the equivalent, if there is such a thing – often with aristocratic heritage and probably voting Tory, who were responsible for organising all the services and information upon which the prime minister of the day depended, and to do so independently and irrespective of the party in power. Personal political preference was not allowed to show, or to influence their judgement. Impartiality was mandatory and only the highest calibre of applicant got the job. Should they survive the – usually – three-year posting, these young men could expect a glowing future with a serious prospect of taking top jobs in Whitehall departments, and eventual knighthoods. The system proved its worth when, for example, Robert Armstrong, who was PPS at No 10 to Edward Heath, remained in post as Harold Wilson took over after the February 1974 election.

This admirable administration buzzes secretly along, invisible to the public and unacknowledged by the media; it should be the envy of the world and probably would be if more generally advertised.

In a way, a private secretary's failure at Downing Street was tolerated with understanding within the civil service, where the stressful hazards of a difficult posting and the unfairness occasioned by temperamental outbursts from some prime ministers were recognised – providing, of course, there was never a hint of corruption. The Private Office task – to feed the prime minister with the very highest grade of information and to co-ordinate his programme with the party, press and public relations departments, the prime minister's family, the diplomatic service and much more – demanded 24/7/52 application. Considerations such as unsocial hours, family demands and even minor illnesses were marginalised as irrelevant.

If you followed the delicate machinations in the *Yes, Prime Minister* series on television you won't be far out.

During briefings from some of my predecessors – Arthur Smith was not among them – total detachment from Private Office was the recommendation. However, its influence both in Whitehall and with the prime minister was almost absolute, and it very soon became obvious that my own responsibilities could not properly be undertaken without Private Office backing. A decision to work in concert with private secretaries and their subordinates, rather than in isolation, soon proved the best way to live happily ever after. Reliance solely on the close support of the prime minister and the vicarious authority implied by our inevitably close association – especially when away from the confines of No 10 – was not something necessarily to be relied upon. Yes?

Within Private Office, wall clocks indicated the local time in Washington, D.C., Peking (in those days), Paris and Moscow. Profound paperwork, including drafts for some of the prime minister's forthcoming speeches, was constantly interrupted by staff comings and goings – messengers, secretaries, drivers, detectives, clerks, curators, ladies with cups of tea – but it was wise not to hang around. Telephones were in constant action, with incoming calls identified by flashing lights instead of an intrusion of bells. Activity, often frenetic, was conducted as quietly as possible. Here was the focal point of the prime minister's official staff, amalgamating data from other Whitehall departments, the Foreign Office, of course, the secret services, Buckingham Palace – the whole world really.

Downing Street was adapted but never custom-built for such intense activity. The secretariat was down in the basement. Paper communications were transferred around Whitehall through puffing and popping old-fashioned compressed air pipes more commonly seen in department stores. In the 1970s not a single computer was in sight. An open office for the PPS adjoined the Cabinet Room, where the prime minister might be working in preference to his first-floor study which was on one side, while that of the private secretaries was on the other. Communication was constant. They overheard telephone conversations and talked to one another to exchange information. The idea was that while each was absorbed in his own batch of tasks, they all became aware, peripherally if not in depth, of what the others were working on. In this way, whichever one was next summoned, he could update the prime minister on all-round progress. They therefore had to be both single-minded and at the same time in touch. Undiagnosed schizophrenia was helpful.

⇒●⇐

Oiling the works with efficient telephone communication was vital for everyone in No 10. In the 1970s this facility was based on archaic old-fashioned switchboards, with plugs and leads slotted home by up to four ladies at any one time. Pre-war GPO headsets left them both hands free for the slotting. Every incoming call, internal or external, had to be answered and dealt with, IMMEDIATELY. It might merely be a cleaner needing to talk to a supervisor; or Buckingham Palace or the ambassador in Washington. There was no question of being put on hold, or of listening to Vivaldi, or hearing automated dialling instructions. Nor was there any attempt to persuade a caller to ring off. The brilliant, dedicated, intelligent ladies handling the plugs somehow rarely kept you waiting, never left a caller in the dark and – uniquely for switchboard staff – were on no occasion the cause for complaint, not even from fractious troublemakers looking for a scapegoat.

The 'friendly' US Embassy in Grosvenor Square sometimes asked these operators for off-the-record help when their own integrated, computerised, automated, infallible system direct from NASA failed to secure contact with – say – the Second US Secretary in Bangkok. Or Vladivostok. Our No 10 ladies would follow a sure pathway to wherever by referring to the stationery office notebook, the bible in which all those little idiosyncrasies of any electronic network were faithfully recorded, and painstakingly updated every quarter by hand with pen and ink. They probably saved us all from the total destruct button on many occasions.

And this performance, incredibly, took place in the triangular attic directly under the sloping, tiled roof. Apparently the demands of security created a need for these special working conditions. I suppose it may have been preferable to the basements in which secretaries in our embassies behind the Iron Curtain had to work with their typewriters, sitting under canvas like Girl Guides. Tents were said to deaden electronic transmissions capable of being intercepted and read by the Russian secret services.

No direct telephone calls, internal or external, were allowed to the staff within No 10. Everything passed through the switchboard. There were no mobiles in those days of course and self-dialling was not available. Call it security or call it eavesdropping, if you will. We assumed every call was monitored.

The cramped and sometimes bent-over circumstances in which these admirable ladies had to work were the probable cause of the permanent list to starboard which identified the taller ones.

Old-fashioned though all of this was, I suppose it was a notable advance from the days when Harold Macmillan was prime minister. He often spent weekends at his country house, Birch Grove, where the only telephone was an upright version with separate earpiece in his housekeeper's office next to the kitchen. On the occasions when he needed to, he ran Great Britain from below stairs.

In the 1970s much of the work in Downing Street was carried on in the most unsuitable, uncomfortable circumstances, which would have been the cause of a work-to-rule in industry or commerce. Central heating was archaic and air conditioning non-existent. An absence of sunlight created a claustrophobic atmosphere both inside and out.

Nevertheless, organised, fast-lane excellence was demanded from all the staff, irrespective of their nominal standing in the pecking order. Incredibly, it seemed to work. Somehow.

Members of the Special Branch team were collectively referred to as 'the detectives' and, while an active part of the total product, they stood independently just outside the civil service arena. However, it was not sensible to remain isolated or dissociated from the collective effort. Our work might have been more practical, less academic, but it was still an essential part of the total No 10 machine, the smooth working of which will frequently be under discussion in this book. As long as our own tasks were not undermined, we pooled our efforts with the others. In the case of the custodians and police officer inside the front door this sometimes amounted, when they were stuck, to help with *The Times* crossword; however, on most days they had the edge.

But it seems wise to point out at this early stage that everyone – politicians, aspiring prime ministers, journalists, interviewers, researchers, critics or everyday loud-mouthed bigots – should have some idea of how our nation is run. It is not all warts and the occupants in No 10 are not fools. Take care before trying to pretend that they are. Until you are in there, you will not have much of a clue. The problem for No 10 personnel is that they never get around to talking about it themselves, but there is no reason why I should not call for three cheers on their behalf.

Of course, not everything was perfect.

In my experience new prime ministers, and especially new PMs' spouses, decide not to live at No 10. It never works. A prime minister's workload is so high that not a minute can be wasted on travelling back and forth. Moreover, questions of security and instant communication make anything other than residence on the spot an impossibility. Newly elected prime ministers also naively decide not to use Chequers at weekends and for holidays. Although Mrs Wilson did put her foot down and insisted upon family leisure time at her bungalow on the Isles of Scilly, Chequers, too, soon became a regular retreat from the harassment that was inevitable within Downing Street itself. Moreover, for the housewife-in-a-pinny image favoured by some spouses, and at least one prime minister, the abundance of skilled and willing staff at Chequers becomes irresistible.

Residence in No 10 can be handed down through the Treasury pecking order if a prime minister decides not to live there. In theory, it could be the home of a Treasury clerk if no one above him wanted it. One example was that of Tony and Cherie Blair who, after the election of 1997, needed more space for their young family than No 10 had on offer. So an exchange was affected with the Chancellor, Gordon Brown. The Blairs got the better of the swap; No.11 is altogether more comfortable, and in my time was also better furnished. It was also a critical few metres further from Private Office and fleet-footed duty clerks, ever-ready to present out-of-hours papers for the immediate attention of the prime minister.

The Right Honourable Harold Wilson, Member of Parliament for Liverpool (Huyton), was in his second prime ministerial administration when I arrived at No 10. The Conservative, Edward Heath, served as prime minister in between and when he left after a narrow defeat in February 1974, the relocation of his grand piano into private premises highlighted one of many problems associated with trying to run the country from unsuitable premises.

His valuable piano was on the first floor at the rear and had to be removed by specialists. The only entrance/exits to No 10 were the recognisable front door, then still in full view of the public twenty-four hours each day, and the back-garden gate onto Horse Guards Parade. It was more of a problem to co-ordinate the resources of the watchful chief security officer himself, the specialist piano removers, No 10 custodians and uniformed police – all in darkness and going about their work in the hope of maximum discretion – than to cross a river in a canoe with a goose, a fox and a bag of corn.

Under normal circumstances and for reasons of security *only* the front door was in use.

It was guarded by armed, uniformed officers outside and in, and under joint control with the doorkeeper, a civilian employee. It was not large enough to get a piano through in the horizontal position. Neither was the garden gate at the rear, the keys to which were restricted to detectives, the housekeeper, Group Captain 'Willie' Williams (the security officer) and a few senior civil servants. Everyone passing through the front door could be monitored. The garden gate was used only by key holders and, to save manpower, was monitored electronically.

Mr Heath's piano was, as I understood it, finally removed on a precision-operated cherry picker. Just before my time, as it was, this was not my problem. But Mr Wilson was another matter. At first, he was resident in a leased town house in Lord North Street which, although outside the immediate range of the private secretaries, seemed to him nicely within either walking or driving distance of No 10. With radio contact we could ensure that uniformed officers were aware of the prime minister's approach either to Lord North Street or No 10, and they would clear the frontage of members of the public and create space to unload the PM and U-turn and park the official limo. There was no guarantee that the press would not intervene and paparazzi trample upon the innocent. For close security it was vital for us to have control over events and quickly to be able to recognise something or someone unusual.

Departure from No 10 was technically easier but was usually handicapped by indecision from the top. In Churchill's later days, when he was well past his best but still the people's choice, he was steered from Private Office – which notified the front door staff that he was on his way – along a line of custodians. The first produced and set his homburg in place, a second slipped him into a warm coat, the next popped a ready-cut cigar in his mouth, and the last one lit it for him just as the front door was opened. Abracadabra, there he was puffing purposefully away as he appeared and gave the 'V' sign to the crowd.

Harold Wilson was not in his dotage but did tend to change his mind at the last moment, and this reflected its way down the corridor, and often back again. If he thought about not leaving but staying, the chain of assistants had to follow suit and unwind too – the housekeeper, custodians, policemen and the doorkeeper, not to mention the driver and Special Branch officer who actioned themselves after a helpful nod from Private Office were then as quickly stood down again as departure was postponed. Or cancelled altogether.

As the prime minister often liked to work from his office in the House of Commons, but eat at No 10, then vote in the House before returning for drinks, departures created a certain mayhem which tended, on days with an otherwise undemanding programme, to come to an end at around 10.15 p.m. – after which the PM was driven to the House for the final call to the division lobby. Only after this and any other appointments in his diary might he head for

Lord North Street. The call upon police resources was inordinate and demanded co-ordinated dedication.

And so there was much to be said for his residence in No 10 itself, and many a prayer was answered when, in the summer of 1974, he and Mrs Wilson decided to move in and also to respond positively to the beckoning finger from Chequers.

———➤•◄———

Before Harold Wilson relocated into No 10, the Special Branch day might start at Lord North Street, where the prime minister's faithful driver, Bill Housden, would already be waiting with the official Rover limo. Bill was usually indoors. As Harold's personal friend – he was a loyal member of the Labour Party and they were on first-name terms, a liberty we never presumed for ourselves – Bill had routine chores to complete before the PM's day could start.

To begin with, every daily newspaper had to be collected from the press office at No 10 and delivered inside Lord North Street in time for the prime minister to scan. The PM devoured, and concerned himself greatly with the contents which often, perhaps usually, motivated his mood for the day. With some reason, he was obsessed with the notion that the press were conspiring against him; it was not unknown for him to plan a meeting with Lord Goodman and authorise action for libel or defamation of character. He was usually dissuaded by sober counsel. With the papers in place, Bill's next task was to play a vital role in the PR department – Mr Wilson's pipe-smoking public relations' image. The favourite pipe and a first reserve were reamed and cleaned and filled ready for action. So were the lighter and a spare, with flints carefully checked. A tobacco pouch was filled with Harold Wilson's favoured weed, together with another spare. A box of matches was laid out as a final resort if the lighters failed. At some early stage in his political career, PR men had advised the importance to the electorate of a dependable, avuncular image, and the associated significance of a middle class, pipe-smoking silhouette.

The paradox was that a pipe was never Harold Wilson's preference. He was very much a cigar man.

The whole ensemble was then stuffed into the prime minister's jacket pockets, giving him visibly Bunteresque contours around the lower central area. It was certain that the first task of the duty press officer – hopefully female – would be to remove these lumps, streamline the image and brush him down if a television appearance was on the agenda.

The work of the day started soon after arrival in No 10 with an informal gathering of the 'Kitchen Cabinet', as the press corps had dubbed it, held within screaming distance of Private Office in a room occupied by his political secretary

Marcia Williams (later Baroness Falkender). Participants included Marcia and her aide, trade unionist Albert Murray (later Lord Murray); press secretary Joe Haines (still Joe Haines); Bernard Donoughue (now Lord Donoughue), head of the policy unit; Bill Housden; the PPS; and the prime minister. If the newspapers had not ruined the start to a prime ministerial day, the Kitchen Cabinet was sure to do so. It also provided entertainment for the ground floor staff. Keeping or reading minutes was not on the agenda.

Invariably, a noisy hysteria would be generated. Within an unfortunate radius, this could hardly be avoided. The men tried to remain implacable but some, volatile characters as they were, could be guaranteed to retaliate to provocation. The prime minister was champion in the Imperturbable League.

It seemed a strange way to run the country.

TWO

He [Bill Housden] wants an OBE or CBE so that he can take his wife to the Palace.

Downing Street Diary, by Bernard Donoughue, Volume Two, p. 699

Having arrived at an understanding with Lord ('Tom') Bridges, it was time to meet other important persons of influence within No 10. 'You can call me Bill,' said Bill Housden, the Prime Minister's number one driver. At the time of Harold Wilson's resignation in 1976, he told me that he deserved a knighthood to go with his existing MBE. He was not joking.

All this was unique in the annals of the Government Car Service, of which Bill was an ordinary member. But having joined the Labour Party and made himself valuable to Harold Wilson for many years, Bill could rightly claim to be the prime minister's personal friend. It was never obvious how Mrs Wilson placed herself in this relationship, but it was apparent that she did not always see the necessity of becoming a close family friend, whereas Harold (and Bill was the only one of the full-time Downing Street staff on first-name terms) was godfather to Bill's children. In turn, Bill supplied saucy magazines for relaxing weekends at Chequers and updates on the football First Division. This dedication was sometimes rewarded with an incongruous appointment as the PM's 'valet' when he fancied official travel abroad. It is fair to say that this did not always meet with the unqualified approval of the organising civil servants; the extra travel and accommodation costs were difficult to hide and Bill was sometimes recast in a more likely role as official baggage master for the whole delegation.

His trusted relationship with the prime minister meant that Bill was not universally popular, in spite of the authority he wielded as a full member of the

Kitchen Cabinet, but he was clever enough to handle the senior civil servants with appropriate respect. Most of the insiders grew to accept Bill but, knowing about his daily contacts with both the PM and Marcia, he was never fully trusted. The position of the appointed number one driver with the three regulars in the drivers' room is always difficult, and although he was the key figure he tried never to patronise his colleagues. In spite of the fact that he knew they voted Conservative he joined in the card school, did his share in the tea club and used his influence with 'the Boss', who permitted them to work without wearing the dreaded official caps which had always been mandatory. From the detectives' point of view he was a critical link – not least because he was the Kitchen Cabinet go-between with the usually phlegmatic Harold and the highly volatile Marcia Williams.

One of the most important routines for everyone working inside Downing Street, and having a need to know, is the distribution of the prime minister's daily diary. This is delivered by hand to each relevant office as early in the preceding afternoon as possible. It is the final guideline on how the staff, as well as the prime minister himself, will need to plan their day. It is, of course, highly confidential. The final version is the product of a year of preparation. A provisional draft goes round twelve months in advance; it is then updated quarterly, monthly, weekly, and, finally, daily.

During Mr Wilson's time, input came to the appointments desk through Private Office. The sources were the prime minister himself and sometimes his family, his constituency and the party, political advisers in Downing Street, the security services, Buckingham Palace, the Cabinet and Cabinet Office, the diplomatic service, the press office and Whitehall departments. Yes, and Bill Housden as well. This was all collated, shuffled, considered, put to committees and passed before the prime minister for provisional approval. The final product was prepared by the secretariat in the Garden Rooms.

From the diary, recipients got to work to make the programme run smoothly. The Garden Room allocated secretaries for any event outside No 10 and prepared travel arrangements with the RAF or British Rail. They were also responsible for accommodation reservations. The travel agents in the Palace of Westminster were often involved because transport for the support staff had to be phased in. Private Office allocated a duty clerk and private secretary. Drivers worked out their roster, recommended routes and calculated timings and notified Private Office. The detectives co-ordinated their duties, helped plan the route navigation and started telephoning district chiefs of police in London and chief constables elsewhere. If travel abroad was involved they might also activate their own contacts or ask embassies and high commissions to do so. One detective would usually be posted to any advance party travelling ahead for the prime minister's visits out of town or abroad. He would co-ordinate security and communications in tandem with all the authorities involved. The very fact that political leaders demanded the right to vary the programme in reaction to developments separated No 10 planning from royal visits, which called for meticulous but inflexible detail. Prime ministers invariably needed imaginative pre-emptive alternatives.

For travel out of town or abroad, security depended upon efficient and positive management of local agencies by the allocated No 10 Special Branch officer. Experience counted a great deal here, as he would often be technically junior in certain pecking orders. Firearms protocol also had to be dealt with. Where the allegedly agreed plan was for local officers to provide the final line of personal protection, our own firearms were not mandatory. We generally conspired to take them anyway – whether strictly legally or not. In Canada, where the Royal Canadian Mounted Police (RCMP) were supremely efficient and authoritative, this was not a problem and we left our guns behind. The RCMP did the same when they came to the UK.

For foreign VIP visitors to London, Scotland Yard insisted that personal protection was carried out exclusively by Special Branch, which had total control over, and responsibility for, their security. This sometimes put us at a disadvantage when our prime minister travelled abroad and reciprocation was insisted upon. It was particularly difficult in Third World, unstable countries where the risk was great and the capacity of the local police was minimal and sometimes undisciplined. Considerable diplomacy – or sleight of hand – was called for. If uncovered, our own last-ditch tactics might be copied by the wild and traditionally trigger-happy men, sometimes posturing as protection officers attached to undemocratic dictators when they came to London.

Very occasionally all this planning went smoothly. More often, last-minute changes at the top unravelled much of it, demanding cancellations and frenetic re-planning, because the preference is that British prime ministerial visits should be both dignified and secure. Our own minimum requirement was to be kept fully updated as the programme developed and redeveloped, so that we could take pre-emptive measures for every contingency. We could then, for example, focus our physical presence around unscheduled disturbances or hitches representing potential danger.

Under most circumstances, our small unit could provide no more than three men to manage any operation, leaving one office manager in London. This called for synchronised thinking and action and we worked to a policy of equality, although the final buck stopped with me. After a few months, rank was disregarded and we announced ourselves as Mr So-and-So from Scotland Yard. In some foreign countries and in areas controlled by our own armed forces, prestige was important and not to be undermined if a perfectly competent officer announced himself to be a detective sergeant. This could lead to instant banishment below stairs and commensurate lack of authority. Although the main thrust was to ensure operational effectiveness, this policy turned out to have an additional bonus.

Our embassies and high commissions abroad were often unaware that the world had changed elsewhere and that Victoria was no longer Queen of the Empire and Empress of India. Politicians were usually despised as upstart social inferiors, while policemen were regarded as Bow Street Runners. If we failed to exert our authority in this outdated environment, we might also fail to assemble enough local support to protect the prime minister adequately. I later found that the Conservative Margaret Thatcher was no better treated than Labour prime ministers. When dealing with a *Mr So-and-So*, as opposed to *Sergeant*, members of the diplomatic service were reluctant to leave themselves vulnerable by underrating our authority and in general the outcome was for us all to be given adequate status and commensurate help.

It was clear to my colleagues that once within the 'abroad' mode they were free to promote themselves on the spot if a clear definition of their rank became unavoidable.

The focus of all this was the diary. And it was here that Bill Housden was so useful. He not only took direct instruction along to Private Office, he was also able to give broad hints of guidelines such as: 'It seems likely that Mrs Wilson will insist that they go to the Scillys before Easter.' As a tipster, such advance knowledge was of the greatest importance to those fitting together the prime minister's programme. It was even more so for us because, during the many hours we had to spend together, Bill would go a lot further. He was a nimble-minded middle-man. Once trust in our discretion was established the information he supplied enabled us to keep ahead of the many internal complexities within No 10, to keep operationally on the ball and to be alert for the appearance of thunder clouds.

It was important to watch him for the occasional, calculated deception – sometimes to test that we were still leak proof and sometimes, with instructions from a higher authority, to deliberately mislead. It was all an intensely political, real-life mixture of pass-the-parcel and Russian roulette.

In return, Bill became dependent upon our unit for many favours, for we often had influence where he had none.

Nobody was in doubt about the strength of the relationship between Bill Housden and the prime minister. For a time, however, where he stood with

Marcia Williams was less than clear. Having consulted Mr Wilson after her elevation to the peerage as Baroness Falkender in mid 1974, the detectives knew her as Mrs Williams, although she was now divorced. Betty and Tony Field, her sister and brother, had associations with No 10, but the family name was never used in Marcia's case. For anyone not in close and regular touch with her, or a personal friend, it was difficult to know how to address Mrs Williams after she became an amalgam of both left-wing Transport House credo and the ultra-conventional House of Lords.

Uniquely, Bill spoke of her as 'Marcia'.

However, warning signals from the Kitchen Cabinet grew in volume and, we noted, increasing confidences from Bill. In spite of the power vested in his special relationship with Harold Wilson, both Bill and Albert Murray, Mrs Williams' assistant in the Political Office, were very much under her control and domination. Ample evidence exists of the commitment the prime minister felt toward her from early days in his political career. With just average secretarial aptitude she secured a position of supreme significance in his blossoming career. She was politically astute, had a sparkling and penetrating wit and useful left-wing insight into the character of others prominent in the Labour Party. On a few occasions before he became prime minister, she travelled abroad with Mr Wilson officially and, among the many conspiracy theories which proliferated around their relationship, was the allegation that they were Soviet agents on the one hand and in the midst of an affair on the other. Contradictory stories also circulated that she had been the key figure in his rise to power. These rumours – and never having been proved, they were little better than that – have been impossible to dismiss, even to this day. It is well established in the public domain that, in all probability, a misguided and unaccountable plan to counter communist penetration at the very top of the governmental tree, led individual officers in MI5 (the Security Service) to convince themselves that she was working for the Soviet Union. With guesswork as their only authority, a group then quietly orchestrated smears against her and the prime minister.

As Harold Wilson's concerns about the media and the Secret Services later matured into near paranoia, I was more than once dragged into events too.

Bill's commitment to Marcia Williams, although not of the same order as that to his boss, was in his own terms no less important. He was unhappy – even after the prime minister's understanding and authority – on days when the official limousine was left at her disposal for morning shopping in the West End. The PM's name was used to ignore parking restrictions. Both Bill and Mr Wilson skated along thin ice when the limo, driven by Bill, was sometimes made available for her social evenings too. With no security risk to the prime minister as justification, how the usual discipline relating to private use of car and driver was covered by Private Office is not known. However, although a great deal of latitude is accorded to prime ministers, it can be taken as a strong likelihood that careers may have been jeopardised. Is it remotely possible that Mrs Williams compensated the Treasury herself?

The dam came near to collapse in January 1975 when Bill walked out on her for constantly attacking him. He thought it must have been because she was jealous of his relationship with Mr Wilson. He also told policy adviser Bernard Donoughue that her style of life needed £20,000 a year and that 'she throws her money around in the shops so much that I sometimes get frightened'. As Bernard's declared income at the time was £8,000 a year, it was unlikely that she got any sympathy from him.

Her political position, although still passionately represented as well left of centre, was in obvious contradiction with her residence in the West End of London and ownership of an elegant detached house in Great Missenden. Her two boys were educated privately. Through exploitation of the prime minister's authority, she took every opportunity to secure her peerage and present herself at upmarket functions in the City and events where she was seen side by side with show business glitterati. Her lifestyle could hardly have been further from that of her devotees in the Labour Party, such as the unacquisitive William Hamling, Mr Wilson's parliamentary private secretary.

While Bill Housden certainly owed his general position to a unique relationship with the prime minister, he was included in Marcia Williams' circle only as a useful functionary.

Mrs Williams' socialite whirl largely centred around the wealthy Jewish community in London. Prominent among these were the publisher George (later Lord) Weidenfeld and Eric (later Sir Eric) Miller, chairman of the building consortium Peachey Properties and financial backer of Marcia Williams' political office. While actively supporting Mrs Williams' lifestyle, Miller was backing his future hopes of a knighthood by covertly providing financial support to the Conservative Party as well. Bill Housden and other attachments were also on a bandwagon, not least with a generous supply of Romeo y Julieta cigars. When a lucky number came his way, Bill lifted a trouser leg or two and stuck them in his socks like a cartridge belt, keeping them safely out of sight while relying on his leg to act as a human humidor to prevent his booty from drying out. As further insurance, Miller sponsored fundraising events for police charities, and there were indications that Marcia rather hoped he might leave his wife and family and marry her. However, this was a bridge too far, and when the Fraud Squad eventually moved in, Eric Miller shot himself. He had received his precious knighthood by then. Curiously for some, including me, the coroner apparently satisfied himself that Eric Miller shot himself in the head – not just once but twice. It sounded like an improbable farewell. Other possibilities were discussed within Downing Street.

Speculation about the death was inevitable but anything which even remotely represented a threat to the prime minister had to be considered. Information and rumour were assembled and filtered through our office from officials, party members, drivers, messengers and police sources. In the race for a knighthood, while he still had vicarious access to the prime minister's ear, was it possible that Miller had not only neglected his commitments to Peachey Properties, but also overspent his available cash flow? Ready money was vital if he were to be seen both dispensing hospitality to influential people and also funding the numerous Jewish and other charities for which he was a prominent sponsor. If he had tried to keep the money flowing and the Peachey Board was now wondering where their cash was going, perhaps he had come to depend upon replacement sources from less scrupulous business colleagues among the Jewish community, in which he was prominent. It would have been very bad news indeed if he had been caught with his fingers in their tills when they were not looking. Was this possibly an early version of the later Robert Maxwell affair? Circles within Scotland Yard undoubtedly thought he had been sailing dangerously close to an ill wind.

If all or even some of this turned out to be true, and the pressures had become too great to bear, Miller might well have thought of suicide as his only way out. However, he was now a knight of the realm and frequently recognised in Downing Street circles. He also had a real devotion to his family. He was a fighter. Therefore, the coroner's decision that Sir Eric had taken his own life needed to be looked at from every angle. Professionally we had to bear in mind the possible spin-off if he had been the target of an organised-crime contract killing.

Outside normal channels, Mrs Williams maintained direct personal contacts with individuals in the Israeli Embassy. These led to invitations to visit Israel and she did not apparently expect to have to fund the travel herself. Her influence here entirely depended upon the close relationship and direct access to the prime minister.

The news as it came to me was that Marcia Williams was ruthlessly self-interested and, although generous to her family dependants in trying to build a social and financial pot-of-gold for the future, she was unconcerned about the jeopardy into which she might be placing others.

Of course, this included the prime minister himself. But, if he was aware of her initiatives – and as the possessor of the only lifebelt on board, no one was more likely to be in the know – Harold Wilson seemed massively unconcerned. Indeed, during their infrequent travel together in the official Rover, a personal relationship flourished. In the midst of cataclysmic worries about the governance of Britain, the trade unions and the future of the Labour Party itself, he was relaxed, smiling and happy. Together they were incisively witty, often at the expense of their party and cabinet comrades. The worries of his world were suddenly lifted and the therapeutic benefits to him of her presence and personality were not disguised.

For the detective witnessing this, the infectious and unselfconscious display of high spirits was difficult to ignore while keeping a straight face. To avoid bursting a gasket it was tempting to join in too. Until he amassed enough evidence, their relationship was at best confusing to Bernard Donoughue, a participant in the Kitchen Cabinet and in daily contact with Marcia Williams. In his *Downing Street Diary* he summarises his bewilderment about her in the Introduction:

> The picture of Marcia Falkender which emerges from these pages is mixed, beginning with great admiration and evolving through sympathy to puzzlement and to eventual hostility. Overall it is not very flattering. As such it may underestimate her abilities – her sharp intelligence, her determination, her great manipulative skills, her shrewd political insight.

Bernard Donoughue and his trusted friend Joe Haines, the press secretary and speech-writer for Harold Wilson, were both in the Kitchen Cabinet. Their respective skills provided sympathetic political support for the prime minister, and they were often at his side for companionable talk over a drink. Nevertheless, they were sometimes excluded from foreign travel on orders from Marcia Williams, or following manipulation from the Political Office over which she presided. This placed Mr Wilson in more isolated company than he preferred when finding time to relax with a drink in the evenings. When she was included in the travelling party, the deputy press secretary Mrs Janet Hewlett-Davies sometimes filled the gap with remarkable equanimity and good humour.

But otherwise, the prime minister might settle to an evening's talk and drink with his civil servants or the hosting protocol officers – not excluding the KGB in Russia – and the detectives. It was here in a matey atmosphere that our behaviour needed to be cautious. It may be relevant to discuss briefly how I had arrived in this inner circle, after progressing from helmeted days pounding the beat around the Elephant and Castle area of south London, followed as a first step into plain-clothes duties by the hot pursuit of flashers across Chislehurst Common. Those were the innocent days when indecent exposure was a popular and almost harmless pastime for lonely men holding pornographic images datelined 'Cairo, 1917'.

My secondment to Downing Street had very little to do with knife and fork know-how. In Special Branch, officers were first picked for close-protection assignments almost at random. Availability and the right rank for the job were useful as a first step, although many were grateful never to be posted on this not always popular duty for the whole of their service. Other than instruction on firearms, we had no dedicated training. My first solo effort as a young sergeant was for an official visit of the President of Iceland – not controversial and unlikely to attract violent intervention. With no useful briefing, I had to ask around for advice on what to do. The immediate need was to attend a meeting of the Government Hospitality Fund with the Icelandic ambassador at Richmond Terrace in Whitehall.

In the chair was the very military, very British old school Brigadier Sir Geoffrey Macnab. I learned later of his risky and patriotic Second World War association with the British Secret Services, but for the moment followed discussion on the proposed programme. It was assumed that my powers would jump a notch or two in the pecking order by giving *de facto* approval on behalf of the commissioner for the use of police resources, including a motorcycle escort. 'Any Questions, Gentlemen?' asked Sir Geoffrey.

The ambassador pointed out that his president had a limited knowledge of English, but would be required to make a speech to City of London dignitaries and businessmen at an official luncheon at the Guildhall, and some help with his speech in reply to the toast of welcome would be appreciated.

'Tell him to walk out briskly from the pavilion,' instructed Sir Geoffrey. 'Then ask the umpire for middle-and-leg. Tell him to hit a few quick strokes to the boundary and then retire gracefully.' Although these guidelines were apparently crystal clear to the other Foreign Office officials, the ambassador remained perplexed, never having seen a game of cricket in his life.

'But you can tell the president not to worry. We have drafted his speech. It is ready for him to read out. We will see that you get it in good time.'

It was the beginning of a steep learning curve. Over the next fifteen years and by a process of trial and definite error, I participated in more than thirty close-protection assignments. In one role or another involving importance and risk they acted as diversions from my normal workload.

The early importance of professional objectivity became obvious on the occasions when I acted as the sole British bodyguard, first of all for Milton Obote, the prime minister of Uganda, and then for the president, known as King Freddie of Buganda, who had been dramatically rescued by a British Secret Intelligence Service from the murder squad sent by Obote to kill him in his palace.

A thick skin was also helpful. During his visits to London to attend the Commonwealth Heads of State Conference at Marlborough House, Milton Obote's team had accommodation in St Ermin's Hotel, near Victoria Street, and were provided with a couple of Daimler hire cars by the Commonwealth Secretariat. With a weekend to spare, Mr Obote spent much of Saturday in Foyles' bookshop in Charing Cross Road, increasing Uganda's national debt by several factors and ending with a massive pile of political and biographical books to take home. With no means of getting them packed into cases for his return flight, he consulted his high commissioner, recently installed from Entebbe and still enjoying London's shops. Unfortunately, he had not yet fully dissociated himself from the Ugandan custom of barter and his recent offers to exchange Ugandan tourist carvings for a custom-built three-piece suit in the Army and Navy stores had been rather abruptly declined. However, when Mr Obote decided to acquire enough travelling suitcases to hold all his new stock of books, his high commissioner recommended a street market he had heard of in East London called Petticoat Lane.

The two Daimlers packed with Ugandans set off from St Ermin's on Sunday morning. I was in the lead car alongside the uniformed chauffeur. We arrived in heavy, mainly static traffic in Bishopsgate and pulled into the small forecourt, then outside Liverpool Street station. It was as near to Middlesex Street and Petticoat Lane as the drivers could get the ten-man delegation.

To cross between the stationary vehicles we followed another Ugandan custom of lining up and holding hands. I took the lead and Mr Obote held my hand in his and that of his high commissioner with the other, while balancing his walking stick of office under one arm. The rest of the delegation lined up and I led this crocodile, weaving through the traffic which, fortunately, was at a standstill. Much of the cockney ribaldry was not easy to decrypt but one bus driver said it all as he slid back the window of his cab: 'Where do you think you are going with that lot, Guv? You'll only get a few bob for the lot of them down the Lane!'

Undeterred, we moved into the street market. Here for a happy hour, Mr Obote selected, examined, tested and thumped a dozen suitcases and concluded hard-fought deals with like-minded stallholders. No doubt the sale was funded by the support fund awarded at the conference. We then crocodiled our way back to the limousines, with members of the delegation holding hands while proudly carrying one or more of their prime minister's cases.

During this particular commonwealth conference, Mr Wilson was in his first administration as prime minister and one of his then detectives, Detective Chief Inspector Dennis Kelly, heard the PM say that although the meeting had been a success there were several of the heads of state that he tried to avoid in dark corridors.

Snap-shoot thinking and a great deal of luck carried me through during these probationary years, as one after another, the men protected here in Britain went back to get assassinated in their home countries.

By 1974, although still without relevant training, the Yard may have considered me a safe pair of hands and ready to take on the Downing Street assignment.

While the main task was always professional, I soon found that an alert watch was essential in No 10 to avoid a litter of dangerous banana skins.

But, as Parliament entered the summer recess, Downing Street was left behind and we set off for the seaside. Although the prime minister did not pack his bucket and spade for the beach, he did take Paddy, his Labrador, to announce that he was going on holiday.

THREE

The climate of the Isles of Scilly benefits from the soothing influence of the Gulf Stream [...]

Tourist publicity in 1974

This may be true if you intend to grow daffodils or early potatoes on the Isles of Scilly. It may be useful if you enjoy walking or watching bird and animal wildlife – but it is all very outdoors, so do ensure you are neither over- or under-clothed; and carry a mackintosh. Be advised there is often no shelter or coffee shop on the outer islands and it can be a very long time before your boat comes into sight. I don't recall seeing any of this on posters.

And if you decide on a swim, do not trust the blurb. Definitely! The detectives soon learned this lesson and concluded that an undercurrent direct from Labrador had a more significant influence on sea temperatures than any so-called Gulf Stream. Swimming was some sort of preparation for an Arctic adventure. A short spell on a sun-drenched, silver-sand beach, and the sight of invitingly clear seawater, persuaded many first-time visitors to strip off and plunge in. The more cautious rarely got beyond ankle depth and only real hearties, once immersed, pretended the water was really lovely.

When her family holidayed on the Isles of Scilly, we kept a sharp eye on Mrs Wilson. The party usually consisted of her and the prime minister, Paddy the dog, and a couple of detectives. From as ludicrously early as Easter, Mrs Wilson might decide to swim before a packed lunch of pasties. And when she went in, Mr Wilson, being a misguided, macho Yorkshireman who really did know better, would feel committed to demonstrate that he was no softie either.

And when the PM swam, we had to go in too. Not because of any written rules, but because, I suppose – no matter how much we might pretend a commitment to play with our radios – an Iron Curtain submariner might just have decided to cruise into New Grimsby Sound, the harbour anchorage between Bryher and Tresco islands, and torpedo our prime minister. A more likely danger was that Mr Wilson would die from hypothermia or run out of heartbeats after overexertion. Moreover, it would have been bad PR for Scotland Yard if the prime minister had been rescued by the Russian spy ship – sprouting aerials rather than fishnets – hove-to just offshore.

One of my colleagues, Detective Inspector Ronald Wickens, a breast stroker of distinction, had recently been the subject of a major internal disciplinary enquiry following trashy allegations in newspapers that he had assassinated an informant down in Banstead. If he was such a hard man, he was – on paper – ideal for these offshore patrols, but after one ordeal it proved impossible to point out the advantages that might accrue to him if he volunteered to swim as a regular assignment. Indeed when I once caught sight of him tentatively dipping a foot in the sea to test for frostbite before refusing to go any further than knee depth, it was as clear as a nearby Portuguese man-of-war that he had not assassinated anyone and that it was down to me to take my turn. A reminder of our disciplinary code and a requirement to follow lawful orders produced a two-word undeleted expletive and sincerely meant advice about what I could do.

We noted with some horror the beginning of the Wilsons' pre-swim routine and, by pretending to help, did our best to make it last as long as possible. A well-gnawed but still watertight tennis ball would be found in the prime ministerial rucksack and Paddy roused from comfortable slumber and was duped into believing the game was for his benefit. Stripped down to his trunks, the prime minister would induce Paddy to the water's edge and persuade him into the icy clear Labrador current with stylish goalie kicks. Off Paddy would dog paddle into deep water, recover the ball and squelch back, smiling with self-congratulation. If we failed to extend this part of the plan, the PM would gradually edge himself into deeper water until reaching critical loin depth. It was now or never and in he went. So did a reluctant detective, while his opposite number gratefully spread his towel and listened for No 10 to call on his personal radio. For the offshore patrol it was now a race between Mrs Wilson and intensive care. She proved irritatingly immune to whimpering detectives. As we towelled down, Paddy would squelch around grinning and wagging and shake himself vigorously, spraying whoever was nearest with seawater droplets. Contrary to all the rules of science, these froze on contact. Following habitually outdated guidelines from the St John Ambulance manual of first aid, we reached for the flask and dosed ourselves with hot, sweet tea.

It was only with great difficulty that Mrs Wilson could hide her dislike of the intrusion into her private life demanded by the prime minister's official programme. Unhappy with life in Downing Street, she was steadfastly a middle-class intellectual, preferring her own agenda, family walks and a simple life. Having bought a small bungalow on the heights looking down on St Mary's with money from sales of her poetry, she was insistent upon private-ish holiday time on the Scillys about four times each year. Harold Wilson tried to fill his time there in-step with her wishes, but it was obvious that he was bored without 24/7 political commitment. On occasion, he conspired with Private Office to cobble together urgent recalls to Downing Street. It could hardly be an average relationship for the Wilsons. As a matter of fact, private life can *never* be normal for any prime minister's family.

The journey from London started at RAF Northolt, where a twin-engined lumbering Andover was lined up. Paddy preceded his master having been collected from his home, the Wilson's country farmhouse near Great Missenden. To identify his place in the seating plan from the rest of us, he was embarked in a special travelling cabinet labelled 'Doggie box' by Leading Aircraftsman Witless. The party invariably consisted of the prime minister and Mrs Wilson, two Garden Room girls and two detectives.

During the first leg down to the Royal Naval Air Station (RNAS) at Culdrose, conversation was a virtual impossibility over the maxi-decibel whine of those prop-jet engines. When not asleep, Paddy – who was alleged by Mr Wilson to have an impeccable pedigree – was sometimes sick. This was not visibly popular with the crew, who might soon need to reconfigure the interior for a royal personage. Paddy's canine credentials were demonstrated by affection for mankind and a testosterone-inspired, implacable hatred of cats.

A quick salute from the commander of RNAS Culdrose, and a plea for more funding, we embarked in two Sea King helicopters – the Wilsons and a detective in the first and the other three in the safety chopper. With ear defenders essential, Mr Wilson might then produce the *Daily Telegraph* and look at the crossword. Although he confessed that he could rarely understand the cryptic questions, this took his mind off a hatred of helicopter flight. For people who enjoy that sort of wretchedness, the flight was usually uneventful.

As the prime minister was saluted off the aircraft, his official world came to an effective end. Once luggage was offloaded from the second chopper, the Wilsons boarded the only private hire transport on the main, blessedly motorway-free island of St Mary's. The PM had first claim on this intermittently reliable, white and rust-stained minibus, run by a pair of local entrepreneurs. We gave a hand with their bags as the bungalow was unlocked and then called in next door, where we were welcomed (in 'Windward') with home comforts by our kind and tolerant hostess Joan Short.

The prime minister was now as far from officials and the diary as it was possible to be and we were all absorbed into his new and not unpleasant routine of holiday domesticity. For detectives there was plenty to get started – meeting the Devon and Cornwall squad of plain-clothes officers appointed to protect the physical security of the bungalow from a nearby observation post and, at night, with regular foot patrols. Patience was called for as our transport entrepreneurs pointed out to their sightseers that 'you are now passing number ten-and-a-half Downing Street' (ha-ha-ha). This robust witticism is not funny at all after the first couple of dozen hearings.

The Garden Room girls worked from a distinguished old Custom House near the quay. They were preceded there by boffins from Home and Cabinet Office, who installed their secretarial equipment and various security paraphernalia. It was my introduction into the high-quality vetting to which the girls were subject. These dedicated young ladies were on duty there as long as the prime minister was out and about and away from his home telephone. Theirs was the responsibility of updating the prime minister on official communications through the encrypted telex network then in use from No 10. They also undertook the morning 'knitting' pattern, a routine in which they reset each day's complex and Top Secret recoding pattern – before contacting No 10 to test it. An engineer from the Cabinet Office, with responsibility to maintain this network infallibly and securely, was the only other Whitehall official on the island. Private secretaries stayed in London.

We settled to the prime minister's holiday routine, which, with the exception of intervals of sometimes frenzied contact with No 10, was not unlike that of any other holiday maker on Scilly. Sometimes members of his family would turn up and, to emphasise the family nature of it all, my wife was invited to join in from time to time. It was agreed with London that all her expenses were down to me. She was often invited to join trips to and walks on offshore islands and most evenings when the whole party might eat at the Sunset Restaurant on the harbour quay. Yes, apart from my security responsibilities, we might have been any old happy family.

Surprisingly, perhaps, not a great deal changed with the arrival of Lady Falkender.

Marcia Williams was not a typically robust outdoor type of visitor but she coped well enough with the Scilly's routines in summer. I don't recall her arrival for winter breaks but at Easter 1975 she set down on St Mary's toytown hillock of an airstrip in Eric Miller's company aircraft. More on party than official business, she was not entitled to financial backup from the Treasury.

She too changed her immediate way of life as she stepped from the aircraft into the minibus. Mrs Williams was wearing a Fulham Road two-piece denim outfit of slacks and battledress blouse – courtesy of Joe Kagan, boss of the Gannex empire and infamous for his successful photo exploitation of Harold Wilson, his most celebrated customer. Mrs Williams had travelled down specifically to map out with Mr Wilson a strategic programme for the forthcoming Common Market referendum – a ploy to wrong-foot the party's left-wing sceptics and dissenters by encouraging a Tory vote in favour. The detectives were not in the know as we waited outside her rented apartment for their talks to end – so that we could escort the prime minister safely back home. By day, she usually joined in the familiar pattern of events and, if ever the PM's eye was caught by an attractive young lady, she and Mrs Wilson might have a quiet laugh together behind his back.

On an average morning, the programme would start with a call from 'Delta One to Delta Two' on the personal radio network established by Whitehall for emergencies, and to maintain contact with the prime minister at any time when he was not near a telephone. When away from the bungalow it was our specific responsibility to mastermind the network, which included the team of local plain-clothes police, as well as the Garden Room girls and the PM himself. As this was sometimes the only contact with potential 'four minute warnings', it was out of order to go to work with a flat battery or leave the set inadvertently switched off. He was Delta One. More an academic than a practical man, Mr Wilson got the clearest pleasure from joining sharp-end activities by bravely playing around with fireworks on Guy Fawkes Night, or pretending he was from Scotland Yard.

His radio call might say that he would leave for the Co-op in five minutes. If earlier than expected, this was often bad news because we were still having breakfast. One hungry, casually dressed detective would then be at the rendezvous point outside the bungalow in good time to join him and Paddy for the ten-minute stroll down the cliff path and along the Hugh Town shops.

Prime ministerial holiday gear was usually the trousers of yesterday's formal suit and a Fair Isle sweater. He had sensible shoes rather than the pre-war white blanco-ed tennis shoes favoured by his successor, James Callaghan. Mr Wilson carried the mandatory rucksack and, wreathed in smoke signals, he would be lassoed, then dog knotted by Paddy's lead and his life hazarded as he unwound with an inelegant pirouette dangerously near the cliff edge. He fully realised that we were there to fight for his life – when needed – and never asked us to encumber ourselves on his behalf or look after his dog. We were grateful for this whenever Paddy decided to go berserk. The PM talked about the early start: 'Well, John. I am reading the history of the Hapsburg Empire. Then, out came the Hoover and it grew increasingly difficult to concentrate on the annexation of Bosnia and Herzegovina in 1908. So I escaped to get the papers. We may as well get the breakfast sausages in the Co-op at the same time.'

He knocked out his pipe before joining the shoppers inside the Co-op stores, leaving Paddy tied to a drainpipe. If granny's favourite cat appeared while he was inside, there was every probability that the pipe might be sticking out at right angles when we came out. With no thought of seeking priority, he queued at the checkout with the rest and humbly paid up. Other shoppers nudged one another, or pretended not to notice him or sent their children along to get their shopping list autographed. People from the south generally ignored him or laughed over-loudly, and told their friends at the Conservative club back home they were near enough to shoot him. Those from the midlands and north treated him as the second coming and returned to the Labour club saying they had almost touched him.

During his 1965 trip round Africa, I had been a makeweight to his protection team and, as he was adored in Gibraltar, ignored in Ghana, and reviled in Rhodesia, I concluded that a prime minister, if not naturally schizoid, would certainly benefit from a touch of bewildered paranoia.

Although goodwill was generally evident, these diverse responses to his recognition kept us alert. The Scillys had a peaceful record and the only significant incident on our warning list was a previous walk up the beach by a demented Irish peer intent upon committing GBH on Mr Wilson over some imagined injustice. We became competent at creating space while hoping not to lose too many votes for him with heavy hands. He generally accepted our judgement gratefully.

After settling his immediate official business at the Custom House, and the walk back home to cook his bangers and bacon, he made a phone call and booked a boat for the return journey to one of the smaller islands. Fully equipped with pasties and thermos flask of tea, rucksack and waterproofs, personal radios and spare batteries, we set off with him and Mrs Wilson, to meet Marcia Williams, before embarking and setting sail. It was also the signal for lurking national newspaper reporters to declare war upon this peaceful scenario.

Fleet Street editors decided that Harold Wilson had some dark secret to hide and that it was probably connected to his relationship with Marcia Williams. The tempting bait created by their holiday together made the Scillys an irresistible assembly point for fact-finding sharks motivated by a ruthless concern to protect the public interest and make the most of generous expense accounts. The urgency of their search came to an end at around 5 p.m. daily, after, that is, the next day's print was already in the editing room. A truce was declared as these predators adjourned to the few bars available on St Mary's for intense and increasingly flush-faced discussion.

On an average morning, with an end declared to any truce, a frenzy developed as the prime minister's party approached the harbour. Dangerously near an inviting push from the quayside, photographers jostled and shoved for their scoop. Health and safety concerns about the public were crudely abandoned. Mr Wilson went into his po-faced mode and ignored them. So did Mrs Williams. Mrs Wilson was not happy with it all. What these investigative reporters and their editors never realised was that if the prime minister did have anything to hide, he was more than content to let this mob surge about following red herrings along a false trail.

The PM's group was likely to include Marcia Williams' two young sons. Here, again, the prime minister was happy enough to pat them on the head, show a misleadingly paternal interest in their comfort and welfare and pretend they were his. Although knowing that their real father was a well-known journalist, some of the rumour manufacturers in Fleet Street still insisted that their father was really Mr Wilson. Followed by a melee of ingratiating, smiling, shouting, and sometimes threatening scribblers and snappers, the prime minister would lead the way down the steps alongside the quay, navigating toward his reserved open boat – the outer of a trot of three. Paddy preceded him, yelping and rampaging across the other two, now with listing bilges full of passengers waiting for the cast off.

Not all these people had voted Labour at the last election. Unaware that Paddy was harmless to humans, many grew frightened and resented this noisy intrusion into their quiet day. A few indicated their feelings with a positive, internationally recognised hand signal, once similarly favoured by Winston Churchill. We gradually scrambled aboard and pulled away, leaving the first two boats free to start off too. We were all fully aware that reporters might by now have insinuated themselves into other passengers' boats in the hope they would arrive at the same island as their prime minister. However, by Mr Wilson's simple stratagem of keeping his destination to himself, their quest was hopeless guesswork. A few determined Fleet Street investigators jangled the change in their pockets to tempt boatmen to help them out; but the Scilly Isles' sailors were too canny to fall for easy temptation. Harold Wilson was a long-term asset to their community and economy.

The Wilsons were good walkers. As we set off from the landing stage, the prime minister – enjoying his captive audience – would give us a lecture on local history. Mrs Wilson was more likely to talk about the flowers and wildlife; both were entertaining company, often settling as they walked along to reciting long excerpts from Kipling or Kublai Khan. The prime minister would also favour us with anecdotes, not always respectful, of life in the Labour Party or in Parliament or Cabinet. Marcia Williams was only out for the day if the sun was shining and – apparently being self-conscious of her legs – never stripped down into a swimsuit when we arrived at the beach. The strip-down, not a process easily disguised, was impressively unfurtive. Although included as members of the family, the detectives always moved aside to set up our lookout post, radio station and weapons' pit – and allow the Wilsons a little space of their own.

One day, on the allegedly sub-tropical island of Tresco, we fetched up at a silver beach on the north-west coast. Bright sunshine and short showers were the order of the day. As we admired the sands and blue seas in a palm tree fringed bay, with an ancient old fort alongside, a brilliant rainbow settled almost overhead like a spectral archway. Mr Wilson noted wryly, 'I suppose that if the press were here today with a photographer, their editor would reject all this as just another Wilson gimmick!'

The weather, though, was often rough and the prime minister's party was reduced to include only his wife and a couple of detectives. Mr Wilson – habitually in Whitehall, hotels or conference centres rather than the great outdoors – was not a man to take notice of the weather centre and shipping forecasts such as, 'Sea Area Plymouth. Westerly Force Six, soon veering and increasing to north westerly, Gale Force Eight or Severe Gale Force Nine. Rain, becoming heavy. Good visibility.' My subconscious rehearsed phrases such as, 'foundered with all hands', or 'failed to respond to artificial respiration', or 'the search for survivors continues' or, worse still, 'next of kin have been informed'. It became clear that this forecast had no effect on stubborn Yorkshire instincts that if the sun was shining we would survive. The local boatmen were wiser and sometimes Mr Wilson could only get one man to take us – David – from the westerly isle of Bryher.

When this happened I saw it as a very bad sign indeed. On one occasion we headed for this sparsely inhabited island after a threatening forecast and, as sun was replaced by lowering storm clouds, found ourselves marooned in cold, heavy rain and increasing winds – as correctly forecast. As we tramped around the pounding breakers rolling in to Hell Bay, increasing in size and unfriendly intensity since leaving New York a week earlier, the Wilsons – trying to shout above the hullabaloo – discussed their diplomatic approach to Sunday worship. They maintained a personal friendship with the Catholic father and also liked to divide their prayer time between the Church of England and Methodist communities on the main island. Tomorrow, they decided, they were due to attend the C of E by rote. Mr Wilson summed up the situation as he saw it, 'That means Hell today and Heaven tomorrow.'

Mr and Mrs Wilson were ill-equipped for this weather. It was an hour or more before the boatman came back to collect us. The wind roared and they got soaked. Mr Wilson's waterproofs remained in the bottom of his rucksack and he was weighed down with the volume of water soaking into his Fair Isle sweater. Mrs Wilson wore an absorbent anorak. As proper shelter was non-existent, we huddled in the lee of a bush; another family with two children were already there and more than a little surprised to be joined by their prime minister. They explained their predicament: 'This is our first visit to the Scillys. Our car broke down at Exeter. We finally got going again and discovered at Penzance that our camping gear had been stolen. When we got here we were unable to find accommodation. We are cold and wet and have nowhere to stay.'

Mr Wilson enquired, 'I am wondering what the pneumonia facilities are like in the new clinic on St Mary's?'

The family were not noticeably cheered.

David eventually appeared with his open-deck, single-screw passenger boat. I counted the lifebelts and would have preferred the RNLI. It seemed a good idea to me to find somewhere on Bryher to B&B for the night. It was now a full force 9 but seemed to be more. How much deep professionalism would I need to allow myself to be lost at sea in the course of duty, when outright cowardice was such an attractive option? I was over-ridden by David's qualified confidence that 'we *should* be able to make it back to Hugh Town OK'.

He kept us in the lee, first of Bryher and then Sampson. Apart from spray and seething rocks and noise, things were not too bad so far. Then he turned our stern to the seas. He was not smiling now. And not talking either. The horizontal flow of spume from high waves overtook us. He spun the wheel. We rolled and surged and pitched and it was a real possibility that the gale would get under the shallow hull and overturn us. Paddy slumbered and suffered from canine *mal de mer*. A wet-through Mrs Wilson crouched under the small open wheelhouse. The prime minister was thoughtful and my colleague, Detective Chief Inspector Colin Colson, struggled like a dinghy sailor to balance the roll and pitch from the highest point in the stern.

I also hooked up my personal radio with the Custom House, giving the girls there our latest position and ordering two lobster thermidors as a last request to the Sunset Restaurant. I also hoped this call would keep the Soviet decoders busy, wallowing about on the listening spy ship. There was also a chance that the Garden Room girls might sense the need to quietly warn the RNLI to stand by for a rescue. However, secure in their cosy, windproof office, they watched David's struggle toward the shelter of harbour without taking an initiative. Fortunately, the local police lookouts did, tactfully calling the lifeboat crew to a first state of readiness without creating alarm. As it was still before stand-down time for the media, they might have sensed a story.

As we struggled our wet and windblown way uphill to the bungalow, Mr Wilson shouted over the wind, 'It is rare indeed to find the gentlemen of the press out searching for the enemies of democracy in conditions such as this!'

<hr />

After an evening meal down on the quayside and, irritated at the lack of uphill pace perhaps, younger son Giles Wilson strode off ahead and then came rushing back to intercept us, declaring with some stridency that a suspicious package was hanging from the back door. Resisting any temptation to initiate a controlled explosion, Ron Wickens and I approached with caution, leaving the Wilsons temporarily under the supervision of the local constabulary. Sure enough a supermarket bag was suspended from the handle. It smelled fishy – and was. The neighbours had caught too many mackerel and donated half a dozen to their prime minister.

Paddy slurped a couple of litres of water and lurched into the bushes to search for trespassers and cock his leg. Mr Wilson pointed out that his dog was simply setting up another vicious circle.

We were scheduled to head back to Downing Street the following day. Outside the bungalow, the prime minister lowered the Warden of Trinity House flag for the final time. The detectives unanimously awarded the Wilson family a ten-star rating for accepting us as necessary everyday appendages in the most kindly way. Neither did they assume – even inadvertently – any need for sycophancy on our part, or indicate that our *proper* place was below stairs.

And now when Mr Wilson talked to me it was with eye-to-eye contact. The prime minister no longer focused on someone over my left ear. Our relationship must have matured.

Once, as we recovered from the Gulf Stream effect, it was announced that the prime minister would be leading a trade delegation to Moscow. January in Moscow sounded threatening. So Arthur Smith and I packed our rucksacks, oilskins and lightweight casuals and – planning carefully ahead – set off for Moss Bros in Long Acre, using the commissioner's account to hire fur hats, waterproof rubber overshoes and gorilla outfits suitable for very sub-zero temperatures.

Versatility was an important asset for this job.

FOUR

We call you two the Angels of Mercy.

Viktor, the KGB liaison officer in Moscow

The media men got to Moss Bros before us and reserved all the best gear. We promised to do better next time.

Clothing suitable for protection duties had never been regarded as important in the supervisory ivory towers of Special Branch. This was a mistake. A balance between formal appearance and operational efficiency was critical, as I had learned in practice.

Some useful guidelines were also picked up from the US Secret Service, who had thoroughly researched the subject as part of their commitment to protect the president. Agents of the Secret Service not only had university degrees but were ordered to retain fitness with regular, supervised workouts. Their chosen dress was expensively casual. Although they tried to remain unobtrusive, wearing just a small identifying lapel badge changed daily, agents were instantly recognisable by various excesses. These included operating anywhere in the world as though they were still in Washington, in numbers disproportionately large compared with other protection agencies, and with an inflexible determination to assert unquestionable American flawlessness, regardless of the undiplomatic damage they did to the US image.

Unless it was freezing or teeming down, they never wore a hat – on the correct assumption that they would be momentarily rendered inoperative if it was tipped over their eyes by a troublemaker. They were always immaculate, recently showered and noticeably aftershaved, and favoured smart lightweight overcoats left unbuttoned to leave them free for a quick draw. Although carefully rostered for breaks they were expected to survive duty standing during a full eight-hour shift if necessary.

It is essential to add footwear to this list. Comfortable shoes with leather soles and heels are best. If a walk across a polished marble floor develops into a Torvill and Dean display, you have got it wrong.

None of this detail takes into account the need to match the protocol for the occasion. Here we were at some disadvantage in No 10. Admittedly the diary outlined the prime minister's probable or possible moves and indicated the destination and type of function – 'lounge suit', for instance. Unlike royal protection teams, however, there were often sudden dashes – to the House of Commons, if an unplanned division was called – and it was no use turning up in a white tie and tail penguin outfit while the prime minister was in a lounge suit. While Scotland Yard automatically authorised funding to hire formal dress, it soon became obvious with experience that this was almost never needed to fit with a politician's agenda.

During his short incumbency in No 10 in the mid 1960s, Sir Alexander ('Alec') Douglas-Home unwittingly oversaw something of a watershed. He was the last of the old school perhaps. Prime ministers until then were still in mandatory dark suits, usually pin-striped, sometimes with bow ties or wing collars, wearing bowlers or homburgs, or even top hats. Sir Alec is reputed to have had something of a cavalier outlook about his appearance, satisfying himself, as just one instance, with a black-tie outfit first purchased forty years earlier at university.

It was Harold Wilson's first administration from 1964 that opened the way for protection officers to stop standing around looking like portly diplomats. Terrorist groups of the 1970s did the rest and the primacy of formal appearance was properly subordinated to the need for active instantaneous reaction to ever-increasing threats.

Harold Wilson's first administration allowed further relaxation to take place. It was, for example, the first to abandon *de facto* rules that Garden Room girls *must* always wear long gloves and garden-party hats when accompanying the prime minister outside Downing Street, and that drivers would wear peaked caps. Holidays with the Wilson family on the Scillys completed the transition, and his close protection team was then able to quit nineteenth-century embargoes and dress more in proportion to current needs.

Not once during six years in Downing Street was it necessary for me to dress up in more than a dinner jacket. It was sometimes different abroad, however.

The bonus here was that we could easily equip ourselves with discreet suits, shirts and ties, which blended well with the need to carry firearms and leave us free for physical combat in emergencies. The commissioner issued totally unsuitable webbing underarm holsters for our revolvers. Not only were they inadequate operationally, they also created a daily demand for sterilisation. At

No 10 we all acquired sturdy, small, well-balanced leather holsters, customised and handmade to fit our belts by an inspired police constable on the front door – Colin Cross.

⟫•○•⟪

All this melded well enough with tropical lightweight suits, but was totally impossible with the survival clothing called for in Moscow. Pistols there were carried in overcoat pockets. You could not exist without gloves, and couldn't fire a pistol with them. Although the US Secret Service – which had recently preceded us to Russia – no doubt called upon the skills of top scientists to fit each agent with heated, lightweight surgeons' rubber gloves for the few days they were there, we decided it was essential to follow the Russian lead. The Soviet KGB were responsible for personal protection in the USSR and had never found the perfect way to overcome the problems of conjoining a necessary state of readiness with severe winter weather. We watched to see how they coped so successfully. As our branch was tasked to work against the KGB under normal circumstances, it was now time to acquire a broad smile in friendly co-operation and a trans-Iron Curtain special relationship – for the moment at least.

On our side, it was encouraging to note that no assassin could possibly survive for long while hanging around in −25°C or less.

⟫•○•⟪

The prime minister's delegation arrived at Vaukovo II, a military airfield outside Moscow, on RAF Special Flight 399 on 13 February 1975. It was the final round trip for their squadron of de Havilland Comet IVs, scheduled for the scrapyard, but her lines still looked rather special as she stood gleaming at the beginning of a welcoming red carpet.

Having struggled into fancy dress and set a tubular-shaped, Finnish Astrakhan wool hat at a jaunty angle, the prime minister led his delegates down to the foot of the gangway. As I stepped onto the red carpet in turn, to my surprise rather than delight, I was seized, hugged and embraced on the cheek by Leonid Ilyich Brezhnev, President of the Union of Soviet Socialist Republics – admittedly in a comradely rather than intimate way – and then by First Secretary and Premier Alexei Nikolayevich Kosygin and Foreign Secretary Andrei Gromyko. It was my first and blessedly only near miss with the vomit-making aroma of aftershave favoured by communist leaders.

I resolved to ensure that I was not rostered to join a reception party when they made a return visit to Heathrow, where parity might be demanded but privacy not guaranteed. Even loyal friends might think I was enjoying myself. At this stage no photographs were taken. The Garden Room girls suffered similarly, but were too well-trained ever to talk about it. Perhaps disclosure was specifically prohibited by small print in the Official Secrets Act?

A disciplined guard of honour performed next and goose-stepped away, followed by a military band. We assumed that, once out of sight, the band had a support team standing by to drench any survivors in warm anti-freeze and hurry them away for intensive care and any remedial first aid necessary to unstick mouthpieces from frozen lips.

Formalities were not yet over. Headed by our prime minister, delegates were shepherded into a carefully orchestrated scenario for Russian television news. About 100 unhappy party officials had been redeployed from heated offices into a couple of open stands near the red carpet. With miniature red or Union flags thrust into gloved hands, they were required to provide background shots of a joyful welcome to the British. This they signally failed to do. But, after our departure they must have been threatened with deportation for life to a Siberian Gulag, because when we saw the edited version a couple of months later during a reception at the Soviet Embassy in London, these grim individuals were smiling and cheering and waving as though their very lives depended upon it. Maybe they did?

I motorcaded with the KGB escort. Ever keen to learn, I saw how they dealt with the problem of having to fire handguns with heavily mittened hands. They pre-empted any likely call for reaction simply by posting one armed, uniformed foot officer for every 10yd of the route through both bleak, windswept, frozen and entirely empty countryside or within the city itself. These officers stopped and cleared the streets of all the few cars that used them and corralled pedestrians out of sight. Our escort rode three-wheeled motorcycles to combat dangerously icy roads and sat comfortably in heavy over leathers heated from the motorcycles' batteries. The journey through the Moscow streets was uneventful. Not even the plump – even enormous – sallow-skinned women, demonstrating socialist equal rights by shovelling great heaps of filthy snow, hardly dared pause for breath and sneak a look.

To our delight the whole area round the official residential *dachas* where we stayed was surrounded by impenetrable security. During an inadequate pre-departure briefing in London, it was emphasised that every move would be monitored, every car and hotel room bugged, and that we would be under constant scrutiny by Soviet security agencies for signs of exploitable human weakness. Conversation with our liaison officer – and all members of the Russian security services appeared to be called either Vladimir or Viktor – was consequently limited. In our official guest *dachas* on Lenin Heights we turned on taps and radios, as advised before we left London, in the hope of disabling eavesdropping systems inevitably planted in lights or sockets, under carpets, or camouflaged as heating units or ventilators. The need for caution encourages a sort of paranoia and furtive, often meaningless conversation.

We had also been warned of a possibility of seduction and compromise by beautiful women agents of the KGB. Any subliminal hopes of victimisation were soon dashed and replaced – in my case at least – by a realisation that any man falling for any of the Russian women we saw would have been certifiable.

Marcia Williams, when she was once accused of having started an affair with Harold Wilson during a pre-ministerial visit to Russia, found the prospect ridiculous, claiming that the last place in the world that anyone would start an affair would be the Soviet Union. She was undoubtedly right.

During his career, both in and out of government, Harold Wilson had made scores of official trips to Russia, and was an old hand at this game of interception and deception – and made the most of it. During relaxing evening stand-downs, he enjoyed company and his close staff were sometimes invited to join convivial, even bibulous conversation. This was invariably in the presence of two or three shifty-looking hospitality or liaison officers from the Russian Foreign Service. Falsely ingratiating and subservient, they were impossible to like.

In impeccable English, one of them would start with, 'and what would be your choice of drinks tonight, Mr Wilson?' Knowing that only *Russian* drink was available, Mr Wilson might choose 'one of your fine Moldavian brandies, I think', and a party would start. Normally reserved officials from Mr Callaghan's teetotal *dacha* next door, would find a reason to deliver some urgent telegram for the prime minister's attention in person, and hope to be invited to join in too. Joe Stone (later Lord Stone), the prime minister's doctor, often bustled in after dining with diplomats from the UK Embassy. Joe insisted, rather obviously, in checking the PM's pulse rate in front of us all, shaking his head and giving a serious warning – always ignored – that 'you really must try to relax and get an early night, Harold'. These, although never riotous evenings, were intensely entertaining and sometimes amusing.

For example, the prime minister, talking to the liaison officer one night, rambled apparently inconsequentially along:

I have lost count of the number of times I have been privileged to make official trips to Russia. And this is my first disappointment at the instant hospitality always provided. Today, before breakfast, for example, I was working on official papers and really fancied a cup of coffee. As I walked about, I said out loud that coffee would be really welcome. But – do you know – nothing happened until my tray arrived twenty minutes later?

The prime minister was pointing Wilsonian sarcasm at the Russian hosts, who were bright enough to recognise that this trip was different. For perhaps the first time, the Soviets were hoping to benefit from the promise of British trade credits, and he was obliquely pointing out that, whether his rooms were bugged this time or not, he knew they always had been before.

It may not be easy to recall now just how grim and intense the forty-plus years of the Cold War were. This visit was somewhere near the middle of it all but there was still no open door to the Soviet Union for westerners. Russian cruise ships had visited the UK for several years to take round-trippers, usually Eastern Bloc refugees from the Second World War, for carefully monitored visits to relatives left behind – but only then after a formidably complicated visa application. Otherwise it was a world of suspicion, espionage, treachery and nuclear threat. Le Carre's novels described life across and behind the Iron Curtain; danger and discomfort in one form or another lurked on every page. Under these circumstances, and with a very limited threat to our prime minister, it was a rare privilege to see something of life without the freedoms to which we were accustomed in the west.

I did once manage to evade our 'liaison' officer and walk from the conference rooms alone. It was my first experience of getting lost and being unable to speak to a soul or read a single road sign. Later, Vladimir insisted on showing me an underground railway station. Just as expected, it was lit by chandeliers, was spotlessly clean, without graffiti, and free from pockmarks of discarded chewing gum. During a visit to Leningrad we stayed in the Astoria Hotel and it came straight from a film set. Faded dark-blue or maroon furnishings proliferated. The room key was too bulky and heavy to be forgotten in some pocket. The sallow, overweight, brutally unfriendly woman spying on our simple proclivities while posing as the *concierge* reported every move. Food was evil and the atmosphere sinister. The plumbing had been designed for a warship and was typified by the occasional, unexpected discharge of scalding water from the cold tap.

Away from the hotel, restaurants, bars or other possible venues for anti-revolutionary mutterings were virtually non-existent, although one pathetic attempt at modern entertainment was organised by the Russian hosts. We were induced into a restaurant – only open to senior members of the Communist Party, foreign diplomats and visitors with American dollars – where we were assured that a pop group would perform. There was nothing at all *pop* about these half-dozen, anachronistic lookalikes of USA 1940, dressed in unlikely zoot suits and playing old-fashioned waltzes. Shopping was possible only in state-run, sparsely equipped, custom-built blocks. Alcohol was comparatively expensive, and committed drunks who were unable to afford vodka lurked in doorways accosting passers-by with a secret sign. Two fingers of the right hand pointed at the throat were an invitation to total strangers to join a consortium, buy a bottle, and drink a share there and then on the street in freezing temperatures. If this totalitarian life was cool, it was certainly no fun.

These are incidental memories from what was in fact a very serious attempt at a high level to relax Iron Curtain tensions by fostering trade. Mr Wilson and his specialist advisers were kept hard at work at long conference sessions and formal speeches and visits. At a solemn ceremony in the vast and impressive area surrounding the Tomb of the Unknown Warrior, Mr Callaghan distinguished himself as the only man present in a trilby. The rest of us took no chances, having been warned that a member of an earlier delegation had recklessly encouraged his brain to freeze after removing his fur hat for three minutes. It was unfortunate for our hosts that the broadcast of solemn music – after audio-tape failure – sounded not unlike an Islamic call to prayer.

For the delegation, the Soviets tried to pull out all the stops. As officials from both sides of the Iron Curtain tended to hide some of their important people as mere minions, the Russians decided to play safe and invite the whole delegation to the Kremlin for a formal luncheon. It was my first experience of a high-level working lunch and an introduction to the fact that politicians nearly to a man have absolutely no interest in the arts, culture or good food.

After a guided tour of some of the historical and political wonders preserved within Kremlin walls, we moved to the dining room. Place settings included a line of seven glasses for each person, a clear indication that further sampling of Russian wines and spirits was impending; water was not on offer and had to be specially requested. I remembered the rules about drinking on duty and decided not to get paranoid about them.

Embassy staff said that *chefs de cuisine* had been specially flown in from Paris. Feeling fairly sure this was not a feast available to the average peasant, I worried about the egalitarian rights of proletarians elsewhere in Russia. Having served in the Special Branch unit at Tilbury docks and sampled the hospitality aboard Soviet cruise ships I was more than *fairly* sure. Let's have a look at the menu, taken directly from the official translation:

Fresh caviar, Kulebyaka pie, fish cartilage and mushrooms
Jellied Bester fish
Stuffed partridge with red bilberries and fresh vegetables
Consommé with a pancake
Sturgeon Solyanka
Soup Stolitchnaya
Baked white salmon with champignons
Roast beef with vegetables
Ice cream Korzinochka

Coffee or tea
Fruit
Petit fours

Start time was 1 p.m. The top table toyed anxiously with toasts of friendship between course after course; but this was a diplomatic affair and food was the last priority. Instead, it was an occasion for protracted speeches: Soviet leaders in Russian and Harold Wilson and James Callaghan in English. The brilliant translator, standing deferentially just behind each speaker in turn, was in my opinion – in spite of faultless mastery of both languages – a mistake on the part of our embassy. Immaculately dressed in Savile Row suit and speaking Old Etonian English, I feared our hosts would see him as an Old Boy class provocation – until he was identified as Viktor from the Russian Foreign Service. The speeches went meaninglessly on and on. While the top table messed about with each plate, the rest of us set digestive tracts into urgent motion. James Callaghan, who liked a nap after lunch, showed distinct signs of weariness as a 5 p.m. truce was declared, just in time for a rush back to the *dacha*.

The staff there, aware that the delegation was heading for a 6.30 p.m. performance of Tchaikovsky's *The Nutcracker* at the Bolshoi Theatre, mustered behind a sumptuous buffet.

The famous Bolshoi ballet is no longer exclusive to Communist Party members and selected foreigners, but in 1975 it was a rare privilege to see a glorious production of the *The Nutcracker* from the president's box. During intervals, all members of the British delegation were conducted to a private room – and yet more food. During the dance of the Sugar Plum Fairy, a delegate, slumbering after an excess of good things, woke with a start and rather too loudly asked the Garden Room girls nearby why the orchestra was playing 'I'm a Cadbury's Fruit and Nut case'? The two tunes, it will be recalled, are not dissimilar.

As the final curtain fell, dangerously excited, flush-faced and normally staid ladies in the British party risked permanent injury, shouting 'Encore!' – and applauding so heartily they nearly dislocated something.

Back at the *dacha*, our faithful staff again lined up behind the buffet. 'Never mind,' said the cynical Bill Housden as he tucked in again. 'What we can't manage they will nick and take home for their family.' Looked at in this way, those of us who were over *la limite* collapsed into bed with a clear conscience, feeling we had done the staff a comradely favour. However, when we left, their equal distribution of wealth dogma overcame any pre-revolutionary weaknesses such as conscience.

They stole women's tights and biro pens and other symbols of western decadence that were unobtainable in this socialist Utopia.

The following morning the prime minister was scheduled for interviews with Russian television and radio in studios adjacent to a transmitting mast nearly 500m high. Our foxy Soviet liaison officer boasted immodestly that this was so cleverly designed the footings were a mere 5ft in depth. Clever this may have been but the restaurant on top – obscured in cloud as usual – was a business disaster. However, the studio was indeed a revelation. Where, I wondered, was the familiar jumble of lights and cables? And why no hysterical director ordering everyone around? Was there anything wrong with a simple rose in a glass vase opening shot – and no music?

Wearing collar and necktie and standing to attention, the sole cameraman patiently waited for the prime minister. Harold Wilson spoke in English, of course, and it must be assumed that the anodyne end product made a change from all those smiling tractor drivers for which Soviet television was infamous. The questions, all pre-arranged between officials, contained none of the snake traps endemic in the UK. Joe Haines, the Downing Street press secretary, complained afterwards that the PM had used the word 'fructify', against his advice. 'I don't care whether they misunderstood it or not,' countered Mr Wilson. 'Fructify was what I meant and fructified was what I decided to say.'

Our negotiators were known as the Sherpas – acknowledging the heights they had to climb during the talks. These 'fructified' into a treaty. The signing ceremony was the first I had seen. With a time and place announced, every Russian with the remotest connection tried to get into the official photographs and claim his place in history. While senior British delegates were automatically included in the shots, I thought their juniors behaved rather well, generally remaining on call but keeping out of the way. Some of the Russians, on the contrary, displayed uncivil determination to get on the record while contriving fixed smiles for the camera, intending to be seen as stern, important and official, but relaxed.

A long table and just two chairs were provided for the two prime ministers. They were ushered ceremoniously in and placed in position by attentive officials, one from each country. Surplus-to-requirement minions were cleared out of the way. The big two officials, looking very, very important, stood behind and outside their two leaders, arranging identical copies of the treaty in a pile, with red tabs prominent where signatures were required. Every precaution was taken to ensure that neither treacherous leader stole a march on the other. This may have been a throwback to the Non-Aggression Pact between Nazi Germany and the Soviet Union in 1939, signed just two years before they engaged in mortal combat.

Each official, keeping a careful eye that he was in synchrony – but neither ahead nor behind the other – then fingered a red tab and opened the appropriate page. Exchanging furtive glances, the first copy was placed before each leader. A pause and nod and together the prime ministers duly signed on. The process was repeated half a dozen times. It was the occasion for smiles, handshakes, speeches and the most sincere and everlasting expressions of mutual trust once again.

Next on the agenda was the determination of junior officials to crowd their way into formal photographs – while looking bored and offended by the unscheduled intrusion into their lunch hour. This was followed by conspicuous loitering for the champagne and canapés. It was illuminating to work out which official was drinking too much, for it appeared that even the most self-important was not entirely resistant to free booze.

I am not absolutely sure, but the last I heard was that not one penny, or *kopek*, of the trade credits created by this treaty was ever taken up. The Iron Curtain was apparently lowered firmly into position again.

Our KGB colleagues relaxed as we boarded the Comet IV on the way home. A smile was definitely attempted and we hoped they had amassed all the data needed for our personal files in their archives. Most of their officers had suffered the violent cold out there in the open, while we remained in modest comfort, indoors near the prime minister. For the last few days, our reappearance had indicated that a move was imminent and they could get some relief from the cold. Vladimir's final words were encouraging, 'We call you two the Angels of Mercy!'

Safely back in Downing Street, the official baggage master for the delegation, Bill Housden, told the other drivers, 'Just wait until I get my memories into print! I've got some really good antidotes to write about from this trip.'

Yes, Bill.

FIVE

They could get married if Clara agreed to bring up any children he fathered with other young girls. Clara had put her decision on 'hold'.

Jamaican Constabulary Inspector Maurice Robinson's
marriage proposal

A large, white American limousine purred up to the Pegasus Hotel in Kingston, Jamaica. With half a day free, four of Mr Wilson's staff piled in. Dressed in holiday casuals, we were taking advantage of the only break from work during the Commonwealth Heads of State meeting in 1975.

The idea was to cross the blue mountains, which separate the humid and overheated south side of the island, and take a look at the tourist north – cooled by balmy trade winds. After negotiating the squalid outskirts of Kingston, the capital, the limo effortlessly eased its way up the winding mountain road. The world began to look rather wonderful.

Then civilisation intervened as we came to the red lake, an excrescence caused by bauxite extraction and processing. This wonderful lake situated in the midst of sub-tropical forest was tainted with toxic chemicals; the trees along high-water mark were dead or dying. This epitomised Jamaica – a mixture of the wonderful and lively, of colour and energy – all in close contrast to frightening decay, crime and devastation.

As we topped a mountain pass, the limo passed through a poor village. Naked children scrambled with cricket bat and ball on a dusty pitch. When they saw this big flashy car passing, they lined up, turned their backs – and bowed. Their bare bottoms were a way of showing their disdain for the haves passing in a big car. It was a hugely political performance. At the sight of this row of dark-brown buttocks, one of the Garden Room girls was threatened with an attack of the vapours.

⟢•●•⟣

After leaving the wintertime deep freezes of Soviet Russia and North America, a diary entry confirmed preparations for the prime minister's next major travel abroad. Long since upgraded from 'pencilled in', the Commonwealth Heads of Government Conference was on schedule to be held in Kingston. Her Majesty The Queen would be there on board the royal yacht *Britannia*.

It was time to take advantage of the commissioner's generosity and kit ourselves for tropical travel. With the benefit of experience, and with the probability that it was a long-term investment, we were authorised to *buy* – rather than hire – two 'fine botany wool' tropical lightweight suits from 'post-Colonial age suppliers, Alkit of Cambridge Circus, WC2 and throughout the Provinces'. Forked sticks to carry messages, collapsible canoes and any other needs were down to us. Nobody would be seen dead in them today, but it was the age of the nylon shirt – easy enough to launder and dry in a hotel room with no electric iron.

These were still the trustingly innocent days before we included a representative in the advance party. So Arthur Smith and I boarded the Comet VI's replacement, a shiny new VC10, with the prime minister and the main group, from the VIP lounge at Heathrow. With a challenging fortnight ahead it was prudent to resist the drinks trolley trundled along by the cabin crew, bright enough really but looking depressed and sallow in drab sky blue. A visit to the flight deck at night was seriously discouraging. Although the tops at their job, the pilots and flight engineer showed their suspicion of anyone even remotely connected with politics. With blue kit melding with green background lighting, they succeeded in looking like recent releases from intensive care. On other trips we had much to thank them for.

The VC10 gave enough space for a forward lounge and sleeping facilities for the prime minister, adequate room centrally for the staff and aft accommodation for temporary support personnel, such as the Royal Military Police.

On special flights when we were joined by old travel hands from the Foreign Office, they turned the cabin into an ad hoc doss house. Rather than eat mass-produced meals prepared hours earlier, FCO men and women burrowed into personal haversacks and produced unappetising gluten-, sugar- and fat-free snacks, vegetarian sandwiches and decaffeinated coffee. Next on the agenda were comfortable lightweight tracksuits, sleeping bags and inflatable pillows. A scramble developed to sequester floor space, stretch out and get to sleep. Cabin staff trying to see to the rest of their passengers were left to pick their way around the jumble.

This attempt to pre-empt jet lag and permit full-scale effort the moment they landed was admirable enough, if night was soon to fall, but reduced the Garden Room girls and No 10 duty clerks to a state of administrative impotence. If the PM's finger beckoned as usual, they trod roughly on their civil service colleagues, asserting priority over the ruthlessly self-interested slumberers cluttering the floor.

After arrival, any residual jet lag was soon dispelled and replaced by sheer terror, as our undisciplined motorcade hurtled into Kingston at reckless and intensely dangerous speed. Police motorcycle escorts are invariably aggressive, self-important and feared, but these lads were the champions. Our liaison officer claimed they were specially selected, but he never explained for what. Clad in all-white leathers, and riding new, white, Norton twin-cylinder solos, they hooted and revved and shouted their way. No doubt the cloying humidity, potholes, dead goats and the cavalier self-assurance of other Jamaican drivers diminished the likelihood of the Highway Code having any useful effect. In any case, it was outright war and even Alkit's lightweights were no help. Hot panic developed into cold sweat and thanks were given to the Almighty – even by avowed atheists in the delegation – as we pulled into the forecourt of the Pegasus Hotel.

We introduced ourselves to Inspector Maurice Robinson, Jamaican Constabulary, our liaison officer. He found the motorcade unexceptional. He did not anticipate compensation claims for the dead goats. It was normal. This melee was repeated more than forty times as other leaders arrived at the airport.

This journey was a distraction from the horrors of Kingston. Humidity, poverty and crime combined to produce a ruined city. Violence was on such an enormous scale that a barbed-wire enclosed concentration camp had been established for those gang members necessarily scooped up by the police to allow some sort of normal life to continue. This was virtually martial law. Any chance of a carefully investigated case being presented fairly in court in the foreseeable future was absolutely out of the question.

Our assessment was that the likelihood of a terrorist outrage here was small but that of a head-to-head attack all too likely. A sigh of relief was possible when we discussed the programme – which was largely to take place out of public reach. The hotel complex was surrounded by police and soldiers and declared a security sterile area. Public venues where the queen and the prime minister would be present were also comprehensively guarded. Although the quality of the various security services could not easily be assessed, they were undoubtedly likely to open fire if needed. This contrasted with security units in countries like Japan, where authority was absolute and police were unlikely to take counter action without direct orders to do so. Probably on paper and in duplicate!

With rooms adjacent to the prime minister and his temporary Private Office, we could retrench and hang up our nylon shirts.

Kingston was a paradox. Squalid and disorganised on one hand, and yet teeming with beautiful, lively, talkative and colourfully dressed people on the other. In one area, hundreds of dispossessed had assembled on a blindingly hot outcrop of rock and set up residence in tin shacks. With all the charm of a landfill site there were no amenities. Living conditions were appalling and proper sanitation absent. And yet they were vibrant and cheerful and seemingly energetic too.

Jamaicans are fiercely independent, as Londoners were discovering. Shopping in a supermarket one morning, a lady from the delegation saw and photographed an elderly man of distinctive appearance. He turned on her, outraged, and gave an outspoken and embarrassing lecture on good manners and the human right of privacy. As she sought justification among us later, it became increasingly hypocritical to try to deny that he was undoubtedly in the right. This strange admixture of independence and the beautiful and ugly was to feature throughout our stay.

One evening, for example, the queen hosted her prime ministers and spouses on board the royal yacht (Dress: Black Tie and Medals). *Britannia* was moored about half a mile offshore. Dressed overall and floodlit, she looked simply magnificent. A vast assembly of locals collected near the purpose-built quayside from which the VIPs were embarked in Royal Navy launches. The weather was co-operative, tranquil and warm and humid, with just a light breeze to extend a fluttering Royal Standard. Onlookers were treated to the sight of recognisable world personalities in the flesh.

The Royal Navy ran a shuttle service from the quay. The impeccably turned-out crew brought their craft alongside with perfect precision and dexterous boat hook drill. In contrast to the squalid decrepitude immediately inshore, it was impossible not to acknowledge inner feelings of pride and outdated jingoism.

The crowds kept it all in perspective. Their colourful appearance was matched by noisy, rhythmic music, singing and exuberance and unreserved, noticeable and often disrespectful humour. Although she might well have been as much loved here as in The Mall in London, this was not the place for Her Majesty to decide on a walkabout among the crowds.

⸺ ❊ ⸺

In Jamaica, and after a year at No 10, I joined a privileged few. It is only a small inner circle, of which I was on the perimeter, that gets a chance to witness and wonder at a prime minister's workload.

For the rest of my time as an outsider inside No 10, the Jamaica experience and conclusions reached never changed. Indeed, with Mrs Thatcher they hardened up, if anything. I have already referred to the inevitable prime ministerial carousel – the election and a honeymoon period, then the next twelve months or so when the mandarins expect their man to be on top of his form, while the public wait and see and the media gear themselves for action. Then along come the first banana skins, seized upon gleefully by the media and HM Opposition. This is followed by tears. Give or take a decade or two and a few name changes and last season's stories can again be recycled as news. 'Undecided' voters may now change sides. It is called the democratic system of government. Please note that the Whitehall establishment is still there.

When this see-saw settles, historians and biographers – benefiting from hindsight, calm consideration and the release of sanitised records – publish balanced assessments and local authorities decide to erect statues. Or not to.

At the Commonwealth Heads of Government Conference in the early summer of 1975, Harold Wilson was still at the peak of his power and competence. I was much impressed. Sadly, it was not to last.

A prime minister's workload is overpowering and personally exhausting. With the benefit of previous experience, Harold Wilson knew the short cuts but, with his exceptional interest in politics and commitment to the job description, it still called for a twenty-four-hour a day commitment. In the months preceding Jamaica, he travelled to the United States of America, Canada and the Soviet Union. Having usually been in the planning stage for months and final agreement waiting only for a rubber stamp, these long-distance visits were probably slightly less exacting than the frequent and more spontaneous local ones to Dublin, Paris and Brussels. The fact that he could call upon special planners and advisers beforehand, and was then supported by officials when away, was merely proportionate to the strain of travel, speech preparation and press conferences when, it must not be forgotten, every word he uttered had to be related to long-term government policy.

In Jamaica, his team included expert advisers on – among others – the media, the Labour Party, Whitehall and the diplomatic service, the armed forces and Constitutional Law. He led from the front, never sparing himself. As far as I remember he never ducked a single session, even when he could justifiably have delegated and spent an hour or two lounging around the swimming pool with a Planter's Punch.

This was no longer the relaxed and chatty man we had known on the Scillys. Mr Wilson was switched on, interested, alert. He demanded briefs and advice from his officials and then, utilising his famed memory to advantage, moved from session to session without a single briefing paper. In between, he wrote speeches, answered dispatches, read papers. He generated confidence and authority.

After each closed session for Heads of Delegation, which included one adviser or note taker, he was surrounded by waiting officials, all pressing for special attention. Some waved messages with requests for decisions on immediate action. They waited for prompt answers. Others needed to know what had happened in the closed session so that telegrams could be dispatched to high commissions and legations around the world. A phalanx of officials dough-nutted round him, including press officers, private secretaries, diplomats and Labour Party advisers. Each was too absorbed in his own special interests to notice Mr Wilson's increasingly worried demeanour. He started pacing up and down. This indicated that after three hours closeted in conference, he needed to find the gentlemen's toilet – sooner rather than later.

As a general rule, after lighting his pipe and rattling out questions and answers, he would set off purposefully along a corridor. Unfortunately, the clear sense of direction displayed on the Scillys was of no use in the confines of a hotel and, invariably, he came to a dead end at some point where security sterilisation called for locked doors. A pause and about turn would follow, with those around counter-marching and reassembling. After other stops and turns, he would find the gents' and bustle in. Questions of protocol now arose for his officials. I had a role to play too.

My task had no specific job description but, clearly, an initiative was called for. I decided – for just as long as the British delegation was hard at work in the gentlemen's toilet – that my first course of action for the benefit of the nation was to ensure that no interlopers from other delegations had preceded us. With this done I took up a bouncer's role, barring the doorway without discrimination to blacks, browns or whites – irrespective of rank or personal immediacy.

This initiative left the prime minister free to select his stall. His staff could hardly just stand around watching and felt obligated to line up as well. Opportunists who most needed his attention tried to edge into urinals next to his. When the stalls were full, something of a log jam built up, but the questions and answers never ceased. One press officer dropped all his papers in the flow in which, in other parts of the world, smokers are implored not to drop cigarette ends 'as it makes them soggy and difficult to smoke'! He was left to rescue them on his own.

Having been the first in, the PM was also the first away to the washbasin. He took out and washed his false teeth, outflanking the others, younger and still displaying a full set of their own pearlies. It had never occurred to me before that world affairs were conducted in such ad hoc, all-boys-together, changing-room circumstances. No longer was it strange that senior No 10 officials excluded women. With teamwork, we Brits had the field to ourselves but, I asked myself, had the enemy bugged the bog? Should I report this potential breach of security for the information of MI5?

It seemed unwise on every count.

On the final day, the Sherpas went into action, pooling many disparate agendas into one acceptable communiqué and statement for a press conference. Preceding evenings were given over to relaxation for some. On Monday, for example, the prime minister watched the ceremony of Trooping the Colour, carried out by the Third Battalion, Jamaica Regiment in the presence of Her Majesty The Queen. She reviewed the troops from a Land Rover, before a large, colourful, boisterous and not always respectful Jamaican crowd who turned the occasion into a dress rehearsal for the Notting Hill Carnival. My enduring impression was that there were simply no military bandsmen in the world to compare with those of British regiments.

An evening of Caribbean dance and music held at the Ward Theatre in Kingston was spectacularly noisy, rhythmic and lively. This wooden edifice was in the last stages of tropical decay and potential collapse. My pleasure was less than complete at the discovery, during a survey of escape routes, that in the event – at times the near certainty – of fire, every exit was firmly locked on *the grounds of security*. These VIPs were not to be infiltrated by unauthorised local gatecrashers but could be incinerated with no likelihood of escape. The officials responsible for this decision were not available.

The prime minister had also agreed to lay the foundation stone for new British high commission offices. It was an old colonial scene, with shady awnings and red carpets. Protocol and precedence were strictly enforced and ladies wore floppy hats, long gloves and cocktail dresses.

There was something haughty and rather sad about many British officials abroad. Although the world had moved along, it had passed them by. They gave the firm impression that they felt rather superior to the locals, to the UK way of life, and every politician. I was later to discover that patronising disdain was not confined to Labour politicians. Mrs Thatcher was in no sense old colonial and they often tried to treat her accordingly – perhaps rather more obviously by male chauvinists than spouses and female officials.

With the stone poised to be swung into position, Mr Wilson was handed a silver trowel. The formality of short speeches was followed by a distinctly British Raj-type function – with cool drinks and canapés served by a staff of black servants to *almost* entirely white VIPs. I did not find the atmosphere easy. At every level, the life of the FCO staff was socially genteel but unhealthily narrow, as some still pretended to the power of empire, while being confronted with the reality of Britain's modest importance as a world power. Shrill voices and pointing fingers were often an identifiable trademark. Much depended upon the example set by individual high commissioners and ambassadors.

I was reminded of a similar outdoor function at the high commission residence in Salisbury – then the capital of Rhodesia – in 1965, when Lady Humphrey Gibbs displayed enviable qualities of cool command to her all black staff. They had gone to a great deal of trouble to prepare sandwiches, lay tables, and set crockery and cutlery in place for a reception around the swimming pool. The best-laid plans failed to take into account my colleague, Dennis Kelly's uncompleted attempt at a double somersault from the diving board. Two rotations might have been impressive; but one and a half represented a massive belly flop and the displacement of much of the pool onto the set tables. Dennis, I remember, surfaced sheepishly with torso nastily red. Lady Gibbs, avoiding eye contact with him did, however, have much to say to her servants, who removed the soggy cucumber sandwiches and sodden white tablecloths at the double – and started all over again.

The final Caribbean flourish came with a barbecue and dance party given by the Honourable Michael Manley, Prime Minister of Jamaica, and his colleagues from Guyana, Trinidad and Tobago, and Barbados, which took place at Jamaica House as dusk fell one evening. Beneath floodlights, five gigantic stages were erected. It was a humid, balmy warm, exotic – even erotic evening, without protocol or formality. Each island showed off its most elegant, energetic and colourful dance troupes. They could hardly have differed more from the disciplines of the ballet seen in Moscow earlier.

With space between each stage, all were in action at the same time. Loudspeakers were set at maximum volume. The sound was deafening and dance and dress spectacular. Rhythms were compelling and even mesmerising. Youngish ladies from the British delegation and our high commission, normally staid, reserved and hiding behind spectacles, were inspired onto the stages to join in, moving in rather sensual gyrations to the drumbeats. For an instant there was a real fear they might start tearing off their clothing too. This was a rave well before the days when it became fashionable fun among young people in the UK. Jamaica House gardens were devastated.

The following day we packed our tropical lightweights and prepared for a cold, grim, windy arrival back in the UK. There was much to think about. In a way our thoughts crystallised around our new friend and colleague, Inspector Maurice Robinson.

First impressions of him had been wrong. An initially sullen demeanour in reality disguised a thoughtful, highly intelligent and quick-witted personality. Under difficult circumstances he had displayed efficient control of his team of plain-clothes protection officers. During many hours away from the hotel complex, poised for motorcade movement from non-security sanitised venues, we had sheltered together in the life-preserving shade of a veranda or isolated tree, learning much of his philosophy of life. We had also been introduced to his beautiful partner, Clara. He explained their predicament.

Robbie's mother held a firm conviction that respectable couples must be married. Robbie and Clara agreed. But it was known that she was not physically able to bear children, and they all wanted a family. Robbie proposed a way out. They could get married if Clara agreed to bring up any children he fathered with *other* young girls. This proposition was received with hesitation and Clara had put the decision on hold. The delay was taking its toll with an anxious Robbie, who was unable to offer any other possibilities if she said no.

This example was typical of the fierce individualism which dominated the Jamaican way of life and – in spite of many difficulties – kept the population sparkling and bright. Their healthy iconoclasm helped those dispossessed living in shacks; and the small boys showing their bottoms; and elderly men demanding their right to privacy with sophisticated argument. It helped to ensure the lively high spirits of men and women whose island was devastated in some areas with industrialisation and decay, and the provocation of a post-colonial existence where the haves and the have nots were still so far apart. It was also related to the pervasive criminality that infected everyone's life so deeply.

This was far from all that had to be weighed up. It was no secret that certain invaluable members of the prime minister's political advisory staff had been excluded from the travelling party after the intervention of the political secretary, Marcia Williams. It was hardly my business, but Bill Housden in his role as valet and baggage master had an inside story to confide.

Having frightened Mr Wilson before he left the UK with inside stories of an impending left-wing revolt among Labour back benchers, Mrs Williams had now telephoned overnight and reduced the prime minister to a state of anxiety and panic.

The PM had left his room in a state which embarrassed even the normally unshakeable Bill Housden. If this was the start of something big we needed to look for further symptoms and be prepared for a roller coaster future.

Although there were no rumours yet in the media, might it perhaps lead to a tactical resignation?

SIX

Winston Churchill advised me to establish a personal link with someone in the Politburo. I have remained in touch with Mikoyan ever since.

Harold Wilson to the author, January 1975

When the prime minister travelled abroad, the role of his protection team was technically modified. Instead of being the last line of physical defence, we became liaison officers and handed over direct responsibility to the host security service.

Sometimes the duty was undertaken by a presidential bodyguard such as the US Secret Service; in other countries, France for example, there was a special unit of the national police (*Services de Voyages Officiels*) responsible exclusively for protecting foreign dignitaries; elsewhere the squad might be directed by the military. The point is that procedures abroad were rarely uniform.

It demanded experience on our part and, as a safeguard, one of the Scotland Yard team usually travelled in advance. This was not only to provide the host country with a programme and details of the composition of the prime minister's delegation, but also to give information on his habits and idiosyncrasies, his blood group, the names of his enemies and other routine matters, as well as to check that his bodyguard-for-the-time-being was up to the task.

This was no problem in North America, or the West German Republic where after the 1970s promptings by terrorists such as the Red Army Faction, the Federal Police had been brought to a peak of efficiency then unique among Europeans. The rapid expansion of international terrorist activities was to ensure, however, that we all rapidly followed their lead.

Our task was to protect the 'Boss' at all costs and this absolute requirement sometimes had to take precedence over diplomatic niceties, personal susceptibilities, and established routines whenever we were dissatisfied with appointed foreign bodyguards. In other words, there were times when we did the job ourselves, if the home team was inadequate.

This was the background as we travelled with the prime minister and his foreign secretary, James Callaghan, for an official visit to Canada and the United States in 1975. Both the RCMP and the US Secret Service were well known to us and respected for their efficiency.

There was a problem, however. In those days, they absolutely detested one another. It started when the Canadians let it be known they were going to play the protection game by firm rules. They would not bring their guns to your country and under no circumstances could you take a weapon into Canada. This did not suit the Americans. During one official visit, when the Canadians laid down the law, the US Secret Service pretended to comply and then shipped in a considerable arsenal through the diplomatic bag. Unfortunately for them they got caught and all hell had broken loose between the two countries.

We were able to sit back sympathetically, even a little smugly, as the Mounties confided with dread tales of misbehaviour by the Americans, and later when the Secret Service complained of lack of co-operation from the Canadians. Echoes from this clash had reached us through diplomatic circles in London while we were still in the planning stage. There was much to be considered before leaving and our role as potential peacemaker was just a small part of a long checklist.

To be effective, proper travel arrangements, food and accommodation had to be guaranteed, and the experienced No 10 machine took care of all that. But clothing was down to us and we were warned by the Foreign Office that North American winter weather represented a serious health hazard. It would be damp, dark, snowy and very cold. We took advice from old hands and Scotland Yard's civil staff – still incredibly known as, 'Clothing and Saddlery Branch' – and made an appointment with Moss Bros in Long Acre.

As usual, the gentlemen of the press had got there first and taken all the best gear but, nevertheless, we hired heavy, wool-lined leather gloves, classic fur hats with ear protection, rubber overshoes, and monstrously large 'Crazy Gang' fur coats reaching to within a few inches of the ground.

Dress rehearsals in our office in No 10 were sweaty, struggling, panting affairs, and much to the amusement of our uniformed colleagues. We found that overshoes had to be strained into place before climbing into a heavy overcoat. Otherwise, attempts to reach down to a foot with coat and hat on led to incapacitating overheating and, eventually, total insensibility. Suitably attired, and fully briefed, we arrived at Ottawa queasy with jet lag.

The 'Mounties' are a super-efficient police service with the great advantage of having coast-to-coast responsibility. This meant, in effect, that just one detective was with us throughout as liaison, and he could call upon local officers according to particular needs, uniformed or plain clothes, mobile or on foot, who all had co-ordinated training and equipment and used identical radio techniques. This produced an efficient operation far surpassing anything we had been able to complement at home, where Special Branch was only one part of the Metropolitan Police, itself one of some forty constabularies – most of whom operated under different and often confusing guidelines.

The RCMP personal bodyguard was chosen for his formidable physical presence; he had an objective, final line-of-defence role and neither he nor any of his colleagues could remotely have been considered 'personal attendants', a professional sickness which undermined the effectiveness of some personal protection task-forces in the UK. In RCMP hands, we were content to leave our firearms under seal with the RAF.

The chief of the Canadian team followed in the first escort vehicle, broadcasting continuously to the whole squad. They had done their preventive work well – checking routes and buildings, making sure bridges and high vantage points were controlled – but all other events were the subject of a cautionary broadcast by personal radio, even providing details of overtaking vehicles or warnings of suspiciously parked cars. This helped to ensure that anything unusual, not already pre-empted or the subject of current broadcast would automatically be treated as suspicious.

It was a valuable technique generating enthusiasm to the whole squad. Even the motorcycle escort – on three-wheelers because of icy conditions, and with electric-blanket type jackets plugged into batteries – were alert and vigilant and making regular passes and inspections along the convoy, instead of forming the usual decorative arrow-formation in the vanguard.

A common denominator in North America was the slow pace of motorcades. Both USA and Canada operated draconian speed limits and urban traffic as a whole moved at an ordered pace as a result. Protection experts had stuffed so much bullet and bomb proofing into the VIP vehicles that they were a straightforward danger in their own right at speeds above 45mph. Instead of the frenetic motorcades to which we had become used to in Europe, screaming, hooting, skidding, hectic affairs, often hazardous even without an enemy in sight, we became accustomed to a new version: a steady, physically protected, highly armoured, vigilant, and intimidating procession of limousines, but with little or no acceleration or fast cornering capability for use in emergencies.

Uniformed Mounties were posted at strategic points, dressed in winter garb, stylish grey fur overcoats and hats. There were few signs of activity from the public, who had wisely retired to the warmth of their homes in the face of tinglingly low temperatures, grey-black skies, and streets lined with heaps of dirty snow. Families skating under floodlights on the frozen river provided an isolated moment of cheer in a winter expected to last the best part of six months.

The delegation was housed in Rideau Hall, the official residence of the governor-general of Canada, constructed in elegant colonial style in the early nineteenth century and purchased for government use some thirty years later.

We were in the charge of Mrs 'Bubbles' Blair, the curator who was in communication – sometimes in secret – with her opposite numbers in Blair House, the president's guest house in Washington, and Chequers. They rarely met but maintained channels of efficient communication to exchange up-to-date information about the idiosyncrasies of their latest guests. The distinguished list of those for whom she had cared included shahs and kings and princes by the score, and there was many a tale she could have told of late night climbs over the dormitory wall by celebrities who should have known better than to get caught – but she was far too discreet to do so.

It was soon time to say farewell to Bubbles Blair and pocket her highly confidential notes for Vera Thomas, the curator at Chequers. I expect it was just a lot of sneaky gossip about our behaviour.

The VIP lounge at Ottawa Airport was overcrowded and we steamed in gorilla outfits as the delay was extended again. Although there were no security scares in Canada it was not too late for drama.

It was only a one-hour flight south to Andrews US Air Force Base where protocol was all plugged-in, and the guard of honour polished, ready to welcome the British prime minister to Washington. Meanwhile, it was a black night at Ottawa, with a steady snowfall and obscenely low outdoor temperatures. The VC10, parked on the apron, had a severe dose of airframe icing and was declared unairworthy by the captain.

Commercial flights were still operating and disappearing into blanket-cloud soon after take off. On the ground, aircraft were kept ice-free either by parking in a hangar or by a de-icing processor built on the lines of a large vacuum cleaner working in reverse and ducting a heated airflow to melt accumulated ice on the fuselage.

Nobody had one to hire at first, and the delegation was an embarrassing ninety minutes adrift as we finally boarded in a hurry, nervously watching ice crystals re-forming on the fuselage of the VC10. After some tense minutes, it was a relief to climb above turbulence to cruise level and divest ourselves temporarily of a half-hundredweight of fur coat and hat.

The aircraft descended through still skies as we strapped-in for the approach to Andrews. Morale was improving. Then, without warning, at 500ft the VC10 was struck by furious buffeting and turbulence. Even the hard-nosed regular globe-trotters from the Foreign Office looked as though this was as near as they would get to an index-linked pension, while the slightly tanked-up journalists in the rear section belatedly tried to promote a working relationship with the Almighty.

The captain fought to hold the VC10 straight for the round-out but, confronted with the yawing effect of a furious crosswind, was forced to apply full power and go around again. Technically this was a big deal.

We all firmly believed that RAF Special Flights had the finest safety record for passenger aircraft anywhere in the world and overshoots are virtually unknown. But residual tension left from Ottawa spread and now multiplied through the whole passenger cabin as we climbed above 500ft into calm air and turned for a second approach.

The captain and his crew now did their own calculations and decided to approach the single runway from the opposite direction, their conclusion being that the severe crosswind would then have less adverse effect. There was not a more favoured cross-runway to choose at Andrews and the captain exercised his right to make the final selection in spite of advice from air traffic control. This was very serious stuff.

The second approach seemed as furious as the first, but somehow the captain held the aircraft straight, just above the runway, until she settled bumpily but safe, with reverse thrust slowing the aircraft in the absence of any useful headwind. With great relief we extracted ourselves from fallen hand-baggage. The prime minister joined spontaneous and genuine applause for the crew. Moving rapidly from cold sweat status, we hurriedly clawed back into our winter clothing.

This was a mistake. The gangway was run-up and, fully Moss Bros-clad, we descended into a temperature of 80° Fahrenheit. State Department officials, Secret Service agents and motorcade outriders were all looking positively uncomfortable in lightweight suits, even with full air conditioning switched on in limousines. We were laughably incapacitated until, secure in the relative privacy of a car we struggled to disrobe partially, but not until the ordeal of the welcoming ceremony was over, during which national anthems lasted an eternity. The hasty guard-of-honour inspection could have been practised in a Turkish bath.

As the motorcade edged onto the Freeway, with warning whoops from sirens, searchlights focusing on black spots, hunting outriders marshalling civilian vehicles clear, and many 'Ten-Four' (i.e., 'Message Received') exclamations from the bodyguard detail into almost invisible personal radios, we were belatedly briefed on the weather. While Canada was getting its expected winter, Washington was under the unusual influence of a super-warm 'Chinook' airflow down from the Allegheny Mountains. This created severe low-level turbulence and perspiringly high temperatures. There was no way we could avoid being overdressed for a few days, but the embassy was good enough to supply a heavy truck with a bucket attachment to get our gear safely back aboard and stowed in the luggage hold labelled, 'No Longer Required on Voyage'.

The dust seemed to have settled but we had not reckoned with our friends from the press. Short of any other drama, Fleet Street criticised the captain's decision to overshoot the first landing attempt. He was relieved of his command, but re-instated after the subsequent enquiry (or was it a full court martial?) declared he had acted correctly.

If there was any doubt, he could certainly have called upon a prime minister, a foreign secretary, and forty members of their staff for character references especially when we learned the VC10 had been within an ace of a fatal, crosswind stall during the first approach.

<hr />

The ceremony of welcome on the lawn of the White House called for precise timing. The efficient Secret Service detail of forty men allocated to protect Prime Minister Wilson ensured that the motorcade wheeled past the heavily guarded entrance precisely on schedule.

President Ford met the prime minister and conducted him to the dais, from which they viewed the crew-cut model soldiers strutting before them. Later there was a visit to Arlington Cemetery to respect the late President Kennedy and lay a wreath at the Tomb of the Unknown Soldier. Nearby is the final resting place of the president's brother, Robert – also assassinated – with a fountain and slate backdrop carved with moving prose commending service to the community and sacrifice for the nation. Underneath is a notice commanding, 'DON'T THROW PENNIES IN THE POOL!'

Lunch was at the Washington Press Club, where the prime minister spoke on British foreign policy as it related to the United States. We met archetypical American journalists – self-styled tough-guys, overweight, aggressively self-confident and gesticulating assertively through barely penetrable cigar smoke screens. A visit to United Nations Headquarters left me with the conviction that the best career for my children, with guarantees of sky-high, tax-free salaries and total security, was that of international civil servant.

By the time the prime minister was left at the White House in 'white tie' for the evening dinner, it had been possible to absorb some of the scope of the security industry in Washington, a city which then had more than a million unemployables and has since become Number One Murder City in the United States. I suppose that means they are also World Champions.

Most shops had bars or mesh over the windows to hinder breakage and theft, and yet violent robberies and gunshot resistance were commonplace. Banks had locked doors, with electronically controlled entrances and protection from armed guards. The acceptance of publicly displayed firearms is absolute.

As I strolled the hundred yards or so back from the White House toward our guesthouse, the police prowl car which had led us to the set-down point stopped to offer a lift. 'Gentlemen,' I protested, 'I only have fifty yards to walk.' 'Look,' said the driver. 'Nobody walks in Washington if they can ride. C'mon. We'll show you the town while they're in there eating.'

Steve Mann and his partner Van Denton generously enrolled me as a third member of the team for the next few hours, and demonstrated tough humour and energetic, laid-back professionalism normally confined to Hollywood or television productions.

'D'ya wanta see the real White House, Jahn? C'mon. We're gonna show you something ya'll never see walkin' around.'

Within a half-mile we entered the decrepit, partly burned-down section of the city. Five-year-old riot damage had been cleared but never rebuilt. The occupants were mainly black and the few white hookers on the streets were transvestite men. The 'White House' was a derelict multi-story one-time hotel. At the entrance two enterprising clerks had erected a barrier that cost clients a dollar to pass. There was no water or electricity and the three of us patrolled through the rubble and faeces-strewn corridors with illumination only from official torches. The building was collapsing in places and few rooms had doors. It was the only hotel in the United States with 'Muzak' and was unaromatically perfumed with urine.

But it was a 'Full House'. Couples were sleeping on filthy furniture, while startled alcoholics slurped from bottles. There were illicit card schools in candlelight, and dark rooms with stunned occupants and discarded hypodermic syringes on the floors. 'Chicks' and 'dudes' were clutching and heaving in doorless cupboard space – homosexual duos careless of interruption.

'What is the city doing to rehabilitate all these unfortunates,' I enquired ingenuously.

'Rehabilitate these M-Fs!' shouted Steve incredulously. 'Ya've gotta remember this is TOTAL WAR, Jahn. The city puts us in the Front Line and we SUPPRESS THEM!'

With whistles shrilling and sirens screaming, we sped off to the next spot on their tourist trail, with three radios blaring and diversions to respond to urgent calls. Policing technique was to saturate the area with 'mobiles' and each unit responded to as many calls as possible. In the UK a car gets allocated to deal with a particular emergency and is struck off the availability list until initial investigation is complete and a report made. In Washington, an emergency call could get a response at times from twenty mobile units, including officers in uniform or plain clothes on mopeds, who were able to thread their way through heavy traffic when larger units were blocked out.

The various vehicles clustered round the suspect building with emergency lights flashing. With no thought of discreet approach, it was as subtle as artillery at El Alamein. A dozen officers went thundering through a building until the immediate emergency was located and dealt with – and then exited in a counter-surge, unless just one was required to make a report. Off went the whole squadron, patrolling and straining for the next 'shout'. Morale was high but all hoped for an injury-on-duty serious enough to qualify for an early pension without unreasonable disablement, and before their turn came on the roster to get shot dead.

'Ten-Four,' responded Van into the third radio, and we headed for a reported homicide. 'You'd better have your gun ready here, Jahn,' cautioned Steve as we de-bussed and swept through a tenement where a grandmother had been beaten to death by her grandson wielding a length of gas pipe – attacked when there was no more cash to give. Light was dim and bloodstains fresh. Witnesses were being grilled and suspects frisked against walls in half-light. Onlookers crowded inquisitively, avoiding eye contact. Within minutes an investigating detective had arrived by moped and taken command and we were released back to the street.

'Let's go Alleycatting,' Steve invited after swerving to avoid 'that goddamn pimpmobile,' a flashy sedan with white-wall tyres, multitudes of chrome modifications, driven by a smooth black 'dude' with white beribboned trilby, smoking a king-sized cigarette.

'Alleycatting' involved leaving the main boulevard to crunch through narrow rear alleys. Garbage was thrown directly from upper windows and never cleared. It piled 10ft high in places before degenerating into some unholy sort of compost. There was rarely enough width for the prowl car, which had to be headed toward the lowest heaps at high revs. Steve stopped at a T-junction and shone the spotlight into a dark area.

'Just look at them Goddam rats, Jahn! They're so big even the cats round here get scared!'

I saw what he meant. Then a firm command – 'Jeez! There's them goddam dawgs again, Van. Don't try to get out now Jahn, unless you want to lose your goddam legs!'

A pack of marauding dogs was scavenging through the garbage. They were strays – ranging from Alsatian down to Jack Russell – ganged up together for protection, apparently friendly to one another but prepared to convert humans into instant Pedigree Pal.

As promised, Steve Mann dropped me at the official White House in good time to collect the prime minister and Mrs Wilson for the return to Blair House. Steve and his partner had succeeded in impressing me with sights rarely seen by visitors to the capital of the 'free enterprise' world. Even US-critical diehard old socialists in the delegation were dewy-eyed with the fine sights of Washington – and there are plenty – and seemed sceptical of the scenes I had witnessed. Many of the embassy staff were frankly disbelieving. 'You must understand we never go to that quarter of Washington,' was their dismissive response.

And so, I suppose, did it not officially exist? Perhaps after all I was a victim of George Orwell's Thought Police in his book *1984*.

The president's guests stay at Blair House in a dignified, elderly terrace opposite the White House. Security is absolute and the American obsession with 'sterile' conditions is nowhere more complete. There is a constant patrol of coloured domestics, dusting and swabbing, wiping and polishing, and patrolling the corridors with replacement towels every time one of the sixteen issued for each guest had been used. The complete range of 'Arden-For-Men' is in the bathroom cabinet. There are all shades of talcum powder, every strength of pre- and aftershave, and deodorant, shampoos, hair creams and lotions for parts of the body only recently discovered.

Bowls of succulent fruit are displayed in all public rooms, as well as in each bedroom, and coffee or cola are always available. It is well known that many Americans, being addicted to fast-food, have lost the use of their taste buds, and the cuisine in these luxurious surroundings is as indifferent as that in internationally despised Metropolitan Police canteens. The gravy is worse.

However, ritual toilet sterilisation and sheet, towel, and bathrobe replacement continue throughout most of each day and much of the night.

The prime minister's rooms were on the first floor. The bedroom faced the road at the front and there was a study and lounge at the rear. On a previous visit there had been a 'scare' when police discovered an armed gunman on a nearby rooftop and, as a precaution, they cleared the front rooms of Blair House.

Bill Housden was with the prime minister that day, sheltering in the study after a substantial lunch with drinks, when the PM's principal private secretary Robert Armstrong came to discuss matters of state importance. Although Bill was, as we know, one of the more important men in the delegation, Robert Armstrong was technically his boss and Bill tactfully withdrew. Without thinking, he exited through the bedroom door to the front of the building and, following well-established precedents, stretched out for a nap on Harold Wilson's bed.

He woke in a sweat, suddenly remembering the 'armed-intruder' warning and feeling horribly vulnerable to an assassin's shot through the window. Instinctively, he sheltered the vulnerable parts of his expansive body and shimmied inelegantly to the floor and the protection of the bed. Following defensive tactics learned from Hollywood films, Bill crawled on all fours toward safety. Keeping his head low, he reached up to turn the handle and ease open the door to the study.

At this cringingly low eye level he saw a pair of shoes attached to sturdy Yorkshire legs as the prime minister admonished, 'There's really no need to go that far Bill. A little curtsey would have done!'

As we packed for departure, newcomers were unsure whether the 'Arden-For-Men' was theirs or not. But Bill was in no doubt. 'If you don't take it the staff will,' he assured everyone from the standpoint of a lifetime of perquisite collection, stuffing aerosols and cans and packets and containers in hand baggage brought along empty for the purpose. With Bill around, you had to be agile, as the prime minister discovered when he looked for some aftershave and found his cabinet empty.

Bill explained to the security operator at the airport when his baggage electronically displayed contents resembling 100 or so variously assorted explosive canisters, 'I'm taking most of this stuff back on the prime minister's behalf.'

One of my colleagues was less lucky. His wife never forgave him for suspected infidelity when he arrived home at Twickenham smelling unusually, indiscreetly and overwhelmingly of Blue Grass lotion.

⟹•⟸

RAF Brize Norton, our scheduled destination airfield, was firmly fogbound and we diverted to Gatwick at midnight. The crew made it clear they were being put to great inconvenience by not landing at their home base. Gatwick Airport sprung to action at the unexpected midnight arrival of the prime minister and put a VIP lounge at the disposal of the delegation. This was just as well, as the RAF crew promptly locked up their aircraft and disappeared to a hotel – their responsibility being technically over.

The main problem was that the road transport was at Brize Norton and the prime minister, his foreign secretary and all their staff, including several knights of the realm, were immobile at Gatwick. Nobody was happy until, in shining armour, the Sussex Constabulary galloped over the horizon with cars and baggage transport and rail information, and quickly sorted out a mountain of problems. James Callaghan commandeered a patrol car to drive to his farm in Sussex and another unit was reserved for the prime minister.

About one hundred phone calls got the weary delegates on the move as official cars painfully crawled from Brize Norton to London for redeployment.

A Black Maria was soon on the scene to get Bill Housden and the No 10 baggage securely back to London; and traffic cops stood by to take Mr Wilson to wherever he decided to go. He finally made up his mind to go to Chequers.

The No 10 duty clerk was told to inform both the curator there and the Thames Valley police unit responsible for guarding the premises. The road journey was likely to take about an hour and a half.

Two uniformed policemen, who had started an average tour of duty patrolling the motorways, finished up with the prime minister and the authority to head for Chequers. With his luggage aboard, the PM and I got in the rear seats. He offered me a cigar and we lit up, safe in the hands of a couple of professionals. Visibility was soon thicker in than out. The prime minister wanted to talk.

For the next hour or so he went into detail of his time as a young minister in the Board of Trade with the post-war Labour government under Attlee. When he led a trade delegation to Moscow, Winston Churchill asked to see him. His message was that the Iron Curtain was being lowered more firmly every day and Cold War was inevitable. He regarded trade between the Soviets and the free western alliance as the only way to penetrate this Iron Curtain and maintain and perhaps even improve relations. He advised Harold Wilson, as an emerging left winger with good socialist credentials, to try to establish a personal relationship with some Politburo leader of influence so that unofficial communication could continue if – as he anticipated – formal diplomatic relations were interrupted.

The prime minister told me that he could see the sense of this and was fortunate in meeting and spending private as well as official time with the head of the Russian talks, Comrade Anastas Mikoyan. They both negotiated robustly, but got on well together socially and, he claimed, they still maintained a personal friendship. So useful had this personal contact become, that he regarded himself as the best agent the Israeli government ever had, because he had never since travelled to the Soviet Union without a list of Jewish-Soviet political detainees for whom the Israelis were asking unsuccessfully for exit papers. In return he was able to offer the Soviets certain 'concessions' on behalf of the Israeli government.

He went no further. I was left wondering why he had decided to give me this particular insight into a small part of his political life. Moreover, it was current stuff and not just for history books. Did he want or expect me to pass this story along? And, if so, to whom? It was not like him to talk about today's affairs without some point. After a talk with Arthur Smith, we decided to do nothing.

Subsequent speculation and disclosure have put this incident into better perspective. Harold Wilson was deeply suspicious of his Security Service MI5, and not without good reason. MI5 was then dominated by right-wing thinkers, some with extreme political agendas, and without the necessary balance of moderates and left wingers. He may have been made aware that individual officers such as Peter Wright, the later author of *Spycatcher*, were assembling an argument that Harold Wilson was a Soviet agent, holding secret allegiance or obligation to communist ideology. The right-wing media were only too willing to disseminate smears against Wilson's character, his relationship with Marcia Williams, and inferences about his disloyalty.

Perhaps the prime minister hoped I would be able to set the record straight within the secret services? If so, I failed to help out. This was probably cleverer than intended because I was in danger of getting well out of my depth in the murky world of Whitehall rumour, secret service paranoia and even international espionage. Usually, undocumented sources are firm in claiming that unpleasant sanctions can be applied very secretly – even to British subjects.

On the balance of probabilities, it now seems likely that the 'concessions' offered by Harold Wilson on the Israelis' behalf were nothing more than large-scale bribery. Would another piece of the mystery slot into place if it were discovered that the late, ill-fated Robert Maxwell, proprietor of the *Daily Mirror* and Pergamon Press, who drowned in unexplained circumstances having fallen from the back of his yacht in deep Atlantic waters, was the cash courier?

Say no more!

———⟫·◦·⟪———

The final act was a call to my office from a bewildered senior officer from Sussex Constabulary asking if any light could be thrown on a complaint from No 10 that police had failed to provide adequate resources for the prime minister at the Gatwick diversion.

This absurd and unreasonable allegation was quickly dispatched to the wastepaper basket. But the incident remained filed in my memory in red, under 'C' for Caution. Senior civil servants, for whom I often had an above-average respect, could behave just as unreasonably as anyone else under pressure it seemed.

But was the pressure in this case due to their personal discomfort at being late and tired, without transport and having to play second fiddle to politicians – or were they echoing a complaint from the prime minister? In either case, it was an attempt to Pass-Very-Dangerous-Parcels into the laps of loyal and unsuspecting policemen.

And a lesson to me to remain vigilant, and to take no one at face value!

SEVEN

Well, I've cracked it today, John. I got right through to twenty-seven at last!

Harold Wilson to the author

Two Rover limousines from No 10 drove in convoy through London's Friday evening rush hour traffic, threading west along the A40. Harold Wilson was a rear seat passenger in the first and I was the duty bodyguard for a weekend at Chequers. In the second, a Garden Room girl had control of the baggage, her secretarial paraphernalia and a secret codebook. Two Downing Street switchboard ladies travelled with her.

Inevitably, we came to an outer lane halt as a pile-up somewhere ahead backed up traffic. The prime minister dozed. As he drooped there was a noticeable smell of burning. Ash falling from his cigar was singeing the rear seat cover. Bill Housden pointed to the inner lane, where a Jaguar driver managed to dodge just in front of a large ballast lorry. Both were forced to a standstill as the queue built up. A very large and very angry driver got slowly and purposefully out of his car, calmly walked back, opened the door of the lorry cab and punched the driver in the face. He lit a cigarette before calmly walking back and climbing into his Jaguar. The lorry driver was either the guilty party in the example of road rage, or unconscious. Situation normal – no panic.

As the Rover left the Metropolitan Police district I cleared our radio contact with Scotland Yard and selected a new channel on the Home Office radio. Thames Valley Police Control Room replied loud and clear. Thames Valley was responsible for physical security of the Chequers estate and our standing pre-emptive arrangements were simple but effective. I notified them in code of the chosen route through their manor, which gate the PM would be entering and the estimated time of arrival. For Chequers weekends this quiet, undramatic approach was favoured over the heavily armed and escorted alternative, calling for multi-manpower, flashing lights and screaming sirens that sometimes merely served to identify the location of a target.

Mr Wilson's week had been harassing. He was becoming more ambivalent about this second term of office, sometimes claiming more time for relaxation now that he had enough experience to delegate much of the workload. On other occasions he would say how much he disliked parliamentary Question Time although by general agreement he held comfortable ascendancy over the Leader of the Opposition, Margaret Thatcher, in the cut and thrust of House of Commons debate. Mr Wilson was also favouring less beer and more brandy. He was looking older.

As early as 1975 a few nods and winks came in our direction that the prime minister might not want to serve his full term of about four years. These, together with other signs of uncertainty and deteriorating health and strength – perhaps more visible to the detectives than others within his inner circle – alerted us to the possibility of change well before it eventually materialised. The fact that the media failed to get wind of his thinking indicated that this was not shared with Labour Party HQ or colleagues, although it seemed certain that Private Office and his trusted political advisers were at least being consulted.

Hanging over all this was the split in the party about Labour's future relationship with the European community, at a time when, paradoxically in the light of future events, the main guaranteed support for remaining within came from the Conservative Opposition.

In retrospect, and with Mr Wilson's increasing paranoia over the British security services and belief in a media campaign against him, it seems unbelievable that not once was I debriefed at Special Branch. Nor was I ever approached for insider information by reporters or journalists. It would be satisfying to claim that the political objectivity within which our SB unit worked was too clearly marked for investigative writers even to imagine that we might be able to provide sources inside No 10. But with the clear relationship between Special Branch and the security services, the detectives *could* have been a critical source of insider information in the media's quest to label Mr Wilson as a communist agent. So either MI5 were *not* conspiring against him or they were content, as subsequently alleged, to invent their own smear stories.

During a walk together later in the weekend, the prime minister made clear his opinion of MI5. After he had outlined his concerns about recent heckling and near violence at a meeting addressed by his Home Secretary Roy Jenkins, I seized the chance to try to explain to him the problems of policing public meetings, thanks to the embargo placed on uniformed officers entering until called to do so by the chairman. Their intervention was then usually too late to be pre-emptive, leaving incipient violence more difficult to control. By the time they were called in, a professional amalgam of political impartiality on one hand, and the firmness expected from uniformed officers on another, was difficult to establish successfully.

For an hour or so we were back to a Scilly Isles relationship. First of all it was impossible for me to judge whether or not he was serious about his expressed concerns for the Roy Jenkins predicament. It was not like the prime minister to talk directly in the first instance. I had to remember that he could have been mildly pleased that the man tipped to step into his shoes was not having things all his own way. Then, as I tried to expand on the police dilemma, he kept interrupting, anticipating – usually wrongly – what I was about to explain. I, too, had a hidden motive and that was to try to persuade him, obliquely and in advance to curtail his own public speaking programme, especially during any forthcoming election or European referendum campaign.

All this fencing proved pointless when he finally pronounced, unequivocally: 'Yes, I understand what you are getting at. If a policeman is firm *or* polite he may well look forward to promotion. If he is both, he will apply for Special Branch. And if neither he will join the Security Service.'

Against this background, relaxed weekends at Chequers became increasingly significant to Harold Wilson. The assets provided aggregated in every direction. There was space and peace, outdoor walks, nearby pubs, churches and a golf course. Communications were first class but duty clerks and private secretaries were left in No 10 and paperwork minimised – although not completely absent. The food was good, rooms comfortable, and staff helpful and plentiful. Mrs Wilson – when she cared to spend time there too – was also removed from all domestic commitments. Family and friends could join in by invitation. An excellent indoor swimming pool had been donated by Walter Annenberg, former US Ambassador, and opened by President Nixon. Facilities for conferences or symposia were first class if needed, and a Garden Room girl was always there to take dictation.

Above all, perhaps, Marcia Williams' home was ten minutes away at Great Missenden. Although we usually got adequate advance notice of walks, or drinks, or church, or swimming, it was for unscheduled trips to see her that the detectives had to remain alert. When the phone call came from the prime minister's rooms after lunch on some Sundays, it was not a good time to be missing. Once at her detached and rather upmarket house, it was one of the very few times that no provision was made for us to wait around in comfort – and that included the otherwise specially privileged Bill Housden.

But do not read too much into this as yet. I remain convinced that the hours spent at Great Missenden or in Mrs Williams' apartment on the Scillys, were invaluable to both of them – obsessed as they were with the real love of their lives – political machination. Moreover, there was a referendum on the Common Market to discuss and plan. It was a bonus to be able to do so out of the hearing of any third party and in total and complete confidence. Of course, if you were looking for an alternative, it was not difficult to come to another conclusion. The media favoured the easy alternative and obliquely tried to make real capital out of it.

—————➤•◄———————

Everyone knows that Chequers is the country seat of the prime minister but not a lot more. Wonderfully situated in the Chiltern Hills and within a ninety-minute drive from central London, it has all the assets of privacy, quiet countryside, comfort mixed with modern amenity, and a real sense of history.

Evidence exists of settlement as long ago as the Roman occupation, but the present south-facing building dates mainly from the sixteenth century. As with so many great English country houses, owners invariably became involved in matters of state, and the complexities of royal succession. In the religious and constitutional aftermath of Henry VIII's death, for example, the owner of Chequers, then William Hawtree, was ordered to take into his custody Lady Mary Grey, a potential claimant to the throne and she was incarcerated for two years in a small upper floor garret, now called 'The Prison Room'. It was sometimes used for guests. Garden Room girls occasionally slept there but resistance became evident as word spread that it was haunted and subject to sudden, unexplained and rather intimidating drops in temperature.

As ownership changed over the centuries, extensions and alterations took place, with the last major overhaul being undertaken by the philanthropists, Arthur and his wealthy American wife Ruth (later Lord and Lady Lee of Fareham). Of all the long-term alterations the most significant was probably the work to roof over the courtyard and the conversion of the space into the Great Hall, overlooked by the Long Gallery.

Before the Chequers Trust was established in 1917 – when the entire property was donated to the nation for the use of the prime minster of the day – the Lees completely overhauled and renovated the building. They acquired every conceivable artefact that money could buy and distinguished the interior with classic good taste and elegance. The standards they set have been faithfully maintained in accordance with the preamble to the Trust Deed – quoted by Norma Major in her excellent publication, *Chequers – The Prime Minister's Country House and its History*, from which the following is an extract:

It is not possible to foresee or foretell from what classes or conditions of life the future wielders of power in this country will be drawn. Some may be, as in the past, men of wealth and famous descent; some may belong to the world of trade and business; others may spring from the ranks of the manual toilers. To none of these in the midst of their strenuous and responsible labours, could the spirit and anodyne of Chequers do anything but good. In the city-bred men especially, the periodic contact with the most typical rural life would create and preserve a just sense of proportion between the claims of town and country. To the revolutionary statesman the antiquity and calm tenacity of Chequers and its annals might suggest some saving virtues in the continuity of English history and exercise a check upon too hasty upheavals, while even the most revolutionary could scarcely be insensible to the spirit of human freedom which permeates the countryside of Hampden, Burke and Milton [...]

Surely there are messages here from the idealistic and generous Lees to today's politicians and their special advisers?

After a lowly start in life, with his family impoverished after the death of his father, Arthur Lee suffered from cruelty and bullying at Cheltenham College. However, he was able to enter the Royal Military College at Woolwich, joining the Royal Artillery as a second lieutenant three years later. In the army he rose to the rank of lieutenant colonel and was posted as military attaché at the British Embassy in Washington. It was at this time that he met and fell in love with Ruth Moore, daughter of a wealthy American banker.

They married in 1899 and, backed by her inherited money, settled in England, where he was elected Conservative Member of Parliament for Fareham, in Hampshire. The Lees first acquired a lease to Chequers in 1909 and after tortuous legal negotiations were finally able to purchase the estate in 1917. The money inherited by Ruth and her sister was used for the purchase and they were effectively the owners. However, in a remarkable display of confidence in Arthur's probity, they gave the house and estate to him. In turn, they drew up a scheme – as a result of which he gave the property to the nation as a country seat for British prime ministers. The sisters were willing parties to this and the family retained the right to live in the buildings too.

The first prime minister to be invited to benefit from the offer was Lloyd George in 1917, during the First World War. He wrote to Arthur Lee in September: 'Future generations of PMs will think with gratitude of the impulse which has thus prompted you so generously to place this beautiful mansion at their disposal.'

The disparity between an unsuitable Downing Street and the wonderfully situated and equipped Chequers was absolute. While some visitors to London may look with derision at No 10, Chequers is the envy of every discerning guest welcomed there by British prime ministers.

On a practical everyday level, much of the land is now let for arable farming. The estate is skirted to the south by a stretch of the Ridgeway Walk, a public footpath. In the 1970s a small rise gave the best view of the front of the house and a vantage point for mortar or ground-to-ground missile attack. It took many months and much concentrated legal analysis before a short diversion reduced the risk of attack and the concerns of patrolling Thames Valley police officers.

With beech woods and coppices spread around the estate, Chequers is in the midst of the English countryside which the Lees thought to be of such importance. It also creates extraordinary difficulties in ensuring its protection from attack. To meet any threat, this calls for extraordinary defences. Uniformed, well communicated and properly equipped police officers conduct vigorous but discreet patrols and lookouts. Although the public are not admitted into the main building, a suitable police response team is posted inside the building at night when the prime minister is in residence. The area round the house is extensively monitored electronically with systems designed by Home Office scientists in various very clever ways. The sensors are directly connected to a permanent mini police station in a suitable building nearby the main house. As a final resort close liaison is established with special military forces.

Metropolitan Special Branch kept Thames Valley involved in necessary intelligence, and liaised personally with the local constabulary. Our task at Chequers was not uncomfortable. We retained overall responsibility for the prime minister's personal safety at all times. The system worked well and was overseen by the understanding presence of Thames Valley chief constable, Peter Imbert (now Lord Imbert), himself a former SB officer with the Met.

The garden and grounds were maintained by a small civilian staff but the inside of the main house was entirely the responsibility of the armed forces. *La suprema* was Squadron Leader Vera Thomas, a spinster lady retired from the Women's Auxiliary Air Force (WAAF). She dedicated herself to self-preservation by toadying to the prime minister while criticising him behind his back – and marginalising his staff. It did not make her popular or an integral part of an otherwise smoothly running machine. She was obstructive to me and my team and we did not get on. Indeed, the only uncooperative staff connected with the smooth operation of the Downing Street machine that I encountered in six years were her and the No 10 housekeeper, Peter Taylor, another pensioner from the RAF. My last-ditch resort in extreme cases was the principal private secretary, whose firm mediation could always be relied upon, but I tried to deal with these two on a person-to-person basis – just about managing to hold on to enough of my own sphere of responsibility to remain on top of the job. It was a surprise to discover after my retirement that these two individuals were equally difficult with Private Office.

Morale among the WAAFs and the Women's Royal Naval Service (WRENs) at Chequers was often lowered by the 'skivvy' status imposed on them and they were generally pleased to welcome more balanced personalities with the arrival of the prime minister and his Downing Street support team.

Vera Thomas delegated through Dot, a brisk, serving Chief Petty Officer WREN, whose friendly help prevented an outright declaration of war with her overlady. The staff, all WRENs or WAAFs, were kept hard at it maintaining in pristine condition a usually empty house, dozens of bedrooms and sitting rooms, conference rooms and passages, ready for the prime minister and guests. Occasionally they had to dispose of saucy books discovered, forgotten, under bedroom pillows. It was all in a day's work and covered by the Official Secrets Acts.

The cuisine was masterminded by a flight sergeant cook from the RAF. He was brilliant, innovative and resourceful – but not always uncomplaining as his carefully planned timetable to maximise selected dishes was ruined by barbarous politicians worrying about incidentals such as state bankruptcy or four-minute missile counterattack.

Walks around the estate were on a descending scale. Harold Wilson took frequent advantage of strolls through the local beech woods and – on occasion – into one of the local village pubs. Many a family enjoying their picnic just off the Ridgeway would look up, guilty and startled with hard boiled eggs and cold bacon butties still in hand, as he burst from a thicket. For an hour or two he was back to the pleasant informality enjoyed with him on the Scilly Isles. But the probability of a call to join the prime minister for a walk round the grounds was less after James Callaghan took over – and non-existent from 1979 when Margaret Thatcher was elected. She made no pretence to be a green wellies prime minister.

For detectives in need of exercise there was always the pool. Or at least there was always the pool until Vera Thomas tried to intervene. Unaware as she was of Scilly Isles intimacies, she saw it as her responsibility to ensure that nothing would interfere with the prime minister's right to privacy when swimming. After alleging that one of my colleagues had left some grit in the shower after his swim, we were banned. However, thanks to intervention with Mr Wilson on our behalf by that infamous non-swimmer, top gun Bill Housden, our rights were restored and standing in the prime minister's inner circle clearly established.

If it sometimes sounds like *The Archers*, it was.

It was not all that frequently that a prime minister could expect to pass an uninterrupted weekend to Chequers just getting fed and fussed over in the company of his family and friends. Government cars inevitably arrived at the back door with messengers delivering red boxes full of papers to be read and dealt with. Official visitors often had to be entertained too and one, on behalf of the Foreign and Commonwealth Office, was particularly memorable.

Memorable for me that was, rather than Mr and Mrs Wilson, who had to meet this husband and wife couple from a self-governing dominion of nearly all white constituents situated on the far side of the globe. They had the reputation of being both boorish and boring and were certainly on the gigantic side when seen alongside their hosts. After receiving them at the front door, the Wilsons walked with them to show the guests their rooms – leaving them to rest and dress for dinner. With a couple of hours to spare, Mrs Wilson was then driven to an old people's home near Oxford. She was overdue for a promised visit to enjoy tea and cakes and exchange expressions of comfort with staff and patients.

I had a word with the visitors' protection team before they left. They were particularly struck with the wife because of her size and strength, demonstrated, it was claimed, with a chestful of swimming medals. Their allegation that she could kick-start a jumbo jet was probably no exaggeration. Her somewhat broken features matched a hugely intimidating stature.

Once settling to agreeable social chat, it frequently happened that Mrs Wilson forgot the commitments of time. Today was no exception and she finally arrived back at Chequers, after a telephone prompt from her husband, with scarcely fifteen minutes to spare before dinner was served. Harold Wilson, already in black tie, met her as she hurried in. 'I'm so sorry to be late,' she said. 'I'll rush up and change quickly. Have there been any alterations to the programme?'

'Yes. There certainly have,' Mr Wilson replied sternly. 'Having seen her now, I've cancelled the wife-swapping.'

———◈———

Prime ministers' travel to and from Chequers was always by official car. The journey back to central London was tedious but usually uneventful. One weekend spent there by James Callaghan and his like-minded, social-democrat friend Helmut Schmidt, Chancellor of Germany, made few calls upon the bodyguards standing by. The focus of prime ministerial attention was to paint the right picture of a prosperous future Britain, in the hope and expectation of German support within the Common Market. Mr Callaghan unashamedly admired the German chancellor and his country's great economic progress – and it showed.

Due to drive back to Downing Street with his host, Helmut Schmidt started his final day with a short stroll in the fresh air of Buckinghamshire and a pinch of his favourite snuff. After breakfast he joined Mr Callaghan in the rather unfortunate Rover limo as the driver headed for London's traffic gridlock.

As the car swung onto the A40 near Beaconsfield, a scarecrow of a travelling woman emerged from her overnight halfway house in a nearside bus shelter, lifted the front of her skirt and stood, urinating like a man at oncoming vehicles. In what I saw as a good cause on behalf of Britain, I created a diversion from this inglorious and hardly typical spectacle by loudly reporting our position on the radio with the set turned off. Most trips were less exciting and generally Mr Wilson would lapse into thoughtful silence. For prime ministers, travel time was generally wasted time.

Once, however, he was uncharacteristically alert. As I glanced in my rear-view mirror – an essential modification additional to the driver's – I saw him actively looking from side to side, interested in what he saw and wide awake. What on earth had brought about this transformation of his travel style? Perhaps he was working out a stratagem for tomorrow's Cabinet meeting. Or developing a statistical argument to put to his chancellor of the exchequer?

Whatever it was my attention was suddenly focused on a call from No 10, with a report that a mass of photographers and reporters were packed outside waiting to waylay him with questions on some parliamentary hiatus. With this news the prime minister decided to abandon the normal approach and leave the car in the carriageway of St James's Park, and walk in the bright, mid-morning sunshine up Foreign Office steps to wrong-foot the media. I warned the police of his change of plan. A couple of SB colleagues waiting inside with junior ministers stepped outside to help escort him through the melee.

I piled out with the PM and covered his approach up the steps while he waved cheerfully to the crowds of visitors – ignoring reporters and photographers shouting questions at him as he walked into the front door of No 10.

As soon as we were inside he said, 'Well. I've cracked it today, John. I got right through to twenty-seven at last.'

'I'm sorry, prime minister. I'm afraid I don't follow …'

Avoiding waiting special advisers and press officers, he talked me along the corridor toward the Cabinet Room. 'Well, this is the way I go about it.'

The prime minister's numbers game in the car was a little more advanced than the average. First of all he had to spot an index plate which added up to number one – either 1 or 10 or 100. Then two – say 2 or 20 or 11 or 101. Three would be 3 or 30 or 300 or 21, for example. And then onward up to the twenties – when things got more difficult. Twenty-one could be 21, or 210 or 777 or 957 perhaps. Things got harder still from then on and the dreaded twenty-seven could only be cracked with a 27 or three nines, of course.

Rush hour on the A40 was his favoured battleground. If this was the way to wind him up into top gear for an unwelcoming Cabinet committee – perhaps it was not entirely a bad thing? But to me it seemed just a diversion – a therapeutic brain-teaser to avoid the really serious issues confronting him, the government and Great Britain upon which he could have been expected to want to set his brain in action.

The *Evening Standard* rounded off the first day of an interesting week with a photo of the prime minister arriving the unexpected way in Downing Street, surrounded by hard men in dark glasses and looking like mafia hit-men, with the headline – 'Democracy? Does it have to be like this?' The hard men were two SB officers, a private secretary, a press officer, one reporter and a member of the public.

Not unusually, the press idea of democracy was not necessarily connected to facts, more to the expediency of sales figures.

EIGHT

*In the evening Robert Armstrong came to see me with the
hilarious news that they had discovered that one of the
female civil servants working in No 10 was a high class
call-girl [...] A strange girl, middle class, pleasant, very well
dressed, perfect manners. But curiously lifeless. Certainly I
wouldn't pay for it [...]*

Downing Street Diary, Bernard Donoughue, Volume 1, Chapter 6

While the telephone switchboard ladies plugged away upstairs in the attic, the Garden Room girls beavered down in the basement.

The Garden Room girls never seemed to object to their title but – on their behalf – I found it derisory and condescending. Even in the next millennium the title stuck and so I must have been wrong. They were a very different collection from the ladies upstairs, being young and, generally, either from landed families or appointed after trawls for bright young civil servants. Those with an aristocratic or landed gentry background tended to be recruited from up-market secretarial schools whereas those trawled had already proved their exceptional secretarial competence and reliability. It was not enough just to have keyboard speed, accuracy, alert understanding and whizz-kid shorthand, although these qualities were mandatory. There was much more to it.

None of the girls were men. This positive discrimination against males may merely have resulted from the title – Garden Room *girls* – although it was used only within No 10 and not formally a civil service rating. Fifteen or sixteen girls were assembled in a sub-ground office from which steps led up to the garden at the rear of Downing Street. The rooms were under the former Lichfield House. Never designed for purpose, they had an inevitably ad hoc appearance, with a jumble of (then) state-of-the-art secretarial equipment, photocopiers, cabinets, desks and electric typewriters. Portable versions were taken when the girls were sent away from base camp with the prime minister. For quiet evenings, while waiting for the call to action, scrabble boards were stacked away in drawers.

Garden Room girls got a special allowance and generally remained at Downing Street – security demands normally excluded them from mainstream channels of promotion. Vacancies for the one supervisory position were filled from their ranks. Odds against selection were something like sixteen to one and opportunities rare. When Jane Parsons retired from the top job in Margaret Thatcher's time, she could quote experience of No 10 from as far back as Clement Attlee. Most of the girls stayed at the job until either they could no longer maintain the pace, or got married.

Within the Civil Service they had some celebrity status. I was told that prior to Harold Wilson's first administration they were recruited exclusively from the upper classes and dressed accordingly, with long gloves and floppy hats de rigeur. Although Laura Ashley dress wear was still favoured, by the time I was at No 10 it was not uncommon to see jeans, at the Scillys or for long aircraft trips, for example. Each girl usually had a personal project for the occasional confinement to barracks without an immediate call for secretarial work – handicrafts being favoured. Visiting detectives could sometimes earn Brownie points by admiring expanding square meters of painstakingly assembled, carefully stitched, patchwork quilt.

The girls had the very highest security clearance. Not to be confused with the private secretaries upstairs – a senior rank in the hierarchy and in the 1970s still the exclusive gift of men – they did not *create* paperwork, but faithfully and accurately reproduced that of the prime minister, his senior aides, and staff in Private Office. With access to the latest government thinking, discretion was paramount and security vetting of a correspondingly high order. They also had the top secret encoding responsibilities.

Miss Jane Parsons made it clear that she did not expect the pristine nature of their reputation to be undermined by male swordsmen and associated scandal. She had once been young herself and was only too well aware of the hardly resistible temptations to which even the nicest young ladies could be subjected when away from home, especially in the heat of the tropics. But even Garden Room girls can be girls as well and an unspoken conspiracy excluded her from hearing much about the welcoming smiles that greeted some adventurers when the lights were turned down.

When the prime minister travelled out of town, or abroad, two girls usually went with his party. Their workload was sometimes exhausting. They were never permitted to absent themselves from their commitment and on aircraft it often meant working with a typewriter on their knees. Air sickness, fatigue and illness were not allowed. Meanwhile the quality of their output had to remain impeccable. A check of the paperwork of one was always read back aloud by the other – and the final product had to be entirely error free.

As Garden Room girls were not on a career-promotion list they remained below ground level at No 10 unless found to be unsuitable. Normally secure in every sense, their offices also suddenly became the front line when the IRA's home-made mortar bombs scored a near miss in the early 1990s.

Only about four of the girls were married. One was 'Lil' from Gravesend, a trawl from the Civil Service, who commanded an impressive early version of what is now known as Estuary English and was contentedly married to a frequently absentee artificer in the Royal Navy. Lil was not typical but – with huge efficiency, experience and a cheerful sense of humour – she melded well with her colleagues and fellow travellers.

<hr />

Together with Mr and Mrs Wilson, and the principal private secretary, Robert Armstrong, I was Lil's fellow traveller in the RAF HS.125 executive jet configured for the queen's Flight which left Northolt Airport on 6 September 1974. The destination was Dyce Airport, near Aberdeen – and Balmoral Castle.

The Queen stays at Balmoral in September each year. The prime minister of the day is unable to have his usual weekly audience in London, and it is traditional for him, or her, to be invited for a relaxed visit to the Castle (with 'spouse') during a weekend early in the month.

Much has changed since my first visit when security considerations were at the bottom of the list of royal priorities. Indeed, preoccupations focused upon rankings in the hierarchical pecking order; inflexible routines and long-established traditions; concern for Queen Victoria's preferences; and a belief in the importance of elderly, anodyne movies. Security was often out of my command, as it was during many royal occasions in those days, and became number one on my checklist of things demanding urgent change.

With the Royal Air Force there were usually no particular security anxieties. But at Dyce, media intelligence had wind of a forthcoming General Election – the second in the year – and their hacks were massed like disruptive hooligans in pursuit of an unpopular football referee. Polling date had not yet been announced and the mob seemed determined to browbeat the prime minister into disclosure even before the queen sanctioned approval.

No steps had been taken by the airport authority to prevent their invasion of the airside apron and, strangely, not a single uniformed police officer was on site. This was all these watchdogs of the public interest needed to take complete control. My hope was that the ringleaders might find themselves shredded through the jet intakes of the taxiing HS.125.

There was, of course, no chance that an old professional like Mr Wilson might inadvertently drop the secret date by mistake. But it was just conceivable that he might recognise a single reporter from a friendly publication – say the *Daily Mirror* – and leak the date to get some sort of tactical advantage over the Tory pressmen, with whom he was engaged in all-out warfare. I later discovered that there was indeed a precedent or two. In the absence of the airport authorities, newspaper and television persons established an impromptu press bureau, setting up recorders and cameras, and surging around without control. This pleased neither me, nor air traffic control or HM Customs and Excise, whose sanitised area was totally taken over against all the rules. Fifty or so microphone and notebook-toting media aces had not apparently been seen by anyone authorised to stop them.

Whether the prime minister was pleased on the basis that any publicity was good publicity, it was a fact that having neglected to take advantage of the on-board Royal Elsan during final approach, he was certainly looking anxious about something. In a purposeful way, Mr Wilson helped me to elbow a path through Fleet Street's irregulars, to find the absentee airport manager, who guided him toward his private facility. In what was becoming a not-unfamiliar procedure I took guard at the entrance to forestall this heaven-sent opportunity to photograph the democratically elected prime minister performing various post-flight ablutions.

We then ran the gauntlet of scribbling notebooks and thrusting microphones to struggle along to two royal limousines waiting to take the PM's party to Balmoral. No police escort was provided for this lengthy, unprotected journey through remote Scottish countryside, or to professionals, potential bandit country. Mrs Wilson decided to take my usual place in front, next to the driver, in a worthy attempt to avoid the car sickness which sometimes plagued her in the back seat, or when too close to the cubic yard of tobacco which her husband would smoke during the journey. It was less than important where I sat anyway. The only radio was out of Balmoral range and under the control of the driver. He was nice enough, elderly and wrinkled – unlike his uniform. Well drilled in the self-effacing disciplines which his role demanded, his driving technique was clearly inadequate to outmanoeuvre terrorist gunfire one-handed, while marshalling a response team through a dead radio network.

It was a long journey, through heavy rain and the tobacco smoke that desensitised the royal interior. The prime minister started to show fidgety signs of a need to arrive as soon as possible. 'How long is this going to take, John?', he asked.

The only person who knew the answer was the driver – and he was not permitted to speak unless spoken to directly, and certainly not to intervene or have an opinion, even on the time of arrival. At least he made no move to speak out. I tapped his shoulder to repeat the question directly. Perhaps his Standing Orders allowed him to talk to someone of similar rank?

Sure enough, while holding a steady course with his right, immaculately-gloved hand gripping the wheel at precisely two-o-clock and, with the left, taking off his cap to hold it respectfully across his chest in what was obviously an 'approved' manner, he answered in clear Queens' English, 'Sirs and Madam. We have exactly ten minutes to go.' He then carefully replaced his cap.

This was not what we were used to, because Bill Housden and the drivers at No 10 had been specifically 'excused caps' – by order of the PM – and regular free-and-frank discussions were held between the Boss and his number one driver on matters of significance – ranging from Huddersfield's position in the Football League to the arrival of a new shipment of cigars or pipe tobacco.

As the cars entered the sweep of the valley in which Balmoral Castle stands, the weather cleared for a moment giving a brief perspective of woods and valleys, glorious lush-green grassland and indescribably mauve-blue heather-covered hillsides. To enter the estate, we were driven across a stylish old bridge over the River Dee, through a gateway and finally along a driveway toward the Castle itself.

This was all pretty impressive, but where were the security checks? As if in answer, the A Division Flying Squad appeared. He was a uniformed Metropolitan Police officer with helmet tipped rakishly askew, riding to intercept our approach on a crazy rusty-red bicycle, featuring half a white mudguard in front and a broken white one at the back. With a defective cotter-pin in the left pedal, a half-turn and miss unstable propulsion was limited to every other rotation only.

At the same time he had to assess whether this was a terrorist convoy or personages worth acknowledging. Easily deciding we were not 'royal', he wobbled well past before deciding on a half-hearted salute – clearly demonstrating his opinion that mere prime ministers were of little significance in general and to him in particular. As we arrived at the guests' entrance, I was physically obstructed by the flunkey. Following our well-established and well-organised routine to see the prime minister safely in or out, I had overlooked the firm rule in royal circles that it is the footman's job. His is a closed-shop task, jealously protected against all comers. I was given an unspoken but perfectly clear indication through a thin-lipped smile that no outsiders were allowed to set an actual foot on the hallowed gravel within sight of the front door.

And so, my personal prime minister, of whom I had intended to take such great care, was whisked from my presence and not seen again for three days. He had left a battleground where the threat was often accompanied by loud explosions. Surely the royal family was not exempted from similar threats just because they were on holiday in Scotland? It was not at all like the terrorists, with whom we were used to dealing, to declare a unilateral ceasefire.

I was de-bussed at the servants' rear entrance. There I met Robert Armstrong and Lil. We were formally given places in the Balmoral Castle pecking order. As civil servants, Robert and Lil were accepted as 'near family' and given places high on the list. But policemen, irrespective of pay-rate or comparative seniority, were encouraged to feel socially superfluous and I was given to understand that although my rating might be just above a corgi, it was definitely well below a royal horse.

On the face of it, the pecking order was a sensible and useful means of organising the household 'below stairs' in relaxed fashion but, in practice, was employed ruthlessly by some of the entourage to secure and strengthen their own position and establish a hierarchy, rigidly distinguishing superiors from inferiors in a way not seen even among the disciplined ranks of the police force. Here at Balmoral, if you were junior enough you ate in a canteen, helped yourself and drinking water was available. I qualified for restaurant status, with service and light alcohol in a mess presided over by Bennett, the Queen Mother's dresser. The importance of this position in the real world had previously gone unnoticed. Christian names were definitely out-of-order. It was not difficult to understand how some people want to break other people's kneecaps. The Garden Room girl, one higher in eating status, had the option of gin and tonic I recall, and above that again, Robert was offered ice and lemon with it.

Bennett's name was somehow always aspirated. His staff showed me to my room and ascertained in this almost exclusively male – if not necessarily masculine – society, that I was anxious to be disqualified from participation in a special inner circle through which singular privileges were available. Lil was not given the same opportunity. The Balmoral household staff with responsibilities close to the royal family all travelled with them from Buckingham Palace. Clearly, this was not an environment in which to spend too long.

I was amazed to find in my comfortable room, thanks to a total absence of street wisdom, letters, envelopes, matchboxes and trinkets – all imprinted with the Balmoral Castle logo, presented on the improbable assumption that everyone staying there belonged to the good guys. It was a treasure house of false identity credentials available on a help-yourself basis. In all my professional service it was unique. Other weekend entertainment was available. This included a film show which members of the royal family and guests attended, to mingle – within limits no doubt – with the staff. It was regarded as disrespectful for guests, irrespective of status and personal artistic taste, to demonstrate independence by disregarding their good fortune and not bothering to attend.

I was getting the picture. The travelling staff – butlers, footmen, dressers, drivers and the few influential female servants accompanying the queen and her family in the United Kingdom, were so preoccupied by elitist tasks and associations that they were unaware, and totally uninterested, in anything happening elsewhere in the real – often unfriendly – world. Some members of the uniformed branch of the Metropolitan Police, responsible for personal protection and defence of the royals' buildings seemed similarly blinkered.

Unfortunately, this narrowness engendered insularity, and produced a hybrid group of eccentrics who gossiped and behaved like a lot of old women, luxuriating in what they thought was a cocoon of everlasting security – although as far as I could make out from the few who would communicate, they were grossly underpaid.

Not only was I allocated to a particular mess – to be confronted with monotonous, unimaginative meals – but also an exact place-setting at the large, rectangular table. This was identified by my personal napkin and ring. Like a bad cheque, the seating plan was not negotiable. A crisis developed when another colleague in transit appeared for breakfast on day two. He was personal bodyguard to the Duke and Duchess of Kent and we had worked together in other parts of the world. It was a good chance to meet up again over cornflakes in an otherwise empty mess room.

It was Tony's first visit to Balmoral as well and he fell into the trap of moving his napkin – which had been placed suitably down-table in deference to his technical juniority – and sensibly taking the empty seat next to mine. It was bad luck when the uniformed flunkey who should have been seated there flounced in to find his place occupied. He lapsed into sulky silence, standing around sighing and looking hurt, refusing at first to take any of the otherwise vacant places.

In our comparative innocence of such important matters, Tony and I did not immediately follow his problem. Finally he snatched his napkin and ring and ostentatiously moved up-table to a more important position. Negotiations proved difficult. He flatly refused to speak to either of us for the remainder of the weekend, declining to unbend even after the usually successful routine of an apology and offer to buy him a drink one evening.

Only one person from my side of the household was normally allowed to approach the front door on foot. He was the Royal Piper and it was to the strains of his diabolical instrument that we were obliged to wake at what seemed very early hours indeed as he crunched up and down the shingle. Access to the front door nearby was never unexpected and then only by car.

My own calls there were few. The only contact with Mr and Mrs Wilson came in the form of notes delivered by footmen. In this way the prime minister informed me that he had just returned from a trip round the estate, alone with the queen, who had driven the Land Rover herself. With no one else present and properly bewildered by the lack of visible security, it was fortunate that Mr Wilson tended to believe that Scotland Yard had command of supernatural powers, depending upon our unseen presence to maintain the safety cover to which he had become accustomed. All I could do was to hope for the best now and add more notes to the growing dossier of things to be attended to in the future.

In the evenings, I declined the honour of watching ancient films and came to know the drivers better during light social drinking at the local pub. Away from the artificial atmosphere of their workplace they were amazingly ordinary human beings. We had many laughs as they taught me the skills of speaking through apparently closed, discreetly curled lips while still looking straight ahead. In spite of the rule not to speak in royal cars unless spoken to they had prepared themselves for those times when it was essential for driver and front-seat passenger to communicate.

We would start off from the mews by car and drive through the woods. Every now-and-then Dave would doff his hat in an 'approved' manner without anyone in sight. His instincts were sure, however, and motive strong, because he firmly believed his job would be in jeopardy if he failed to salute even the youngest 'royal'. The muttered word – 'Children!' – would come from curled lips as he saluted an apparently empty driveway. Another clue to an imminent sighting was Tripod, a three-legged corgi. He was usually the last of the thirty-seven on the estate. As he limped around behind the rest of the pack, Tripod was a good indicator for a timely salute – because where there were corgis there was usually an owner as well.

The highlight of the Balmoral weekend was quiet evening drinks with some independent-minded colleagues from A Division of the Metropolitan Police, and drivers, ghillies, river-fishing bailiffs, dog-trainers and the countrymen who formed the human and healthy-minded element of that extraordinary Castle. They were highly skilled, underpaid, and as proud as could be of their standing near the royal presence.

I could not say, however, that I felt similarly drawn to the travelling flunkeys, footmen and dressers, who had found a protected haven from the rules of conduct which applied to the rest of us. Theirs was an unhealthy world.

A second note from Mr Wilson confirmed that – apart from the enemy – only he and I were aware of the need for personal VIP protection and planning. Our Special Branch strategy – imperfect though it might have been – was to work from worst-case scenarios drawn up by risk assessors, modified by current events and precedents, and then to prepare a commensurately balanced response. With politicians it was simply not possible to cocoon them with inflexible, overpowering defences and some compromise was needed. Conforming to this pattern, the PM informed me that he would attend the Crathie church service on Sunday morning, together with the royal family, and depart for Dyce Airport and London the next day. Without his initiative, I would probably still be waiting. For such trips, I had to get to the front door, first setting off on foot for the Royal Mews at the rear to pick up a duty chauffeur.

The royal family and guests traditionally attended morning service at nearby Crathie church. For them, this entailed a drive from the front door of the Castle, through the grounds to the main exit, along a short stretch of public road and then, still by car, into the churchyard for disembarkation and a few steps into the main door of the church.

Visible security forces consisted of uniformed officers of the Metropolitan Police within the curtilage of the Castle and church and, usually under the direct command of the chief constable himself, members of the local constabulary for the short trip along the public road. Such overlapping responsibilities were adequate to cope with the many good-humoured onlookers who bussed out to see the queen and her family, with various VIP guests, at an unusually intimate distance – but pathetically unsuitable to resist attack by trained assassins or kidnappers.

What were personal protection officers doing? A drill had been arrived at over many years and, as a benefit to terrorists on reconnaissance, was precisely followed. We all met at the rear of the Castle half an hour before the service started and walked in an informal gaggle along the route to be followed by our 'targets' in limousines – in reverse order of precedence. We stood waiting for our respective VIPs near the church doorway. The Queen arrived last and left first. As they were driven in, the personal protection officer stepped forward and opened the car door – there being no flunkey around – bowed as they descended and arranged rugs as instructed.

This was a laughable way to undertake protection responsibilities. Somewhere there was an iron curtain between the risk assessors with whom I dealt and those advising the royal family. Because the programme was so casual, it had to be hoped that the enemy were fooled into believing there was a trap somewhere, and we were just decoys for a camouflaged, well-armed and specially trained team of marksmen waiting to spring an easy ambush.

As I moved to join the prime minister and Mrs Wilson in church, I was gently restrained. Detectives, it seemed, were not allowed within – even if the IRA were. So a seat in the car seemed advisable for the duration of the service while uniformed officers patrolled? That was equally forbidden. Well, a stroll along the pea-shingle path, to reduce the chance of exposure from heavy rain and Gale Force Eight? I failed to take into account the adverse effects of communicating with the Almighty over crunching gravel. A small area of grass was our allocated waiting room; and there we stayed – almost completely useless.

Arrival at the front door on Monday morning was not accompanied by the usual routine checks for lurkers by doormen who would appear instantly and bar any exit. Instead there was a dogged wait in position by the car until Mr and Mrs Wilson appeared. As she waved goodbye on the doorstep, the queen looked nothing less than amazing, with immaculate, trim 1950s hair-do and heavily made-up, court-occasion face, superimposed over country-casual Scottish tartan kilt with brogues, giving the impression that top half and bottom half were separately constructed.

At Balmoral I was in danger of getting the sack either from doing the job effectively – to the displeasure of the royals – or by not doing it at all. And that would have been my proper fate had the prime minister known how miserably I had failed to provide him with any effective security cover. Fortunately for me, he did not, and with some positive measures orchestrated by Private Office, the SB team was never again to be so seriously disadvantaged. Although we also acquired clout where it counted, our weakest arena was still with the royals. There were still limits, but protection officers *might* then be able to do their duty and, if necessary, lay down their lives unimpeded by a modest rating in the pecking order.

During the Balmoral weekend, Mr Wilson told Her Majesty of his wish to announce a general election for Thursday, 10 October 1974. In spite of all the prime minister's care and attempts at deception, Fleet Street printing presses were already tooled up with accurate leaks.

Mr Wilson, with two or three speeches scheduled for each day, was the big gun in the Labour electoral armoury. For a month the prime minister spearheaded the Labour Party campaign in a fast-lane effort to improve the number of their seats in the House of Commons. Arthur Smith calmly co-ordinated his SB team, now working more with the party than No 10, as well as the constabularies. Transport and accommodation was provided from party funds but official cars were used for good reasons of security – at a price per mile. Air travel was essential to maintain pace with the PM's frenetic schedule, but the RAF were disbarred during the campaign, so the Labour Party secured the exclusive use of a commercial HS.125 based at Luton Airport.

Security planning was set back when Hertfordshire Special Branch discovered – through a very secret source – that the family of one of the air hostesses kept a close friendship with a known Irish extremist, recently released from prison for IRA activities. The source was so vulnerable that the prime minister could only be given a cursory brief. Hertfordshire SB established an observation post on her home and set a surveillance team to follow her. The thinking was – this was before suicide bombings became fashionable – that providing she was on board the aircraft when scheduled, an assumption had to be made that it was also safe for the PM to be on board. In spite of the logic of this threat assessment the seat reserved for a detective became less sought after.

To the consternation of chief constables, who were not in the know, two policing operations were prepared for each day when air travel was involved. Although the police service was committed to the protection of threatened government VIPs, there was no visible enthusiasm for the overweight posting of men, either by policemen themselves or their ratepayers.

On day one, the hostess telephoned her flight office to report sick, and plan two was stood-to with policemen put on the alert for a car journey. However, the surveillance team saw her leave home carrying a flight bag, and followed her to the airport. As soon as she boarded, plan two was cancelled.

It was on this stop-go basis that while the prime minister got more tired, detectives became exhausted – anxious about the flights and physically extended bustling the PM through crowds. With this peripatetic existence, it became increasingly confusing to remember which shirt had been worn before. It was a slight understatement at the end of the programme when Arthur Smith made a, 'No untoward incident' report to the Yard.

The prime minister was in Liverpool for the final count at this Huyton constituency and then retired to the Adelphi Hotel to follow the results of the election on television, with telephone updates from Labour HQ at Transport House. With an overall majority of just three and a lead of forty-two over the Tories, the celebration was muted. A flight was arranged for those he wanted to be with him and there was something of a dispute with Marcia Williams over seat allocation. Nevertheless, Bernard Donoughue was aboard. He noted in his diary: 'Drove out to Heathrow with Joe [Haines] and Mrs Wilson. When we reached the small Hawker Siddeley the other four were on board – Marcia, Jean Denham and two secretaries. Marvellously smooth flight and marvellously beautiful hostess. Marcia was very jumpy on the flight, swallowing sedatives washed down with brandy.'

You were not alone Bernard. For different reasons, perhaps, the *marvellously beautiful hostess* made a real impression on us too!

NINE

Everything at Passchendaele was different [...] The entrenching tool was strapped to the front instead of the rear, to protect a certain part of the anatomy which it would be indelicate to describe.

'Passchendaele', from *Fifty True Stories of the Great War*

As a boy I was appalled to read in *Fifty True Stories of the Great War* the horrors and injustices suffered by British soldiers on the Western Front during the First World War. The Battle of Passchendaele in 1917 was just one terrible example.

The author, whose name I have forgotten, described why everything there was different for Tommy Atkins. Four hundred rounds of ammunition were carried instead of the usual two hundred; and four Mills grenades instead of two. Everything that could be doubled up was, leaving the front-line soldier floundering and immobilised in the all-consuming mud of Flanders' fields of battle.

From an early age, therefore, my vote could not necessarily be counted upon when the British roused themselves for war. On protection duty I tried never to overlook the importance of entrenching tool precautions. I learned that it was often more important to keep one eye on the safety of delicate parts of the anatomy when working in areas of limited insurgency, rather than in the more recognisably hostile countries with whom we were engaged in the Cold War.

In the mid 1970s Ireland was the most significant area of limited insurgency within the prime ministerial remit. Ulster was surreal – stranger than fiction, a mix of peace and beauty and calm and terrible violence. Danger came from the

IRA and paramilitary units, but the response was hampered by disagreements between various authorities charged with the task of restoring permanent law and order to that unhappy province of the United Kingdom. At a governmental level, most British politicians and their civil service executive favoured a diplomatic resolution. These efforts so patently failed, or were abused on so many occasions, that many soldiers left to hold the real front line and suffer real casualties, unashamedly espousing the politically catastrophic Bloody Sunday alternative of vigorous counterattack. With the army preferring an overwhelming armed response, the fact that they were frequently under-resourced became a seriously divisive issue. So great were the tensions – although I did not know it at the time – that the Wilson Cabinet actively considered the possibility of separating Ulster from the rest of the United Kingdom on a self-governing basis – a policy which, although vehemently denied in public – was openly feared by Ulster Unionists.

Such division at the very top inevitably fed downwards. Moreover, the Royal Ulster Constabulary (RUC), so long the feared and hated enemy of republican sympathisers, also pursued and favoured a strong arm policy but operated with secrecy and some discretion. Neither the army nor the RUC approved the methodology of the other. Moreover, the army suspected the RUC of leaks, perhaps even of penetration by clandestine republicans. Although it was reasonable to assume that military intelligence was working in concert with army command, the mistrust between the agencies was compounded by the secret services, MI5 and MI6, who recruited their own agents and worked to their own, often uncoordinated agendas.

All this led to utter confusion when the prime minister had to visit the Province. For instance, Mr Wilson maintained a tradition of cheering up the troops with a pre-Christmas visit. Political and publicity imperatives ignored the inherent distrust which soldiers have for politicians, and it does not really matter which party they represent. Soldiers saw themselves presented with an impossible task created by politicians, left unsolved, and then handed over to the army to sort out. This point of view might have been unfair and oversimplified, but it certainly seemed reasonable enough to the men patrolling the streets, getting abused, provoked, sniped at and blown up.

One trip took place before Christmas 1975, when normal arrangements for personal VIP protection were set aside, although, outrageously, I was never included among those with a need to know. It seemed likely that a hidden committee masterminded the prime minister's visit, with the honourable but naïve intention of working to a secret programme until the very last minute, by keeping it from Special Branch in London and the RUC, as well as the press and public. With no mastermind present on the ground the outcome was chaotic, with spheres of responsibility no longer evident. The various agencies necessarily involved, such as our SB and the RUC, had to set about overlapping tasks in their own, separate ways, with normal courtesies of liaison necessarily abandoned; the army seemed to have protection priority in some public areas but then disappeared from others. Not even oblique briefings were presented by the missing overlords.

Assuming wrongly that Downing Street detectives were in the know, but not letting on, the RUC were uncharacteristically suspicious and uncooperative. Inefficient personal protection was the unprofessional outcome.

None of this prevented the media from knowing about the visit. Some reporters clearly benefited from advance nods and winks while others had to depend upon last-minute notification. The visit was largely a public relations exercise and the interest of newspapers and television channels were high on some priority list. In the absence of the invisible mastermind, it had to be assumed that the buck still stopped with us when things went wrong. As the senior personal protection officer, I would have been a star witness at an enquiry into a disaster – and then undoubtedly found personally responsible.

This was unacceptable and the entrenching tool was carefully placed for future visits to the Province.

The final approach with the RAF to Aldergrove Airport with Mr Wilson and his small team, honed my understanding of surface-to-air (SAM) missile threats. The IRA was reputed to have plenty of them and tension built up as the captain started the let-down procedure to low altitude. Thirty years later it must have felt similarly intimidating as Baghdad Airport swung into sight. No time was wasted either in the air or on the ground, and with a satisfying dash and shudder, the RAF parked the HS.125 in a remote corner of the airport.

Northern Ireland was not officially at war – such words were discouraged as overblown pessimism. Nevertheless, someone had decided upon the necessity of surrounding the parked aircraft with light tanks and weapons carriers, armed and alert soldiers and RUC dogs and handlers. Their barking Alsatians were said to be able to distinguish between terrorists and good guys but, from my own experience of police dogs in London, I decided to proceed without provocative eye contact. Remembering Passchendaele I kept the prime minister between them and me. In grim weather and surrounded by this show of force, it would have been more clever to volunteer for duty only within the soothing influence of that 'Gulf Stream', as claimed by the Isles of Scilly tourist office.

Mr Wilson and our team were swooped away by helicopter to Ebrington Barracks at Londonderry, together with Merlyn Rees, then Secretary of State for Northern Ireland. A heavily armed convoy escorted the prime minister into the city centre where, with checkpoints and extensively bomb-damaged areas, life should never have been described as *normal*, although a bustling population hurried busily about. Soldiers served under grim conditions. They were billeted in battered huts – none too clean and with zero opportunity for relaxation and comfort. When stood-to, the risk was high. The prime minister spoke to a section of young men as they set off on patrol.

Mr Wilson was convoyed to Strand Road police station which, with protection devices, anti-missile netting, sandbags and shrapnel damage, looked more like a combat zone observation post than a cop shop. It would have been pointless to walk in with a lost dog. Continuing this jittery journey, the motorcade climbed to the heights of Fort George, overlooking the Bogside. Mr Wilson bravely disembarked and walked briefly around, trying to look relaxed for the cameramen now trailing along, as he peeped nervously through a gun slit – but not long enough to risk a sniper's bullet.

After lunch at Stormont Castle, the prime minister was again rushed off by helicopter, this time on a long cross-country journey to the remote border camp at Ballykinler. The pilot nervously initiated a series of swoops and low-level dashes to confuse the IRA, if they were down there watching and waiting. I was convinced this was for real. The prime minister met soldiers of the Ulster Defence Force and the Queen's Lancashire Regiment unfortunate enough to be posted to this vulnerable and frequently attacked outpost.

My own uncle, David, an uncomplicated and gentle Scottish highlander, had been posted to Ballykinler after the Easter Rebellion of 1916. He never did understand the provocation represented by a draft of Scottish and largely protestant law-enforcement units. But, after initially enjoying freedom from the whizz-bangs and the Western Front's weekly 10 per cent casualty rate, experienced uncompromising hatred from the Irish. Things, it was clear, were not all that different nearly sixty years later. The camp was now hugely protected with earthworks, electronics and lights.

Just outside was the rubble of a building recently destroyed by a large IRA bomb – to the delight of the soldiers within, whose line of sight had previously been dangerously obstructed. Their frustration had been exacerbated by a local Planning Department, which refused them permission to pull down an ancient building. The IRA had effectively completed a clearance which the army had fruitlessly sought for years.

Tense but unscathed we started – prematurely – to breathe more easily as departure time approached. Approached and passed by. Winter darkness started to fall. Still we waited as the prime minister and officers talked away while fog drifted in over the hostile hills intervening between us and our RAF flight waiting at Aldergrove Airport, thirty minutes away. It was now that a little knowledge was dangerous. I knew that our helicopters were not equipped for night or blind flying. To maintain safe orientation, the pilot needed to see where he was going. As every minute passed this became more difficult and the flight deck crew were not alone in feeling anxious. As the prime minister belatedly climbed aboard, smiling and waving a farewell as he donned ear defenders, he was coolly greeted by a set-faced pilot and observer. And me.

It seemed paradoxical to have survived a vulnerable day with a vulnerable VIP, only to finish up colliding into a remote Irish hillside in the dark long after the IRA had retired to a warm pub. After climbing away, the pilot was forced to descend dangerously low to keep the ground within sight as fog and darkness closed around and thickened. A church steeple passed above, followed by a rapid, breath-taking ascent to climb above power cables. Temporarily out of sight of the ground and disoriented, the pilot must have considered a safer option of landing in the nearest field he could find with his spotlight. Although we were now miles from anywhere, in an area short of dependable faces, there was no danger of the enemy finding us any more than a friendly mobile army unit. I kept a firm grip on my entrenching tool. Like a tooth drilling and filling session in a dentist's chair, the journey seemed longer than scheduled, and I wondered just what course of action that great outdoor man, Lord Baden-Powell, would have recommended?

Dib-dib-dib was as far as I could get.

After a careful let down the helicopter passed some cottage lights and the fog grew more patchy. Finally, the runway lights at Aldergrove flashed into view and the pilot beat up the airfield and landed promptly alongside the waiting RAF aircraft. The accompanying gunship – which had set off from Ballykinler with four soldiers – was missing.

Safely back in No 10, the ticker tape reported the death of two soldiers from that Londonderry patrol, and then of the deaths of the four aboard our back-up helicopter – which had collided with those power cables.

In a brief debrief I was able to report that we had experienced no untoward incidents. Scotland Yard, Home Office, and anonymous unaccountables were happy to read it. The army report would have differed.

Seven years later I discovered what had happened. By then I had retired to become the chief instructor of the Metropolitan Police Flying Club at Biggin Hill. The pilot of the prime minister's helicopter had retired too, and was re-employed as a commercial pilot. Coincidentally, I was invited to join him for a test flight in a new Squirrel aircraft and the subject of Mr Wilson's 1975 Christmas visit to Ulster came up.

In view of the adverse visibility he had briefed the pilot of the second helicopter to take special care and remain visually in station with his lead helicopter. Then to navigate independently over power cables, the main known obstruction. It was essential to cross only with a pylon in sight and to pass well clear before letting down to see the ground again. It was not as easy as it sounds and unfortunately the gunship pilot lost sight of the pylon, caught the tail rotor as he descended too early, and the aircraft crashed upside down with fatal results. The score for this day of pre-Christmas celebrations was: IRA – Six, British Army – Nil.

I kept the entrenching tool handy for the next emergency ...

Although probably bathed by the same Gulf Stream benevolence as the Isles of Scilly, Irish weather often seemed grey and wet, cold and uninviting. There was no let up in the usual grim forecast as, once again in 1975, the prime minister was flown to Dublin for the funeral of the Irish President.

Life at Downing Street was a constant learning curve for me, and the president's name, Erskine Childers, sounded familiar. Surely it was not just coincidence that the iconic novel, *The Riddle of the Sands*, a sort of yachtsman's bible, was also written by an Erskine Childers? These were the days before information technology came on stream and things took longer to unravel.

The fictional *The Riddle of the Sands* was written in the first decade of the twentieth century. It described a real-life cruise by two archetypical Englishmen sailing the *Dulcibella*, a sturdy wooden yacht, southbound along the German North Sea coast and down the Friesian Islands. So accurate were the guides to navigation that many yachtsmen still followed Childers down the coast, using his book as their pilot. In 1982 I was one of the lucky ones to do so, having been commissioned by a dedicated Norfolk doctor and his family to skipper their chartered Moody 35ft sloop.

Some claims were made that Childers' journey had been undertaken on behalf of the British Secret Service but, in any case, he discovered secret German naval preparations for war. As the British authorities took little notice of what he was telling them, he wrote this novel as a successful wake-up call to the British public. *The Riddle of the Sands* became an influential best seller.

The author, (Robert) Erskine Childers, was orphaned at an early age. He was brought up in County Wicklow but received a formal English education, developing skills as a yachtsman as he matured. He volunteered to serve with the British Army in the Boer War and then secured an important post in the British Civil Service as a clerk in the House of Commons. In the First World War he served with distinction as an observer in British seaplanes and motor torpedo boats.

Childers, a protestant, passed as conformist, imperialist British but, particularly after marriage to Mary (Molly), a radical and strong-willed Bostonian American, he took an increasing interest and concern in Irish campaigns for independence.

Almost incredibly, however, after trauma following the 1916 Easter Rising in Dublin, he became a principal publicist for Irish independence. He organised and participated in firearms smuggling by boat for the Irish Volunteers (later the Irish Republican Army). He was eventually caught by the British and in 1922 was shot for treason. He declined to be masked or bound and shook hands with each member of the firing squad before he died, almost uniquely, as an English martyr to the cause of Irish nationalism.

His elder son was named Hamilton Erskine Childers, and taking the name revered by many Irish republicans, served as Erskine Childers when he was appointed as the first protestant President of Ireland in 1973. He died in office two years later.

With this background it was not surprising that the funeral ceremony in Dublin attracted heads of state from across the globe. Security assessments were unclear. Not all republicans favoured the Childers' legacy without question and the occasion could have been seen as an opportunity for a publicity outrage. An assembly of such dimensions was a tempting target for extremists who were in any case busily in action on both sides of the border. Their campaign of murder, extortion, robbery, firearms smuggling and explosions was orchestrated across to the British mainland and into Europe and the USA. Nevertheless, it was a funeral and hardly an occasion for violence, perhaps? The most likely target, it was agreed, was the British prime minister and unfortunately, of all those present he was the only man scheduled to travel with the cortege in a green Jaguar. This easily identifiable car, heavily protected, was used normally by the British ambassador. That it was vulnerable became clear soon afterwards when it was blown up by the IRA and the ambassador killed while being driven in it.

The usual arrangements went ahead with the *Garda Síochóna*, the Irish police, who were well acquainted with the special technology of the Jaguar. They posted one of their officers next to the driver and he handled the radio. I followed in the next limousine, an elderly Austin Princess, reserved, amongst others, for Lord Louis Mountbatten. After an impressive church service, the long motorcade set off at about 300yd per hour. It was less – or more? – than several limousines were capable of and some chaos was evident as radiators boiled and embarrassed occupants hurriedly debussed.

The green Jaguar was easily identifiable. Six hefty plain-clothes police officers were posted to walk, or run, alongside. They had come dressed for the weather rather than the occasion and presented a motley collection – some wearing sheepskin jackets and warm roll neck sweaters, and others in light coloured suits and fancy brown shoes. Properly ready for action, their cold bare hands changed to an unhealthy red colour as they marched along. Prudently, the prime minister did not wave to the crowds.

My learning curve went steadily on, I had assumed this to be a solemn occasion. But the occupants in the back of the Austin Princess rather irreverently took advantage of this unplanned chance for bilateral discussion, light-hearted assessment of world personalities, current affairs, and the exchange of humorous anecdotes. As they left for the reception, the scene was more like a worldwide assembly of political leaders, renewing old friendships and developing new lines of contact, rather than a respectful presence to honour a man of distinction.

It was a real insight into the hard-nosed world of international politics – but perhaps Erskine Childers would have approved?

⟫·◦·⟪

For protection duties in the island of Ireland, either north or south, the respective host police services never quibbled about our firearms. Instead it was simply assumed that they were discreetly carried under the armpit, or wherever, with no questions asked. This was a reciprocal understanding. Although now happily almost forgotten, in the mid 1970s the IRA campaign had escalated to warlike status. Elsewhere in Europe firearms protocol was a constant problem for armed officers travelling abroad, as I was reminded after a couple of days with the prime minister in Luxembourg.

I was the advancing officer and, to remain incognito and avoid wave-making, I travelled out with a return ticket on British Airways (BA), unarmed. The prime minister flew over for this European Community (EC) meeting in an RAF HS.125, configured with only five seats. After his disembarkation, my colleague, Peter Smither discreetly passed on my handgun, which had travelled with him as arranged – unquestioned as usual. So far, so good.

After the EC meeting, which lasted a couple of hours overschedule, I had a liaison planning commitment for future travel in Amsterdam and was driven there and on to Schiphol Airport in a UK embassy car. Having missed my flight, the plan was to transfer the BA ticket to the first available Heathrow flight where transport back to Downing Street would be waiting. Of course, the plan was too simple. Flights were being cancelled, crowds waiting, and transfers almost impossible. Nevertheless, I managed to wangle myself onto a flight that was already technically full, and joined the queue at security.

It was only then that I realised that I was still armed, having forgotten to hand my weapon back to Peter as he reboarded the RAF aircraft in Metz (near Luxembourg). With terrorist campaigns now originating indigenously in both

Germany and Italy, as well as with the IRA, airport staff were justifiably jittery. Watching the queue ahead, and counting, it seemed that one person in four was pulled aside for full searches, as well as those who *bleeped* positively. Positioning accordingly, I decided to try my luck but, to be on the safe side, slipped my official Warrant Card into a top jacket pocket, ready to identify myself. Metropolitan Police Warrant Cards were pathetically old fashioned and, with no photograph attached, totally inadequate both at home and away.

Perhaps I could brazen it through the electronic security screen undetected? So I moved forward with the queue, counting carefully and kindly waving people ahead to avoid being number four. It was all pointless because I *bleeped* like a reversing refuse truck. As I was singled out and moved aside, I reached for my Warrant Card as hands slipped under my jacket and discovered the Smith & Wesson.

Elsewhere this would have caused a panic. But here at Schiphol it was treated as just another routine – although it was difficult to impress the officials of my status and position equipped only with an indifferent ID card. Instead of an arrest and big fuss, I was politely, if firmly, moved into a small room, satisfactorily identified and then offered options. Favourite was to separate revolver from bullets, secure them in two special containers and arrange a security escort to the BA captain for personal delivery at Heathrow. This was unexpectedly civilised. I was released and made my way into a tourist-class seat, unfortunately right in the middle of the very full passenger cabin.

As a regular traveller, I knew the drill for rapid departure at Heathrow. My small case was under the seat and the idea was to make an early dash for the Customs area and my transport. Halfway across the North Sea, the opportunity was presented to make necessary arrangements with the flight crew when a hostess walked down the centre aisle, demanding in a very loud voice: 'Would the passenger with the … Would the passenger with the – er – *article thingee* deposited with the captain, please make himself known?'

Discretion was abandoned as I declared myself, and an understanding captain agreed to my request not to let the two special containers cross the tarmac with other luggage unescorted. If he could get them to the enquiries counter near the luggage carousel, any risk of the gun going adrift would be minimised. All was agreed and, with the help of his cabin crew, I made an early exit.

But, of course, he had an aircraft to fly in bad weather, and through a busy circuit and with a couple of other things to think about. I was first off and first at the enquiry desk.

An unhelpful member of the ground staff had no special containers and was uninterested in finding them. I joined the throng at the luggage carousel, keen to avoid the S&W getting lost or, worse, falling into the wrong hands. I waited impatiently until every other piece of luggage had been collected and was left as the last passenger. I made yet another trip to the enquiry desk. 'Could these be what you are looking for, sir?', asked our unfazed official, as he bent below the counter and produced the missing packages. Perhaps he had recently been stopped, searched and beaten up? If not, should I arrange it?

Guessing that my car driver had now headed back to town, I allowed myself an ill-tempered final salvo and broke normally inalienable rules. 'I am from Downing Street.' I spoke too loudly. Perhaps I shouted? 'I promise you that no one from No 10 will ever, EVER travel with British Airways again!' He seemed grateful to hear this. The good news was that my loyal driver was still waiting. I was not pleased with myself.

But a lesson was learnt. I never got myself into such an unprofessional snarl up again.

TEN

Very confused, completely disordered.

'Chaotic', as defined in *The World Book Dictionary*

If the Royal Canadian Mounted Police were the best protection team in the western world, the US Secret Service were arguably the best equipped and certainly the most numerous. They turned up in force with President Ford at a top western nations' summit in Paris in 1975. We learned a lot from them, much of it worth avoiding at all costs.

Their Motorola satellite communications network was ahead of its time and the envy of the protection world. By talking into a small microphone hidden up a sleeve they could keep in touch with Momma back in Washington, as well as with every member of their operations team. Well, but discreetly armed, they were carefully selected and comprehensively equipped and trained. Although originally created to protect the US dollar from forgers, Congress now also allocated to their agents the additional task of protecting the president.

As usual, whenever he left the White House in Washington, a fleet of specially adapted bullet-resistant limousines, with back-up teams of support staff, agents and supplies was flown in ahead of President Ford's arrival in Air Force One. The supplies included a complete medical unit equipped with bottles of blood and all the intensive care essentials necessary to bring along part of the USA in style. When abroad, the White House team was actively supported by the resident US ambassador and his staff. All this ensured that no reliance needed to be placed upon resources of the host country, in contrast to the inexpensive Whitehall and Scotland Yard policy on behalf of No 10. Much of what the prime minister's protection team was able to achieve on the ground resulted from effort, experience, personality and a percentage of calculated mendacity. We saved the Income Tax payer at least a penny in each pound.

The bad news was that in the mid 1970s the US Secret Service had yet to acquire any diplomatic skills. This led to misunderstandings and resentment as they tried to take over the host country. Their only imperative was to preserve the president alive *at any cost*. With caucasians preferred, it seemed that not one of them spoke a foreign language to ease a way through, although there must have been a Spanish speaker here and there.

The sum total was an intact president and chaos all around. In 1975 the Secret Service put on a special performance at the Château de Rambouillet, to the south and west of Paris. In days when European concerns over terrorist outrages were paramount, they showed distinct disinterest during advance planning meetings held by French government officials. In the US, where any individual differing from the mainstream was still labelled *a commie*, the Secret Service saw protection mainly in the limited terms of forestalling another Lee Harvey Oswald – or whoever had assassinated President John Kennedy. The American antidote to trouble was an early demonstration of shock and awe tactics by 200 tensed up agents trying to look relaxed as the president and Secretary of State Henry Kissinger arrived.

Although especially vulnerable to another outrage from the German Baader-Meinhof gang, just two officers protected the Chancellor Helmut Schmidt. Our British protection team, intended to fend off the massed ranks of the IRA for Harold Wilson, totalled Ron Wickens and me. The French hosts provided a single officer to liaise with each delegation. Ours spoke neither English nor German but – while modishly dressed and on alert for good camera angles – dexterously tongued yellow *Gitane* cigarettes through febrile lips. The stage was set for the curtain to go up. The audience was not to be disappointed.

<hr />

The UK delegation (UKDEL) was welcomed at Orly Airport by official hand shakers, a guard of honour wearing medieval helmets and military bandsmen in peaked kepis and shabby, hairy blue serge. The Brigade of Guards would have ordered a thorough brushing to improve their turn out. After performing an uninspired 'God Save the Queen', the bandsmen – who must surely have been part-timers – moved around talking and absent-mindedly scratching their private parts as the prime minister inspected the guard of honour. Suffering a touch of dandruff and bulging at the centre, with pockets full of pipes and tobacco pouches, Mr Wilson, not himself a man of military bearing, did little to improve television images of the proceedings. Neither did the pairs of security officers dodging between ranks with radios blaring – or capering French pressmen waving cameras and notebooks who were given exclusive access.

Although traditionally respected for adding last-minute style to an occasion, rather than engaging in the more boring long-term planning favoured by the British, the French organisers certainly got off to a bad start at Orly Airport.

A shuttle service helicoptered the delegations to the small Château de Rambouillet, situated in park and woodland and fenced in with rings of tight security patrols and checkpoints. With limited accommodation, only heads of delegation and a handful of senior aides could stay inside the chateau, with all support staff booked into hotels within a radius of about 10 miles. They could only gain admittance into the security-sanitised main building on production of an official pass.

It was now that fault lines in the planning started to show. The Americans had insisted that every person in their delegation, including 200 protection officers, should have a pass. As space within the chateau was so limited the French had capped the total number of passes and the only way the Americans could be issued with enough was for all the rest of the – much smaller – delegations to give up some of theirs. It does not need Sherlock Holmes to point out that this left the British and Germans, for example, with fewer passes than people. Conspiratorial initiatives were agreed in UKDEL that the first Brits to arrive would collect their passes and smuggle them out to others waiting to get in. The result was that some delegates moved around in the chateau without a pass.

It might still have worked, but the US Secret Service made sure it did not. The organisers' intention was that – as well as attending formal sessions – heads of delegation were free to move around and engage in informal bilateral talks. But when President Ford walked along a corridor from the conference room to get a cup of coffee, he was doughnutted by a scrummage of twenty worried bodyguards, flattening delegates from other nations against the wall and interrogating them if they failed to display a pass. After senior diplomats of both the German and British delegations were given this third degree, strong protests were lodged at top level and a crisis declared. Hopes for western *entente* or signs of an emerging special relationship were endangered.

France and the United States did not in those days see eye-to-eye over the North Atlantic Treaty Organisation (NATO), and French diplomats had engaged in a show of independence from the mighty dollar. French security organisers were on a learning curve, but determined on a show of strength. One of the first lessons they needed to learn was the importance of photographs on passes. In place of security experience their personnel stood around smoking cigarettes and trying not to look embarrassed, while posing in the fashion favoured in contemporary spy films. However, our protection duo from Downing Street benefited from a developing relationship with German counterparts thanks to the fact that they spoke no French and their liaison officer spoke no German. We were able to help them understand one another for the first time. The chateau featured Napoleon Bonaparte's ablutions' area, which was in the British delegation rooms. To strengthen this useful link we let Helmut Schmidt's two Hamburg bodyguards in to have a look. Other foreign delegates – calling by to see just how small Napoleon must have been to fit into this inconvenient mini-convenience – were rigidly excluded on security grounds.

Among the excluded were the Japanese police. They had brought no more than about ten men with them to protect their prime minister but – attempting to emulate the Americans – covered twice the distance and passed much of the day excitedly gabbling into personal radios. There was nothing they could do to look as tall as westerners. During the next four years' service at No 10, I had no reason to change my admiration for the efficiency and friendship of the Germans or to re-evaluate the first impression that the Japanese were massively incompetent, overdisciplined and dragged backwards by the terror of losing face.

From time to time, my colleague Ronald Wickens and I were able to retire to the prime minister's suite, where the worthy Bill Housden distributed hospitality provided by the French. Nearby, Garden Room girls and Private Office staff were kept hard at work to the amazement of their Foreign Office peers, still working at an unhurried, Victorian quill-pen pace. We kept alert for the development of hostilities between the French, now preparing for action, and US Secret Service and State Department agents, soldiering doggedly along without heeding flashing red lights.

Trouble broke out on the final day.

———⊰•◦•⊱———

International Sherpas drew up a compromise communiqué. The leaders signed the agreement and it only remained to hold the press conference and we could all go home. Only the French knew that it was not planned to be held within the chateau but in the Mairie, 250m away across *La Place*, the town square, where the media were already in occupation. In this way the French reasserted their authority, but failed to take into account a heavy downpour of rain. As no cars were stood by, the leaders had no option but to walk across, cold and ill-clad, exposed not only to the elements but also to the public, enterprising photographers and any opportunistic terrorist who happened by.

Spectators were cleared from the centre of *La Place* by local *Gardiens de la Paix*. President Ford surrounded himself with fifty Secret Service agents and strode away, followed 20yd later by Mr Wilson, his two SB officers and French liaison. Heavily outnumbered, he dropped back to obtain some parity with the Americans and joined Helmut Schmidt and his team of three. Eight of us hurried along to get ahead of Henry Kissinger and his fifty State Department agents. As the least suitably dressed for the weather, our prime minister got high marks for Yorkshire determination as the leaders were ushered for a snapshot with the lady mayoress. It rained more heavily.

Media men had their own entrance and staircase to the first-floor assembly room. The leaders went into the main entrance and up narrow, private stairs, together with about 125 assorted policemen. The Secret Service had not yet caught up with the plan, which was for the leaders – once on the first floor – to be fed through folding doors to face the media on a narrow rostrum already prepared with microphones and floodlights. Thanks to the lack of advance knowledge, and as there was not one Secret Agent placed to watch the pressmen, all fifty of Mr Ford's detail tried to join him. French security forces, easily recognisable in long trench coats left open and still smoking, were determined to stop them. With the Germans, we too were powerless and had to hope that the French intended to show the Americans that France was not America and did have the assembled media men and women under properly vetted supervision.

Things started to get much worse when Mr Kissinger turned up to be fed into the press conference and on to a place on the rostrum. His support team were also trying to go with him, and deploying force to do so. Had this been a football match the riot squad would have been called in.

Push soon came to shove when the lightweight folding doors failed to take the strain of heaving bodies and gave way, cascading dozens of struggling plain-clothes policemen onto the rostrum in full view of television networks transmitting live to a worldwide audience. None of the Americans had mastered the French password, which seemed to be *Merde alors!* World War III was imminent until – in unholy disorder – a few agents of the Secret Service burst through to supervise the media men, while the rest were firmly ejected behind the folding doors by the now triumphant French.

Back in No 10, the press office told me the spectacle had not required sub-titles to follow, but had not been a pretty sight. The next day the prime minister unusually failed to report at the Kitchen Cabinet. He was suffering from a heavy cold and Joe Stone, his personal doctor, was called. The detectives took our suits to be cleaned and pressed.

Even as early as the spring of 1974, following his re-election, Harold Wilson confided to his new parliamentary private secretary, William ('Bill') Hamling, that he did not intend to serve another full term of office.

During 1975, the last complete year of his final administration, Mr Wilson discussed the exact date within a small, private circle of confidants. Amazingly, the progress of his convoluted thinking and frequent changes of mind never leaked out. Harold Wilson had picked his cronies well, and it was not until the end of 1975 that the clues we had been witnessing materialised into some sort of certainty – courtesy of our own special mole.

A prime minister – not having the day-to-day responsibilities of running a department – has considerable licence to decide how to spend his time. His preferences are reflected in the diary. As the prime minister wound down, delegated more responsibilities to the Cabinet and made time for some private life, the frequency with which foreign travel commitments were included was surprising. Jamaica, Washington, Helsinki, Paris, Brussels and Rome were, I recall, included with others in the 1975 list – and then at the end of summer the prime minister made an official visit to Romania. He was the first post-war British prime minister to travel there.

International discussions were not necessarily a vacation and could be really hard work for him. Although I was close enough to the fountainhead often to be present at his pre-talk briefings during outbound flights, I was only occasionally an insider after we landed. However, either as direct close protection officers or in essential liaison with those who were, the Special Branch team had to be party to (nearly) all the agenda undertaken outside the conference room. We travelled with the prime minister whether the programme was formal or informal. This was often more hazardous than the protection, especially in Iron Curtain countries.

It was a fact that although the prime minister could expect abundant comforts and attention, such official trips as these were no rest cure for him. Romania was another good example.

Mr Wilson was greeted at Otopeni Airport outside Bucharest by a very smart guard of honour. Any thoughts that they had relocated from Paris for the occasion were soon abandoned. These official events were the Romanian soldiers' only task in life. Impeccably turned out, they were exceedingly good at drill – although they had adopted the unfortunate goose-step, which always seemed to me – as a former Royal Marine – to look ridiculous. Mr Wilson slouched among the lines and it was tempting to hope he would add substance to the occasion by giving one a dressing down for dirty boots. Looking not unlike battery chickens waiting for their feed, they were trained to swivel their heads and look *at* the inspecting officer as he passed by. After a successful inspection, the officer in charge strutted across to the VIP party, waved his sword threateningly close to the PM's face and shouted something aggressive. It must have been the usual 'Permission to carry on, SIR!' – and off they goose-stepped. The guard of honour was awarded a generous seven points out of ten by critical British veterans comparing the performance with their own heroic days of National Service.

The prime minister's party was driven away from a magnificent display of saluting by prettily tasselled British military and air attaches, and taken to President Ceaușescu's guest residence just outside Bucharest. There we were treated to saluting of altogether grander dimensions. No doubt the heavily armed patrols of police and soldiers, posted around the distinguished, single-story residence – architect-styled for the modern communist epoch – showed off the Russian influence. Certainly they conformed to inflexible disciplines of communist equality by standing rigidly to attention and saluting anyone who was, or might ever have been, higher than them in the pecking order. If an assassin had vaulted the surrounding electric fence and negotiated his way through the barbed wire defences, it seemed unlikely that any of the guards could have shot him. It would have taken far too long to unwind from their upright saluting posture, cock a gun, take aim, and fire as well as working out whether to salute him or shoot him.

Perhaps it was unfairly provocative for the swimmers among us to try to co-ordinate a racing turn at the end of the long sub-ground indoor pool, with a salute from guards – frequently of strikingly hairy appearance – patrolling outside the picture window overlooking the trees and gardens outside.

Interior decor was modern and featured classic Romanian artefacts and splendid wood, glass and leather fixtures and fittings. Mr and Mrs Wilson had a large suite, complete with an enormous jacuzzi-cum-swimming pool, good for about three breast strokes. They were also blessed with a substantial Al Capone-type barber's chair for personal grooming. Most importantly, the PM's travelling valet Bill Housden (who else?) was soon able to establish a hospitality area, courtesy of the president's personal servant and – we had no doubt – KGB grass; an ingratiating, overweight, shiny and unsavoury man nicknamed 'Highball' – a reflection of his unnaturally high-pitched voice. He reeked of that especially communist aftershave which must have inspired so many counter-revolutionaries. Within the definition that describes 'the ability of being everywhere or in an indefinite number of places at the same time', he was ubiquitous. Highball was ever-present with a tray full with long glasses of cool lager and short ones with hot schnapps.

God was denied any recognition during proceedings around the Tomb of the Unknown Warrior, which was inscribed: 'The Memorial of the Heroes of the Struggle of the People and Homeland – For Socialism.' Outside the comfort of the president's guesthouse – and there is much in the assumption that the poorer the country the greater the ostentation – life in the city appeared to be grim. After circulation of this advice from the British Embassy, we unanimously voted to eat in whenever possible:

> The pleasures of eating out in Bucharest are not among the city's major attractions. Menus, although often appearing to be very comprehensive, are frequently limited to chicken or pork in various disguises. Red wine and beer are often unobtainable at all, even in the very best restaurants, but one can occasionally get an excellent dish of venison or sturgeon. Except for the Restaurant *doi Cocosi*, bread is almost always stale. Service varies between slow and atrocious.

The *Bucharesti* was described as having faded velvet seats, rickety tables and no ventilation. It was best avoided in summer. 'The *Pescarus* is very slow and often with unpleasant service. Watch for grossly inflated bills.' When it came to detail the writer had second thoughts about even the *doi Cocosi*, previously applauded for *not* having stale bread: 'The place is so draughty. The Loos are ghastly. The *Hanul lui Prepalec* is a seedy but fun place, except in September when the caterpillars drop by their thousands into one's food.'

Please say no more!

———⟫-◦-⟪———

After an official dinner, and signatures of agreement to a trade deal, in the palace of the former King Michael, the prime minister returned to the official guesthouse. Bill Housden, who had been left there all day, collapsed to the floor as he tried to stand up to greet him. Joe Stone was called and a frenetic scene developed as he tried in a panic to revive the unconscious Bill. With no flicker of response, a cold, blue-eyed KGB doctor, who had probably been watching from behind his one-way mirror, emerged after a couple of minutes, coolly felt Bill's pulse, took his temperature and blood pressure, listened to his heart and rushed Bill off to intensive care. My colleague and I decided to sign on the KGB panel while we were there. Bill returned a couple of days later as the delegation left for home. He brought with him a sealed medical report.

The Wednesday before departure day was devoted to culture. It involved an early start and embarkation onto the president's private aircraft, an aged, rust and oil-stained, bald-tyred and clearly unairworthy Russian Antonov. The seats were all full and the pilot, who must have failed all attempts to pass even elementary tests on weight-and-balance calculations, had hangers-on standing behind him and the co-pilot. As engines started up, a dozen British journalists persuaded him to take them as well. They stood in the centre gangway waiting for free drinks as the Antonov bump-bumped along the runway. As he finally got airspeed and pitched up the aircraft's nose, the standing journalists were accelerated into an unhappy heap near the tail – making for a yet more precarious flight envelope.

Happily for them Highball then grinned from behind the pilot's bead curtain with tray held high. After such irresistible provocation, nothing could now stop Fleet Street's finest from levitating *en masse* from the crush in the tail in which they had been pinioned since soon after take-off, and getting the first helping irrespective of their modest rating in the travelling party's pecking order.

Finally the aircraft wheezed to 10,000ft as the air conditioning failed and heat and humidity aboard were soon compared unfavourably with the Black Hole of Calcutta. Mercifully, perhaps miraculously once on the ground, the prime minister's party and Romanian officials boarded the waiting motorcade.

This comprised Soviet-made wrecks, probably recycled from a crusher, occasionally black and frequently rusty. The luxury of decadent extras such as windscreen wipers had been abandoned. Retreaded tyres were from the Antonov source. Seedy chauffeurs displayed instant recklessness as – escorted by cacophonous motorcyclists, we spluttered away to make up missing hours from the scheduled programme. An admittedly joyous day followed, waving to children lined up from school to flutter Union and Romanian flags; to visit splendidly refurbished monasteries run by nuns for a single monk – whose allegiance was clearly more to the communist philosophy and the tourist board than God; watching energetically dancing villagers and fields full of happy peasants gathering the harvest in classic early twentieth-century labour-intensive mode. The harvest went into horse-drawn wagons and only an occasional museum piece internal combustion-powered wreck was on site to give them a hand.

Although none of these peasants looked unhappy, ten years later they were among those who showed they must have been by summarily executing the president and his wife after the collapse of their regime.

A degree of complacency set in after a multi-course lunch and we headed back toward Bucharest. The prime minister's limousine (*sic*) was no better than the rest and burst a rear tyre at speed, slewing off the road and taking an adjacent motorcyclist with it. The brave fellow aboard wrestled with a sudden cross-country challenge before trying to mount a large bush, losing control and upending spectacularly. As I piled out with Mr and Mrs Wilson, grateful to find that toes were still moving (thanks for that tip, St John Ambulance), and in spite of a sheepish official's reassurances, it was clear the prime minister's car had no spare wheel. A frantic hunt revealed that neither did any of the others.

The solution was to remove a working wheel from another car and leave it and the occupants behind. Two Garden Room girls firmly refused to be shanghaied in Dracula country and spread themselves over back-seat passengers in the remaining, semi-roadworthy transport. I feel sure the chauffeur of the now three-wheeled Russian limousine must have been rescued after the counter-revolution.

As the British delegation left with the RAF the following morning, the guard of honour seemed more pleased, and officials promised everlasting allegiance and friendship. Highball distinguished himself by some skilful theft. No doubt the president had ordered him to find some decent aftershave? It was not a sad departure and, once safely airborne on the RAF Special Flight, we were free to give our opinion of the Romanian government official handout for visitors to Bucharest:

> The Garden City is a harmonious mixture of various architectural styles belonging to different epochs. A European metropolis with an intense life both day and night. A meeting place for businessmen and tourists from all over the world. The Romanian capital offers multiple possibilities of spending a pleasant and bracing sojourn.
>
> Bucharesters' temperament, their cheerful, open nature, the proverbial Romanian hospitality, accompanied by the traditional welcome greeting, all these are arguments increasing the temptation to visit the City of Bucharest!

The public relations team that wrote that must have been trained in a capitalist western city, surely?

—————⟫•⟨—————

In gratitude for their co-operation while he was away, Bill Housden never failed to take back a present or two for the telephone girls under the roof in No 10, and anyone else who had helped him keep in touch with his family while abroad. He also handed over to Private Office the sealed envelope from the Romanian medics. It stated that tests showed heart and liver ailments, blood disorders and gross obesity. By any guidelines, Bill's days as the prime minister's official driver were over.

Not at all. Harold Wilson's influence overruled any objections and Bill remained at the wheel. With this new hazard added to our lives, the detectives set up practice car seats in our office and worked up a checklist of procedures when Bill next collapsed, on the assumption this would be during a high-speed motorway convoy. This was how it went:

Throw your self across Bill to hold him in place
Steer with the right hand
With the left, select neutral with the automatic gear lever
Apply the handbrake
Pray aloud

It was not as easy as it might look. We all survived and Bill did not finally keel over to join his friends in that Great Car Pool in the Sky until months after his master had gone into retirement.

It gave us an opportunity to wonder at God's ways.

[…] he [Wilson] will not go down in history as one of the great prime ministers, but if it had not been for that woman he would have gone down as the greatest.

Lord Goodman

For some reason Marcia was always very friendly to me. She said she would come along and pick me up to attend the cremation [of William Hamling, MP]. When she arrived she asked, 'Has Harold arrived yet?' I was astonished. She then asked if I would do them a great favour and come and work for them at No 10 […] I always felt that she was ill at ease – even shy maybe […]

Kath Bishop, Labour Party worker

Harold Wilson wrong-footed the media by unexpectedly resigning as leader of the Labour Party and prime minister in April 1976. Not a single Wilson watcher outside No 10 was in the know. Speculation mounted and guess workers went wild. Smears and rumours proliferated.

Marcia Williams and temporary civil servants Joe Haines and Bernard Donoughue had to go too. Harold Wilson was not saying why he was standing down and so it was no surprise that many malevolents who had been poised to strike had a field day – Labour personnel as well as media men and women.

The relationship between Harold Wilson, the prime minister, and his political secretary Marcia Williams, provided the easiest target.

Nearly thirty years later, on Friday, 18 March 2005, the *Daily Mail* was still at work. The headline read: 'What did this woman have on the Prime Minister that could have destroyed him?' Alongside was an eye-catching photograph of the PM and Marcia Williams captioned, 'Influence: Harold Wilson in his office with Marcia Williams'. Printed meaningfully above was the sub-title: 'Sexual intrigue, mystery pregnancies, and KGB links have been unearthed in newly released Downing Street papers.' This build-up must surely have been intended to rekindle old, unproven prejudices and misconceptions.

It was the work of a few moments to discover that Geoffrey Levy's article was little more than a rehash of already well-rehearsed innuendo. Included was the hardly secret, single and almost irrelevant fact that the 'unearthed papers' were no more than the routine release of correspondence about the death in 1970 of Mr Wilson's former principal private secretary, civil servant Michael Halls, and his wife's attempt to claim compensation. The total package presented to undiscerning *Mail* readers probably bordered upon the libellous. As Harold Wilson was dead by then and Marcia Williams incapacitated with a stroke, can it be doubted that legal advisers at the *Mail* – depending also upon the likelihood that few of their readers would fully absorb the content – had concluded that legal counteraction was a strong improbability.

The fact is that although tens of thousands of words were written about this bizarre relationship – both before and after the resignation – and the effect it may have had on the decision to quit in 1976, neither Mr Wilson nor Lady Falkender have ever gone public. I think I can almost guarantee that while some insiders – of whom I was one – were nearer to the truth than any journalist, only perhaps a dozen people were *fully* in the know. I was not one of those special few.

Harold and Marcia first met at a Transport House function in 1956. It is a fair bet from what I saw later that he discovered a singularly dazzling star in an otherwise seriously dull firmament of Labour Party damsels. Marcia Williams' many detractors have never disputed her wit, her political perception and the unqualified joy which radiated from Harold Wilson when they were together and on happy terms. She was his one-woman intelligence service, watching and reporting every move by significant members of the Parliamentary Labour Party. She advised and recommended and acquired enormous importance at his side.

The date of their 1956 meeting significantly disposes of the mish-mash of fact and fiction which still clouds their early days. They could certainly not have been co-conspirators during his tenure at the Board of Trade under the post-war Attlee government of 1945–50, when Mr Wilson was rumoured to have been a Soviet agent after negotiating the sale of advanced aircraft jet engines to the

Soviet Union. He did lead the British team in Russia, but reported back daily to the Cabinet. In turn, they relayed his new instructions and the final sale was their collective decision. Incidentally, it will be recalled, he told me it was during these protracted talks, headed on the Soviet side by Comrade Mikoyan, that he followed Churchill's advice to set up personal contact with him as a member of the Comintern. Mikoyan was his Soviet contact for the indefinite future.

Much has been alleged about a sexual relationship between Harold Wilson and Marcia Williams. Whatever it had amounted to in early days, it was certainly not a factor during my time in Downing Street. Although in Labour Party terms she dazzled a little, Mrs Williams was no irresistible raving beauty. She was vastly self-conscious about her legs, which seemed to me to be no better or worse than anyone else's. She had prominent teeth, which did not enhance her appearance. Richard Crossman, in his diaries, did credit her with wearing attractive gowns, but it must not be forgotten that – at least until the appearance of Neil Kinnock as the leader – smart appearance was seen as some sort of treachery to working-class tradition. It was more important to project a working-class image than do anything to improve it. Women in the party – except for Barbara Castle – wallowed in a sort of plump, breathless dowdiness, which typified them as party faithful who refused to tart themselves up like Tory matrons.

The *Daily Mail* article referred to Marcia Williams' repeated threat to destroy Harold Wilson with one phone call. This claim did nothing to help her quench the smouldering fires of suspicion. Her alleged statement that they had once engaged in a short and unsatisfactory sexual relationship may or may not be true. Other reports that she had actually told Mrs Wilson some of this are unconfirmed. As we have seen, they were not unfriendly to one another while holidaying on the Isles of Scilly. I am sure it was not a part of the prime minister's relationship with her during the 1974–76 administration, and my predecessor who served during the 1964–70 term had no concrete evidence to the contrary either. If a liaison could have taken place during a visit to Soviet Russia, as is sometimes alleged, Mrs Williams may successfully have poured cold water on the possibility with her derisory riposte that Russia during the Cold War was the very last place any couple was likely to choose.

Indeed, I concluded that Mr Wilson did little to discourage these rumours and, by treating Marcia's children very much as his own when in public, for example, was happy both to add virility to his image and lay a false trail over any misdemeanours in which he really was indulging himself.

However, there was some doubt and differing descriptions of events leading to the 1961 divorce proceedings between Marcia and her husband, Ed Williams, an aeronautical engineer employed by Boeing in Seattle, USA. Harold Wilson's supporters for his future leadership of the Labour Party did apparently contribute to the cost of legal proceedings and if Mr Williams was persuaded, or induced in some way, not to involve Harold Wilson, this may have been of significance in the Wilson/Williams relationship. In those now forgotten, narrow-minded days could this have been the threat of which she was warning? If so, it would hardly be headline news today. It was before my time but in any case we are unlikely to want to hear more detail now.

In 1963 Hugh Gaitskell, leader of the Labour Party in Opposition, suddenly and rather mysteriously died. It was almost obligatory that this sad event generated stories of conspiracy by Russian agents. The main contenders for leadership were James Callaghan, to the centre-right of the party, and Harold Wilson – the preference of Bevanite hard liners. Comprehensively unconfirmed rumours were circulated that Gaitskell had been murdered in order to let Harold Wilson – favoured by the Soviets and unencumbered as he then was with any scandal – into the now vacant Labour Party leadership.

Bill Housden always insisted that the Wilson campaign was orchestrated and timed to advantage by Marcia Williams. If so, Mr Wilson may have felt obligated to her for the rest of his political life. If he was so cleverly helped into power by covert Russian intervention, the Kremlin must have been greatly disappointed in him. Certainly during his final administration it was his clashes with trade union leaders, his moves to remain in Europe and a steady drift away from the left of his party that so infuriated many Labour hard liners and crucially divided the party. The final outcome was twenty years of Tory rule.

Can there be any doubt that Marcia Williams was her own worst enemy in many ways? It was surely a mistake to adopt such an uncompromisingly belligerent attitude toward the civil servants in No 10, to alienate Labour's special advisers and press secretary Joe Haines, and eventually the prime minister himself. In doing so she exposed an aspect of her character and personality that she would have done well to keep under control. If she had a chip on her shoulder – an inferiority complex perhaps – which manifested itself in demonstrable hysteria, was it perhaps overcompensation for her own inadequacies and insecurity? She found herself working closely with all-male elitists and may well have believed she was being patronised. If so, her all-out and virtually daily assault upon them – although probably justified in her own eyes – was the very worst way to handle them. It also proved counterproductive to the feminist cause. She was there knowingly after all, having worked in No 10 during all of the first Wilson administration.

Mrs Williams was admittedly under pressure. She took on board a number of commitments to her family, not least her brother Tony, manager of Harold Wilson's political office in Opposition until 1973 and then an unsuccessful land deals speculator. She maintained her own high standard of living and, as Kath

Bishop discovered, had a kind and generous side to her character. As we know, Bill Housden remained concerned, too, about the extravagance of her frequent West End shopping sprees.

She amassed formidable opponents. Unfortunate words were spread about her and the prime minister from a number of sources within the party and without. Freelance members of the Security Service were also at work, from a political position well to the right of the mainstream Tory Party. Newspapers and television revelled in all this and fanned the flames for public consumption. The media infuriated both her and the prime minister. In the end she even succeeded in losing the unconditional support of her strongest ace, the prime minister himself, upon whose back nearly all her future standard of life depended.

It was also a mistake to benefit financially and socially from close proximity to a number of Jewish businessmen and showbiz entrepreneurs, although she might well allege anti-Semitism in reply. While they provided her with a temporarily glitzy way of life, their own dubious activities and connections more or less guaranteed that their backing was finite. They may have shown her the highlights for a time, but it was clumsy to drag Harold Wilson into the act too. When he retired and honoured them with peerages and knighthoods, their misdemeanours and suspect contacts across the Iron Curtain followed him around too – sometimes adding to the improbable likelihood that he was a Soviet agent.

I was a personal witness to an average example of the curious relationship between Baroness Falkender and Prime Minister Harold Wilson. On the Isles of Scilly the three of us travelled by boat to a virtually uninhabited island. The sun shone and it was their 'happy hour', with laughs and jokes and fun and wit. I gave them space so that they could discuss their favourite subjects: politics, the party and future manifestos and legislation. I took a radio call for Mr Wilson from the duty private secretary in No 10, Robin Butler. Reception was clear but intermittent because of intervening high ground. I found a spot where two-way communication was uninterrupted. If I recall correctly, the airline and travel company, Court Line, had gone bust and the Treasury was asking No 10 for guidance on a rescue package.

Instead of sticking to one place, the prime minister paced up and down while dictating his instructions. Communication consequently failed several times and he handed the set back to me to sort out. Finally, I pinned him to one spot and the call was gradually wound up. Unfortunately, while concentrating his mind on the issue, his body suffered an audible attack of Gale Force Ten flatulence from a southerly direction. For several seconds this was synchronised in step with his pacing. As he handed back the two-way radio, the previously pale but happy Mrs Williams – now very red indeed – gave him the biggest rocket of his life. 'DON'T YOU EVER DARE TO DO THAT AGAIN! DON'T YOU EVER PRESUME

TO … !' It became very personal and direct and I withdrew to a safe haven. The prime minister said nothing in reply. No apology and certainly no explanation. He remained absolutely set faced as she raved. This was the downside of their day. Either he had learned to control himself in a hard school – the Kitchen Cabinet – or he was transfixed with terror like a rabbit caught in car headlamps at night.

On the final morning of the Commonwealth Conference in Jamaica, Bill Housden confided to me, it will be recalled, how Marcia had repeatedly telephoned Mr Wilson from London. She warned him of an imminent left-wing coup to depose him while he was still abroad. Bill said that so great was the fear she induced in him that the private bathroom had been left in a state that embarrassed even the undeviatingly loyal Bill.

The enigma of the relationship between Harold Wilson and Marcia Williams is no closer to a solution today than thirty years ago. I remember, during the Common Market referendum campaign of 1975, that a small group of the fascinated – trustworthy officials, civil servants and party implants in No 10 – were gathered for a couple of hours in the bar of a midlands hotel. From one of the No 10 drivers, to a press officer and onward to a senior private secretary, we all had direct experience of the two of them. One by one we expounded possible explanations for the prime minister's dedication to her and his steely-faced acceptance of the tantrums, which Mrs Williams took no trouble to disguise. When we had all done, the private secretary – quiet until now – summed it all up as he saw it: 'The only reason remaining for his willingness to be humiliated in front of us all *is that he must enjoy it!*'

There was nothing more to add.

＝＝➤◦◄＝＝

Lady Falkender's big-time proposition was that she was related to the queen. According to an entry in Bernard Donoughue's *Downing Street Diary* for 2 March 1976:

> He [the PM] wanted Ken [Ken Stowe, his PPS] to ask if she [the queen] were willing to 'receive' Marcia. The latter believes that the Queen won't because Marcia is related to the Queen – being, so she claims, a direct descendent of an illegitimate child of Edward VII. Her chosen peerage title is her statement of her claim to be of Royal blood.

I represented no threat to Lady Falkender's special relationship with the prime minister – and so we got along well. Indeed, I once enjoyed her invitation as escort (or was it *prince consort*, perhaps?) to an evening party at the Chelsea flat of Lord Weidenfeld, head of the publishing empire. I was undoubtedly the least celebrated celebrity at an event held for the world's special people in London. However, had I been aware of her claim to royal descent, I might have felt obliged to resign from her supporters' club.

In spite of all this, genuine people such as Kath Bishop – and many others – will always recall Marcia Williams' many kindnesses.

Should it now be left to the reader to sort out?

'One of Harold Wilson's reasons for resigning from the premiership when he seemed to be secure in the post for many years ahead was that he wanted people to ask: "Why did he go?" rather than, "Why did he stay?"' (*The Politics of Power*, Joe Haines)

The only real surprise about Harold Wilson's resignation in 1976 should have been that it was not a surprise at all to an inner circle that had his absolute trust. Members included his wife, Mary Wilson, and their family and a few close friends such as his legal adviser Lord Goodman; top civil servants and party advisers in No 10; Joe Haines and Mrs Janet Hewlett-Davies in the press office; and Lady Falkender and Bill Housden, of course. Much to the PM's satisfaction, his iron curtain of secrecy confounded the media.

Following the laws of equal and opposite reaction there was a downside too. The media – and therefore the public – were caught unaware and surprised; it was often assumed his decision to quit was suddenly imposed upon him. In turn, this implied urgency, even panic, and that led to the further belief that there was something catastrophic lurking around. The popular assumption was that something Mr Wilson needed to hide was about to be made public.

In fact, as early as the General Election of February 1974, Mr Wilson had privately assured Mrs Wilson that if elected he would work toward a two-year deadline in office. He also told William Hamling, his trusted parliamentary private secretary. Mr Wilson had been deciding on the precise date for several months before he finally left Downing Street for the last time in office on 5 April 1976. As there was no warm-up period for newspapers and television journalists to discover real facts, they disseminated unimaginative inventions using hints and rumours. Newspaper proprietors and readers enjoyed an intense period of speculation. The Stock Market tottered for a few days. Marcia Williams' special role was rewritten; the Soviet agent rumours presented again; and heavy hints about corruption circulated in Fleet Street taverns. Ever the master of deception, Harold Wilson was no doubt delighted to see them hunting around, safe in the knowledge that they were far from working out the truth.

By looking to find one single, overriding reason for Mr Wilson's unexpected departure from No 10, journalists and reporters headed along a false trail. While trawling for a mysterious, hopefully undiscovered secret, they largely failed to understand that there was not one reason, but several. The columnists depended mostly on recycled copy. Mr Wilson's imperturbably studied calm diverted them from the additional extra.

However, his well-rehearsed phlegmatic and avuncular pipe-smoking image of mature dependability and reliability – cultivated through all his political life – was not a fair representation of the fallible man underneath. The detectives were the one group who knew the facts.

Apart from that undertaking to Mrs Wilson, the simple facts were that everything was going wrong for him and he could no longer stand the strain.

The trail of clues started for me during the run-up to the Common Market referendum held during the early summer of 1975. As a former left-winger, Harold Wilson was undecided whether or not to recommend remaining inside the Market, and yet economic and business issues demanded an early decision in order to organise and clarify the direction of their future strategy. The people of Britain were also demanding a hand in the choice. Labour hard-liners generally opposed the Common Market and so Conservative support was needed to ensure a majority of 'Yes' votes. Failure to arrive at a majority one way or another was holding back the nation's economy, and it showed. Politically, the government had much to lose by further prevarication. In order to secure his own political future, Harold Wilson was in the anomalous position of needing Tory support to remain in charge.

Although he was all tooled up as the leading government spokesman, the prime minister had to decide the line to take one way or another. His initial speeches were anodyne and indecisive. It was here, it seems probable, that private talks with Marcia Williams may have been critical. If she persuaded him that he could depend upon enough Tory 'Yes' votes it would account for his decision to champion the Common Market positively. If it worked, then the Tories would indirectly strengthen his position in Parliament as well.

This would be a numbing example of the abandonment of conviction government in favour of political expediency, and the influence of opinion polls. To some detractors, Mr Wilson would seem to have sold his political soul.

In my opinion the truth – while undramatic in national terms – was intensely personal. Shall we try to see just why?

<hr>

The campaign was orchestrated rather inadequately from Transport House, where an office was set aside for Harold Wilson and Marcia Williams. With friendly encouragement, they called me in one afternoon. I was needed, and offered a comfortable chair. Mr Wilson wished to make a formal report about alleged criminality. For some years he had suspected that his records and tax returns had been tampered with and a number of them stolen. Now there was evidence – he said – that more had been burgled from an office rented by Lady Falkender. He suspected unauthorised secret services activities and nominated the South African Bureau of State Security as the most likely suspects. As a police officer it was obvious that the information given was imprecise to say the least.

I agreed to report what he had told me but was not enthusiastic about the next step – which would certainly be for the investigating officer to ask me the questions I had put to the prime minister and which had been avoided or answered without clarity. One of the vague inferences was that MI5, the British security service of which he was in charge, might be looked into at the same time. If this was to be an Official Secrets' Act enquiry there was nowhere other than the scene of the alleged crime for an investigating officer to start looking for evidence.

The unfortunate Detective Superintendent Roy Ranson (who subsequently led a murder enquiry involving the missing playboy Lord Lucan), head of A Division CID, was given the enquiry, which dragged on pointlessly for months – before finally disappearing following a couple of minor convictions.

However, the police investigation had apparently worked political magic at the right time. It transpired that Mrs Williams had learned the day I was called in that an allegation about her would be published the following day, and by warning the editor that the case was already *sub judice* – which it was not – publication at a critical time of the referendum had been successfully forestalled. I am afraid this was another example of the ruthless way in which Lady Falkender used the prime minister on incidental matters affecting her, and diverting him from running GB Ltd. The fact that the police service had also been used for personal purposes was unlikely to win many of the 100,000 votes commanded by its personnel.

Mr Wilson's fear that his own security services were working against him became paranoiac. It was true enough that a number of its inadequately supervised personnel, headed by Peter Wright, author of the highly contentious book *Spycatcher*, had convinced themselves after largely unsubstantiated whistle-blowing from Soviet defectors that a KGB agent was in place – first in the Treasury and later within No 10 itself. This group failed to establish evidence that the supposed agent was either Marcia Williams or Harold Wilson (or anyone else for that matter). Nevertheless, these secret service agents felt justified in questioning their loyalty in the eyes of many people, by the deployment of rumour and invention in stories to the media and the eager listeners in right-wing circles.

With Lady Falkender and Harold Wilson in secret service and media firing lines, they both became more and more obsessed with the content of the daily newspapers and supposed anti-Labour bias on television and the radio. There was some justification, but their concerns grew disproportionately out of control – often to the horror of party advisers and private secretaries worried about any detrimental effect on Britain's governance.

I believe that Mr Wilson became seriously concerned about his ability to govern at all. The Labour Party was in disarray, with Transport House and many constituency parties at loggerheads with Downing Street and the Parliamentary Labour Party. The UK economy refused to climb from decline. Sterling rates and balance of payments deficits were implacably troublesome. With a slender majority in Parliament, survival in the division lobbies was an everyday cliffhanger.

Mr Wilson was acknowledged as the master of Prime Minister's Question Time in the House of Commons each Tuesday and Thursday afternoon. He was well briefed beforehand by his officials and advisers during a working lunch in Downing Street, and his extraordinary memory and quick wit had always enabled him to outmanoeuvre the Leader of the Opposition, Mrs Margaret Thatcher. However, he was drinking brandy during lunch instead of beer, and then *more* brandy, and he started to complain that he no longer looked forward to Prime Minister's Question Time; indeed that he hated it.

In spite of Mr Wilson's stoic, calm appearance, he was a man who could see his whole reputation heading downhill. Most of his adult life had been a story of one success after another: as an academic prizewinner at Oxford, as a popular leader of the Labour Party and, finally, as prime minister. It was an astounding record for a man with his humble background. However, it was all crumbling while he was still a youngish man and he had run out of incentive and stamina.

Although he covered up brilliantly, I am sure Mr Wilson had completely lost his nerve. It was easy to see plenty of evidence. He was drinking more. He suffered unpleasant stomach disorders and fell asleep frequently during car journeys. He looked older and took less exercise. During his last year, I never remember him swimming at Chequers and his walks tended to aim for a local pub. He was certainly not well. Bill talked of heart disorders as well as the stomach problems which – sometimes embarrassingly so – manifested themselves undiplomatically.

With the Labour Party fragmenting and the nation's economy collapsing, Harold Wilson must have seen that his reputation as the leader of a white-hot technological revolution, and the longest-serving prime minister since the Second World War, was being displaced by evidence that he had instead led the Labour Party into oblivion and the country into decline. Although he tried never to let it show I have no doubt that he was simply terrified by all this. Here was an honourable man, abject with fear, and compounding his problem by pretending to the world it was not happening.

Added to this was his relationship with Lady Falkender, who relentlessly added to his pressures. She undoubtedly terrified him even more with threats of party coups and conspiracies against him. Mr Wilson gradually turned against her in a private way that he had never dared to initiate previously. He was helped by loyal sympathisers, who could see much of what he was going through. He conspired to spend more time with Mrs Janet Hewlett-Davies, Joe Haines' deputy in the press office. She was an attractive career civil-service professional, who provided sympathetic female company and the warm understanding that he had once enjoyed with Marcia Williams. However, this relationship did not please Lady Falkender.

With evidence that his own faculties were on the decline at the early age of 60, surely there is no mystery about his resignation. Where he had once revelled in the cut and thrust of Westminster and anticipated a respected academic retirement, it was now all going so sadly wrong.

Controversially, Mr Wilson had elevated Mrs Williams to the House of Lords in June 1974. Behind the No 10 scenes in 1976, a terrible scramble for honours took place among some of his political cronies as he finally decided on a date for departure. Some must have felt uncertain about a future in the hard world outside without him. The very last two-finger gesture that Harold Wilson and Marcia Williams were able to make to the media and the establishment was the list of names favoured for royal recognition by Mrs Williams. She wrote it on lavender notepaper in her own hand. It was in effect her resignation from his service and his replacement as a pension fund with commitments levied upon her wealthy friends to ensure she was not left in the wilderness when she no longer had the vicarious influence and power that she had enjoyed in Downing Street.

Although a few names had to be deleted as unacceptable, many of the others were those Jewish businessmen and showbiz entrepreneurs who had toadied to her while she was in No 10 and who had often contributed to Harold Wilson's office funds. Some were also prominent in secret service records and some secured privileged admission to Scotland Yard's criminal records too.

Can there be any doubt that for Harold Wilson – an honourable man completely uninterested in money himself – retirement was simply a blessed relief from it all? Perhaps the scriptwriters of *Yes, Prime Minister* came near to the truth with the claim that 'the greater the office, the greater the paranoia'.

TWELVE

These have been the most difficult three months of my life!

Sir Kenneth Stowe, PPS to James Callaghan

James Callaghan was appointed prime minister in April 1976, following Harold Wilson's voluntary resignation from office. He was chosen for the job neither by the queen nor her people, but by the Labour Party. His arrival at No 10 Downing Street signalled the temporary end of close co-operation between the prime minister and his officials, as well as the social ambience that prevailed during the final weeks of Harold Wilson's administration.

Although he made the mistake of ignoring the advantages of living in No 10, and the comfortable weekend and holiday facilities at Chequers, he was far too experienced to fall into the traps laid for him by press and television crews when he arrived at No 10 for the first time. With his lengthy background as a senior Labour politician and previous government appointments as home secretary, chancellor of the exchequer and, more recently, foreign secretary, he also clearly determined to assert new authority over Private Office. Ken Stowe carried bravely on from the Wilson administration and it was here that he found himself in the firing line.

Reporters and television crews, wreathed in encouraging smiles and shouting words of friendly welcome, were coiled for action as Mr Callaghan's official car was driven into Downing Street. He knew that the smiles and welcoming words were in reality attached to hard-nosed men and women charged by their editors to discover and record weakness, idiosyncrasy or careless comments, which could then be used against him as soon as the honeymoon period was over. Being fully aware of their relentless preparation of pots of political boiling oil for him to pour

The famous front door of No 10 Downing Street. (Author's collection/Ann Warwicker)

Harold Wilson. (Author's collection/No 10 Press Office)

Prime Minister Wilson, with his Labrador Paddy and yours truly, sets off along the cliff path from his bungalow towards the Co-operative store in Hugh Town, St Mary's, Isles of Scilly, to buy his breakfast. (Author's collection/Arthur Smith)

Harold Wilson and his daughter-in-law relax with friends on the Isles of Scilly. I look on, glass in hand. (Author's collection/Arthur Smith)

Harold Wilson and I leave No 10 for the House of Commons. (Author's collection/ *South Wales Evening Post*)

The prime minister enjoying relaxed hospitality at the holiday home of the Liversedge family on the Isles of Scilly. (Author's collection/ Arthur Smith)

The comedian Tommy Trinder and the prime minister leave the stand at Craven Cottage (home of Fulham FC) in good spirits to meet the teams at a charity-friendly organised by Eric Miller (in the light trench coat). I am stood just in front of him. (Author's collection/*Daily Mirror*)

Arthur Smith (right) and me with the Soviet KGB liaison officer, who introduced himself inevitably as 'Viktor'. (Author's collection/ Arthur Smith)

Prime Minister Harold Wilson at the Soviet's Tomb of the Unknown Warrior. (Author's collection/Arthur Smith)

Janet Hewlett-Davies, deputy press secretary at Downing Street, walking in the grounds of Chequers with the prime minister. I've taken up my customary position. (Author's collection/Janet Hewlett-Davies)

Prime Minister Harold Wilson manages a brave smile during a walkabout in Liverpool docks in 1974. (Author's collection/Liverpool Dock Authority)

Harold Wilson looking troubled during a photo opportunity on the ramparts of Derry during the height of the Troubles. I'm stood furthest right. (Author's collection)

Mary and Harold Wilson and me after voting in the second General Election in 1974.
(Author's collection/*Evening Standard*)

In 1975 the prime minister spent the day at the Royal Naval Air Station, Yeovilton.
(Author's collection/Ministry of Defence)

With Best Wishes for
Christmas and the New Year

Audrey ~ Jim Callaghan

10 Downing Street,
Whitehall

Prime Minister James Callaghan and his wife, Audrey, pictured on their Christmas card in 1976. (Author's collection/James Callaghan)

James Callaghan and US President Jimmy Carter in a melee of US Secret Service agents, British protection officers (me included, right in the middle) and the public during the president's walkabouts in the north-east of England. (Author's collection)

Me receiving a commemorative medal from Pope Paul VI. 'You know, my son, they were right. We do have similar noses […] ' (Author's collection)

A precursor to the infamous 'winter of discontent', this image was taken as school children, parents and teachers combined to protest directly to the prime minister against education cuts in the Rhondda. (Author's collection/*Western Mail & Echo*)

A red-carpet arrival to welcome the prime minister, typically Pakistani, saw his Scotland Yard Special Branch protection team fall naturally into the best defensive positions. (Author's collection/Pakistan Information Service)

Prime Minister James Callaghan gives impoverished Bangladeshi peasants (and me) a lecture on the benefits of mechanisation and modern fertilisers. It was unfortunate that none of his listeners spoke a word of English. (Author's collection/Colin Colson)

After defeat in the 1979 General Election, James Callaghan bids his final farewell to the media and public waiting outside No 10. (Author's collection/*Hoad* magazine)

After a complex programme of departures and arrivals between Downing Street and Buckingham Palace, Margaret Thatcher (with me right behind her) arrives at No 10 for the first time as prime minister. She was also the first woman ever to do so. (Author's collection/*Financial Times*)

To my huge relief, the *Financial Times* loyally decided not to publish this image after a storm-blown entry to the Russian exhibition in London. (Author's collection/*Financial Times*)

The prime minister's farewell to the domestic staff at the UK High Commission after the conclusion of the Commonwealth Heads of State conference in 1979. (Author's collection/ UK High Commission)

Margaret Thatcher is greeted by the Japanese prime minister at the 1979 summit in Tokyo. (Author's collection/Japanese Information Office)

The state dining room at No 10 in 1977. (Author's collection/James Callaghan)

The elegant pillared room to the rear of Downing Street, formerly part of Lichfield House. (Author's collection)

The state drawing rooms in Downing Street, formerly part of Lichfield House. (Author's collection)

Nos 10 and 11 Downing Street by night. (Author's collection)

over himself, Mr Callaghan easily sidestepped their booby traps. It would take two years before the media finally got him.

James Callaghan prepared himself for the task of dealing with No 10. Here he was ambivalent. He understood that some senior civil servants tended to view politicians as mere *arrivistes*, temporarily interfering with Whitehall's established right to govern the country in their own covert way – sometimes with barely concealed derision for their temporary political masters. He went into action with all guns firing. Mounting an assault upon well-honed systems of administration and information exchange, he laid down certain new rules. In his middle-sixties, he tired easily, but knew how to handle this and declared himself unavailable for work commitments after lunch until he had managed forty winks. This displeased Private Office who habitually depended upon ready access to the prime minister at any time. Although Mr Callaghan did usually read official documents, paperwork was sometimes not returned, and then went missing until rediscovered later stuffed into some forgotten pocket. Pending trays proliferated as decisions on behalf of Private Office occasionally went into limbo. The prime minister also expected early nights fitted in with relaxing, family downtime.

The Private Office, kept at arm's length in many ways, did not yet feel strong enough to administer corrective slaps on the wrist. They had never experienced paperwork log jams with Harold Wilson who, for better or worse, dedicated all his working day to the cause and involved Private Office in much of it.

At the outset Mr Callaghan's private secretaries were largely excluded from political debate, as the new prime minister pointedly separated Labour Party matters from the official side. Annoyingly for Private Office, he made no such distinction with his special advisers, who were brought into both sides of consultations. This was bad news for Whitehall, used as it was to a compliant and – at least on the surface – trusting and co-operative Harold Wilson.

The special advisers were appointed as temporary civil servants at deputy secretary level, and as such carried considerable weight in No 10. They were headed by Bernard Donoughue, retained as head of the No 10 Policy Unit, and Tom McNally (now the Liberal Democrat Lord McNally) who replaced Marcia Williams as political secretary. Tom had been Mr Callaghan's political adviser in the FCO.

Bernard Donoughue writes about these days in detail in his book, *Downing Street Diary*. Tom McNally did once get a rocket for impertinence when he offered unwanted advice, but with this exception Mr Callaghan treated his special advisers with respect. Although resistant to committing himself on paper, the new PM did display worthy new, overdue, standards of efficient government by his commanding presence in the Cabinet. Welcome decisions were soon evident, often on matters long outstanding. Bernard Donoughue soon gave credit to Jim

Callaghan's firm but democratic management of Cabinet and the ceasefire which he orchestrated with Labour Party HQ at Transport House.

An apparently deliberate act of provocation by the new prime minister was inferred by the appointment into Private Office of a young diplomat from the FCO, who had shown clear sympathy and high standards of care and efficiency while in Mr Callaghan's Private Office there. Against all normal conventions he was imported to No 10. It was feared that he had been put there as the prime minister's mole and, in spite of his juniority, to monitor what was going on. It was a difficult position for this young man with, on the one hand, potential career backing from the prime minister but on the other, and more immediately, the displeasure of his civil service colleagues.

They made their feelings clear by not giving him a desk or telephone for a week, leaving him standing around looking cross and superfluous. In due course he appeared to meld with the other private secretaries and survived the full length of Mr Callaghan's term of office. However, after Mrs Thatcher's election success in 1979, I heard he was posted to a remote embassy somewhere in deepest South America.

A subtle outbreak of hostilities was signalled between officials and the prime minister and his political advisers. Noting that James Callaghan seemed to be taking a different line with his own Labour Party staff appointees, a coalition of mandarins called upon all Whitehall's accumulated skills to reassert their influence.

Private Office mounted an impressive counterattack by an excess of compliance and co-operation, dedicating themselves to all-round, unrelenting service to Mr Callaghan's every need. So high were their standards anyway that in terms of sheer professional efficiency they had little more to offer, but on a mundane level all the stops were pulled out. Each of the four limousines allocated to No 10 was systematically withdrawn and the interior fumigated, dabbed and sprayed. Cigar and pipe tobacco burns in the back seat were carefully patched. The fact was that Harold Wilson had not been the only smoker; he allowed both Bill Housden and my colleague, Arthur Smith, to light up their pipes when under way. A programme of sterilisation was overdue.

Although not at first occupied by the Callaghans, the prime minister's official flat was also spring cleaned – curtains, carpets and furniture. Accessories were added at Mrs Callaghan's request. Her chosen paintings were withdrawn from public emporia and hung as directed. One night the prime minister's red box even included papers from the Royal Parks' authority on the names and origin of species about which he had shown no more than passing interest during a walk through St James's Park. A quiet programme of paperwork overload was instituted in the knowledge that it was not the prime minister's strong point.

The prime minister was a man notably concerned about wasteful spending, and here Private Office was on strong ground. The mounting cost of protecting his Sussex farmhouse – where the Callaghans were determined to spend free weekends and holidays – and the small Kennington flat that he initially favoured over the apartments in No 10 was absorbed by the Home Office. Sussex Constabulary placed an emergency portacabin control room, not unobtrusively near the driveway and in sight of the farmhouse. State-of-the-art electronic warning systems were installed too. The attitude of Sussex Constabulary was that they had the highest police rate in the country and they had no intention of reducing it. But the tab eventually fell to the Home Office, who passed it through to No 10 for the information of the prime minister himself.

I was reluctantly but inevitably drawn into all this. The Callaghans owned a modest south-east London flat in Kennington which I remember as an ex-Greater London Council flat on the first floor, with a cold, sunless concrete passageway and no lift. It had originally been taken as an overnight sanctuary, a halfway house sleeping pad for the long nights occasionally demanded by parliamentary affairs. The prime minister and his wife intended to live here and the local M Division chief superintendent asked me to go along with him to arrange the security survey.

The flat was sparsely furnished. It had bachelor hallmarks, such as spilt cooking fat spots over a cheap carpet. Piles of reports and old newspapers were littered around. It was cold, with no central heating, and it was gloomy.

'Well!' said the chief superintendent. 'This can be a rough area. We will need a PC outside twenty-four hours a day. We must see that physical and electronic countermeasures are installed as a priority. It must all be properly co-ordinated with emergency response. This will cost a packet. Who is going to pay?'

After a moment's thought he added glumly: 'You know – this place might be alright for a prime minister, but I wouldn't let one of my PCs live here.'

———⇒⊳•⊲⇐———

Previously an influential member of the Wilson Kitchen Cabinet, the Government Car Service driver Bill Housden was not retained and he left No 10, and the state affairs over which he appeared to have had some standing, to remain as Lord Wilson's driver in retired obscurity. He was replaced by Joe Hazard, a small, bright, wiry Londoner. Joe had been brought up in a hard school in the East End, had some reputation as a bantamweight boxer and was a survivor. He was devoted to 'Else', his wife, but had no interest in the drivers' room card school and solutions to the *Daily Telegraph* crossword. Although he never fitted in with the three other drivers, Joe was not unpopular. They dominated him with previous experience of No 10's protocols, while he thought that as he was now the PM's chosen number one – he was in charge.

Joe could possibly have been illiterate and never read a map. Fortunately he had a comprehensive knowledge of London and the Home Counties and was usually able to plan the route for longer journeys well in advance. This took place with the other drivers, who were invited to discuss, for instance, the best way to get to the Adelphi Hotel in Liverpool. Joe would add their ideas to his own experience and quick wits – avoiding the use of road numbers or place names, but by remembering to turn left at the roundabout where the White Horse pub stood high on a hill and right at the Dying Duck T-junction. This was not an infallible system. Joe was aware of Mr Callaghan's vulnerability to car sickness, expertise at back-seat driving, determination to follow motorway routes whenever possible, and explosive exasperation when things went wrong.

Joe was never to aspire to Bill Housden's ruthless skill in fixing himself up with food and drink, and came to depend on the detective for the day, both to help him with long-distance navigation and revictualling at regular intervals. But SB morale dropped inevitably during many a melee with a high-spirited crowd pressing to see the prime minister, when Joe's little face appeared with the silently mouthed question, 'Where shall I be eating?' It was not uncommon to find him walking a red carpet strictly reserved for VIPs, looking for a detective to lean upon for his lunch.

Favouring gold wristwatches, bracelets and necklaces, Joe was easily identifiable with a metal detector and tinkled if he took a bend at speed. He gave alert and competent attention to his real job, dependability, speed and safety on the road, and a lift home at night if you were stuck for transport.

In between the civil servants and the political advisers were semi-independent regulars, including detectives. Within the party the prime minister was known as 'Happy Jim', 'Lucky Jim', 'Honest Jim', 'Big Jim', or even 'Stoker Jim' – although I never heard him addressed directly with this oblique reference to his wartime service in the Royal Navy. He soon vetoed any unlikely mateyness from my team with, 'Just because I am singing don't make the mistake of thinking that I am happy!' As a one-time MP representing the Police Federation, Mr Callaghan held a low opinion of the police service in general, and his previous SB protection teams in particular. Perhaps he thought he had detected a tendency towards corruption and racism within the Metropolitan Police, and the traditional conservatism within the security services – of which SB was part – that accounted for their determined conviction that all *pinkos* were simply covert communist agents? If so, he had the wrong man with me.

Bernard Donoughue writes that the new prime minister's character had three layers. On the surface was simple, honest, bluff Jim; below that was a very cunning and secretive politician; and finally, under that was somebody who did really believe in simple and honest virtues. Joe Hazard was aware of a fourth layer. James Callaghan was also dominated by an uncontrollably bad temper. Others within a close radius were wise to discover at an early stage that they were not exempted. Our own standing outside the civil service, and on an independent ladder of promotion, was some reassurance. In daily contact with him as we were, the probability of an occasional tantrum provided the detectives with a special challenge. The prime minister told me that some people called him a bully. He tried, illogically, to defend this proposition with the ludicrous and clearly preposterous counter claim, 'but I only bully my equals!'

Mr Callaghan's first trip down to his constituency in Cardiff provided the chance to test his patience. The duty detectives barely survived this first real test and it was fortunate that our team were quick learners.

—————⇒⋅●⋅⇐—————

Top civil servants work to a three-year schedule with new prime ministers. Having entered No 10 wreathed in smiles, it takes a full year to train a new incumbent; this may be followed by a usefully efficient and co-operative year. The third promises inevitable decline. This is the time to watch for thin lips and drawn faces – followed by tears. Within Whitehall this process is regarded as almost inevitable.

As they had collective organisational experience and access to a wide spread of facilities, Private Office expected that the prime minister would want to comply with their recommendations when travelling officially. They also had every reason to anticipate his compliance on security, the use of government resources such as the Royal Air Force, co-ordination in planning the programme and an understanding of close protection disciplines and police techniques. With a touch here and there, most PMs are happy with this. However, from the outset, James Callaghan refused to fit to the expected pattern. As a result, Mr Callaghan, after objecting to the expense involved in being driven down the M4 motorway, insisted on showing the flag and travelling by British Rail for his first semi-official constituency visit to Cardiff.

In spite of a detailed briefing, it is apparently difficult for a newcomer to the top slot in No 10 to absorb the importance of modern government communications' systems – that the now obsolete Home Office radio installed in official cars was critical both to Private Office and the man with whom the buck stopped. By ensuring the very promptest contact with No 10 and the Ministry of Defence, the special radio and the official cars were essential not only for official travel but also for private or party programmes – when arrangements were already in position for mileage payments to the Treasury. With the Cold

War rumbling, communications were an integral ingredient to defence and, by ensuring effective government from the centre, were a routine part of Whitehall's administrative machinery.

Urgent defence decisions were impeded and operational difficulties magnified when advance communication was not already in place and prompt contact with their man became essential. Special arrangements were soon put in hand at the private flat in Kennington. For the prime minister's proposed periods of relaxation at his farmhouse in Sussex, among other expedients, the very highest level of security clearance for Garden Room girls was pre-arranged. With top-secret hardware, they kept watch on the encoded telex machines specially installed at police HQ in Lewes and then, as no private secretary was on the spot, took IMMEDIATE papers to the prime minister in person – waiting for his decisions to feed back into the system. Frequent knocks on the farmhouse door signalled farewell to the hallowed prime ministerial privacy.

By later standards this must look appallingly antiquated. After one security assessment, the prime minister minuted that heaven should be thanked that we were in a Cold War with the Soviet Union and not the real thing.

Private Office therefore favoured official cars for journeys such as this one to Cardiff. By using British Rail, other agencies had to be called in. Either a special coach or a purpose-adapted compartment had to be laid on, with fully security-cleared British Transport Police to travel and operate a Home Office radio, and stationmasters unwrapped and warmed up as hand shakers. Without the official car, there was also a loss of flexibility, security and communications at the point of arrival. In this case, Private Office decided that even if the train was used, official No 10 limousines would have to be on the spot in Cardiff as well – in spite of the cost to the nation and the Labour Party.

Perhaps 'Sir Humphrey' also seized the opportunity to activate a stratagem of his own too? If so, was it intended to add yet more leverage to undermine the Callaghans' determination to avoid No 10 and Chequers and travel in private or party transport? Two drivers were instructed to drive their official cars to Cardiff overnight and rendezvous with the prime minister and his party at the station. However, to maximise the advantages on offer from Downing Street, nothing was to go wrong.

Joe was in Downing Street in good time on the morning of departure to take the prime minister and a detective to Paddington station. In the hope of avoiding early morning gridlock in the West End, Joe – sensibly but unusually – elected to head along Whitehall and cut through the archway and on to Horse Guards Parade, using the Mall and Hyde Park Corner route.

It was unfortunate that the Horse Guards' Corporal of Horse – on foot in his cape under the archway – was not aware of the significance of a small, approved light in the front windscreen of the official car. Unaccustomed to traffic transiting his sacrosanct territory, he crashed his spurs and presented a threatening sword, demanding in approved parade ground tones, 'Who goes there?' He had no authority to deviate from his Standing Orders. Valuable minutes were lost defusing him.

With the late arrival of the prime minister at Paddington, train departure was delayed. Following established protocol, the prime minister was met by the duty stationmaster. Youngish, long-haired, with an unfamiliar but mandatory bowler hat perched like a black bath bun at an angle, he was not impressive. The Inter-City train made a late departure. The close-knit programme carefully honed in Private Office began to slip. Worse still, the train broke down near Swindon. The public address broadcast – not a masterpiece of British technology – whirred away in unintelligible high-pitched decibels, sounding – as the distinguished American travel writer Bill Bryson would have explained – like a Mexican singer with his nuts jammed in a drawer. With a replacement power source eventually shunted on, the train bumped along at half speed.

Arrangements in the carriage were neither discreet nor conducive to the scrutiny of paperwork. Although first-class seats had been reserved, a private compartment was not hooked on. With luggage and red boxes stacked at one end, under the supervision of a Garden Room girl, the detective formed the only breakwater from autograph hunters and passengers processing up and down to the buffet car or, with incrementally increasing frequency, on the pretext of hurrying to the unisex toilets.

With an open red box on the table in front of him, the PM adopted the huddle position to reduce the chance of his affairs of state being read by inquisitive British Rail passengers, not all of whom had paid a first-class fare. It is a fact that well-meaning people like to touch prime ministers, as we had already found on the Isles of Scilly. This had to be prevented, even if votes were lost.

It was virtually impossible for the prime minister to dictate to the second Garden Room girl sitting opposite with shorthand notebook and sharpened pencil ready on the table between them. She avoided eye contact by concentrating on the *Daily Telegraph* crossword on her lap. This young old hand from a county family had seen it all before and Mr Callaghan was lucky that she stuck to the crossword during long periods of underemployment instead of producing either her travel scrabble or needle, thread and growing patchwork quilt. It was unlikely that she voted Labour.

The prime minister could not be described as 'Happy Jim' when his train finally pulled into Cardiff seventy-five minutes adrift, and with his programme corrugating. Worse still, he was forced to cancel his afternoon nap. He did just manage a brief, reluctant smile and unconvincing handshake with the stationmaster. Mr Callaghan hurried down the platform, ignoring the Garden Room girls' frenetic commitment to oversee a safe unload and assembly of official red boxes and his personal luggage – and not to miss a place in the convoy either.

Help had been thoughtfully provided by British Rail, who allocated a porter. He struggled, red-faced, back and forth and set off with a heavily unbalanced trolley, urged on in pursuit of the prime minister by increasingly strident Garden Room girls. When these iron-wheeled trolleys gain momentum into the fast lane they are – not unlike a supertanker at sea – difficult to stop, and it was bad luck when an unsuspecting lady member of the public was mown down. She suffered unpleasant lacerations and bruises on the leg requiring medical attention. Having lost patience, the prime minister instructed his driver to get on with it. A gaggle of helpers were left applying bandages.

After a brief wash and brush up at his maisonette, Mr Callaghan – already over an hour late and still enquiring gruffly where his baggage was – tried to make up time on the first leg of his constituency programme.

He was due to officiate at a pre-lunch ceremony in the small factory of a local Labour supporter, situated on a new industrial estate on the edge of town. Dignitaries and their good ladies had been in position for some time and were tiring, the local press strutted around looking for 'exclusives' and a red carpet was already unrolled and hoovered. The Right Honourable James Callaghan was on his way at last. Curtsies were perfected. Mrs Callaghan had wisely opted out.

The motorcade was led by a discreetly unmarked red Ford Escort with inadequate radio communication, driven by a police officer in plain clothes who knew the way. The first No 10 limo followed with the prime minister. A Special Branch car containing three local officers was next. It was followed by the second Downing Street limo with the duty Garden Room girl in the back seat, with red boxes and her electric typewriter. A locally allocated government car brought up the rear.

In busy traffic the lead driver, overexcited with his great responsibilities, jumped a red light and, in a melee of traffic congestion, the Downing Street number one driver safely repositioned to the inner lane and waited for the lights to change. The following cars failed to spot this manoeuvre and gonged and flashed their way past the waiting outer lane and followed the lead car across a dangerous junction without spotting the prime minister's car. He was left behind with a detective and driver. Neither knew the route.

The driver of the lead car finally realised that he had lost everybody and pulled into a layby, where he was soon joined by the stray cars from the motorcade. Thinking that the prime minister was there too, the lead car set off again, was waved past the barrier of the VIP ceremonial area and he and the SB car pulled aside to let the No 10 limo set down the PM. Directed to the red carpet threshold and, thinking Mr Callaghan's car had somehow preceded him, the driver of the second No 10 limo pulled to a standstill and before the expectant audience out stepped a Garden Room girl with her typewriter ready to plug in. The ceremonial choir started up and petered out in disarray. This was not the prime minister at all.

Meanwhile, in the outer world, the detective in the PM's car was inviting pedestrians to tell him how to get to the VIP address. After vague guidelines and with his driver now under instruction in distinctly positive terms, Mr Callaghan directed the real prime minister's car, finally arriving at the barrier. Here a suspiciously confused security guard, certain enough that he had just waved through the prime minister, refused admittance to a *doppelganger*. After a long phone call a local police inspector strolled unhurriedly down. Finally satisfied that while one prime minister was impressive, two were an impossibility, he signalled an over-casual go-ahead.

After a bad weekend in Cardiff, it was agreed that the prime minister would abandon British Rail and be driven back to Downing Street. The weather was foul and after a motorway hold-up in heavy rain, followed by a long diversion, the limos – in danger of running short of petrol – swung into a filling station near Heathrow. Out jumped Ian Bryan, the duty detective, to keep watch. He saw a man wearing a blue anorak, jeans and a knitted bobble hat squee-jeeing the windscreen of a car. The prime minister's Rover was filthy and Ian suggested that the employee might like to help out? 'Jeezus,' exploded the American tourist. 'I've just travelled fifteen hundred flaming miles from Texas. I haven't been here for half an hour when some nut asks me to clean his prime minister's car! What a country!'

Back in the sanctuary of Downing Street, Mr Callaghan's first task was to tell a private secretary to instruct all the drivers that he wanted to be driven away without delay as soon as he was aboard. ALWAYS! This ill-considered decision would lead to chaotic confusion in several countries. He also insisted on travelling by motorway wherever there was one to reduce his decidedly un-macho bouts of occasional car sickness.

But, by default, the result of this chaotic weekend in Cardiff could hardly have been more useful. Prayers had been answered.

We set up firm new pre-emptive disciplines at both planning and operational levels and, wherever possible, never relied upon others whenever we could do it ourselves. With the backing of Private Office and the authority of the Cabinet Office, and with concerns now on paper, we took on new responsibilities, adopted advanced planning strategies, rarely travelled single-handed and, wherever possible, made an advance visit beforehand to every location outside No 10 and parliament. This demanded new resources and considerable and energetic dedication on the part of the Special Branch unit at No 10. The Private Office orchestrated much of this. Our greater liaison with them helped us to get things done properly and gave them a direct link with events outside Downing Street. While security now demanded prevention rather than last-minute kick and rush, the presence of armed officers was the final line of defence for successful close protection. It was soon possible to compare our work favourably with that of foreign colleagues.

Even so, it was impossible that everything could go smoothly all the time. But for now, Mr Callaghan buttonholed me. 'I suppose it wasn't entirely a bad police operation, but don't expect a pay rise this year.' He was not joking.

South Wales Police Special Branch rang early the following day. Their chief constable – desperate not to miss a knighthood – had concerned himself that all may not have been well over the weekend. 'Leave it to me,' I advised. 'I'll do my best to sort it all out. But do tell him to stop rolling cigarettes in public. The prime minister cannot stand people who smoke.' The chief did get his honour in the end.

However, there was never enthusiasm within the No 10 team for weekend visits to Cardiff and, particularly, the annual Bank Holiday festival at Splott, a Labour Party stronghold and a *must* for Cardiff MPs.

There must be something about the name?

The first three may have been the worst months in Ken Stowe's life. But by then the unrelenting pressure, quietly applied by the civil service to the prime minister, produced a transformation. He and Mrs Callaghan moved out of Kennington and into No 10, Chequers replaced the farm at Lewes, and the use of official limos became *de rigueur*.

The prime minister was becoming ever more dependent upon his Private Office and the No 10 infrastructure. The private secretaries were consulted with increasing frequency, even on party matters, and with both his and official backing, Special Branch was soon providing high-quality close protection.

With the final score of Callaghan 0, Whitehall 1, a team effort was now possible. Walking the Sussex Downs one weekend, Mr Callaghan confided, 'If only I could be a benevolent dictator I really think I could get this country going again, John!'

That may have been as near as he was likely to get to a sense of humour, although now, as history shows him to have been a man with remarkable political aptitude, it makes interesting speculation. For the moment, however, he was free to concentrate on the great issues of state and not mess around working out the best way to get to Splott.

THIRTEEN

Incidentally, the PM had earlier decided to return today. But this morning on his way to see the Pope, he looked up at the blue sky and said, 'I think we will go to look at the Bay of Naples' – and went off to Positano for the weekend.

Downing Street Diary, Bernard Donoughue. Friday, 23 September 1977

James Callaghan insisted on spending the summer 1976 recess at his farm near Lewes in Sussex, where he had entered into a partnership with the experienced John Gingell. John shovelled the muck and the prime minister gave him advice.

This decision required massive demands on his support staff. Ken Godbeer and I made an early reconnaissance, closely following technicians from the Cabinet Office who had already established sophisticated communications between police HQ and Whitehall. Accommodation for the No 10 staff was found at Shelley's Hotel, and secure rooms and a garage rented in an unused house nearby. Security liaison with Sussex Constabulary was encouraging. Aware that the prime minister and his family intended to stay at the farm without intrusion from the public or interruption by Downing Street, the assistant chief constable in charge directed a large portacabin to a prominent spot on the entrance drive, as well as a posse of policemen equipped with county-wide communications and modern security paraphernalia, including adapted single-shot Sten guns. The automatic version was still prohibited to the police service.

From then on the Callaghans could watch television in cosy privacy in the evenings, but if they ventured outdoors would immediately be confronted with armed police and aggressive dog patrols – as well as urgent response teams with front-line commitments when their warning sirens, bleepers and flashing lights were activated by secretly hidden electronic warning devices. It was not what the family had intended, but Sussex Constabulary had no intention of downscaling their responsibilities by letting a prime minister or his family get kidnapped and forwarded in pieces by registered mail to No 10 together with the usual 'demands'. The prime minister also intended, at times, to drive his own Rover saloon instead of using the (expensive?) official limo. His own car was not equipped with radio communications and if we had notice we would fall in and follow, together with a police van and barking German Shepherds. This was less than discreet but the picture grew worse if he tried to escape without us. We then had to find him and this called for widespread trawls through country roads by every police vehicle in the area. Under no circumstances did No 10 intend to allow the head man of their world to be out of touch. As we know, he had the final word over Britain's nuclear arsenal.

With his vast experience of government, Mr Callaghan really should have known better. After a couple of attempts to take the grandchildren on quiet picnics to Cuckmere Haven, a local beauty spot, Mr Callaghan got the message. However, Mrs Callaghan did not, and remained bewildered after Joe Hazard and I arrived one morning to take them to an appointment at Leeds Castle. As this was on the manor of the Kent Constabulary, complex arrangements were agreed with them in advance for a preferred route, communications channels and quiet police backup to ensure the PM's safety.

Mr Callaghan quietly let me go ahead with our plans, but Mrs Callaghan could not understand what was happening. After a while her conversation with him became more than a little tedious. This is a verbatim account of how it went: 'What are they going this way for, Jim? Don't you think the other road is quicker?' After a pause, 'The other route is certainly prettier, Jim? I do hope we can go back the other way,' and, 'Well – I'm surprised we found it at all coming this way.' Unusually, the prime minister did not try to interfere.

He normally had a provocative habit of congratulating Joe when the detective had done the navigation, but today he was unusually sensitive. When we got to Leeds Castle in good order and on time he said, 'Well done John. That was a tricky journey.' Mrs Callaghan was never really in contact with the real world of a prime minister, but she did possess the kindest and most thoughtful nature. One day when Ian Bryan shut her fingers in the door of the official Rover she said, nursing her red and swollen digits, 'Let's agree it would be better not to tell Jim what has happened.'

Life for the duty Downing Street driver, the Garden Room girl and the detective was not unpleasant during the summer weather of 1976. The tab for hotel accommodation was processed through Downing Street and Home Office, and the commissioner of police paid a subsistence allowance to help out with meals away from home. Private Office gradually increased Mr Callaghan's burden through their link person from the Garden Room secretariat, and the prime minister was confined to his office more often than he had ever expected. Unfortunately for him, Whitehall did not share his opinion that governance of Great Britain could come to a standstill during parliamentary recesses. One afternoon when the prime minister was safely embedded with red boxes, his three staff decided it was opportune to carry out a necessary reconnaissance to a forthcoming venue not far from Shoreham Airport – just past Brighton. Shoreham Airport was the home of a branch of the flying club of which I was a member and part-time instructor. It was not a problem to show them around the county from a height of 1,500ft or so. Unfortunately, when she saw him that evening for dictation and red-box delivery, Vanessa, one of the Garden Room girls, told Mr Callaghan how much she had enjoyed the experience. When I called to see him that evening to work on his programme he said, 'Vanessa tells me you have taken her for a flight from Shoreham, John. When can you take Audrey and me?'

'Prime minister – there are all sorts of rules about these things I'm afraid.'

'Look here, John. I *am* the Prime Minister. I *make* the rules.'

Faced with the logic of his point of view I suggested, 'How about four o'clock tomorrow afternoon, Prime Minister? Joe and I will pick you both up at 15.00 hours.'

'OK then. Do fix it all up.'

'Yes, Prime Minister,' was all I could think of.

I was pretty deeply into the mire. As far as I knew there were no rules because we were intending to create a precedent. But a prime minister's safety is, of course, of paramount importance and I was there to ensure it. Instead, I was intending to take him for a flight in a single-engined private aircraft, rather than the normal multi-engined official types. Indeed, in those days it was exceptional to resort even to British Airways.

The technicalities of the operation were not complicated. I knew Patrick Copping, the chief flying instructor at Shoreham. It involved a telephone call to book the flight, a request to check over the aircraft for me in good time, and to prepare the necessary membership forms ready for a couple of signatures – and to do all this without a word to anyone, especially the media.

The real problem lay with Downing Street and my loyalty to Ken Stowe, the principal private secretary, who would certainly be the main target in any enquiry to establish the cause of the prime minister's death – an improbable likelihood though it was. I decided to take another chance and not tell him. If I did so he would have to say a firm 'NO!' and exacerbate an already difficult relationship with Mr Callaghan. If I could keep it quiet, it would be down to me alone. I explained this to Vanessa and she boldly played along, although Ken Stowe was, of course, her overlord.

It all started smoothly at Shoreham. Joe parked discreetly and the membership forms were signed and handed over. That not only made the flight legal but covered insurance obligations as well. Mrs Callaghan climbed into the rear seat of a sturdy French Rallye training aircraft – the MS 150 – and the prime minister sat in the front right-hand seat next to me. We taxied away to the holding point of this grass airfield and went through engine and pre-take-off checks. Everything was 'in the green'. Air traffic control radioed permission to line up and take off. There were no other aircraft in the circuit.

With full power selected, away we went. Unfortunately …

With over 400 hours in-command logged up, and somewhere in the region of 1,000 previously uncomplicated take offs, just why did this one have to be any different? But after passing the halfway mark the MS 150 would still not unstick! The take-off run had to be abandoned and we taxied back to the holding point. I switched off and jumped out to see why. This could not have been good for the passengers' morale, but they resisted the temptation to abandon ship too.

Of course, there was nothing wrong with the aircraft at all. It was simply that the management at Shoreham had not cut the runway grass for a week and the friction disallowed sufficient take-off speed. Let's try again – this time from a couple of yards further to the right. Sure enough, off we soared to enjoy a splendidly untroubled hour of flight over Sussex.

The drama was not yet over. As we passed over his farm, Mr Callaghan exploded. 'Just look at that wheat field. It's all patchy. Must have been badly drilled in the autumn. Wait till I see John Gingell!'

And so we said farewell to John Gingell and another carefully nurtured relationship. However, the good news was that the Callaghans and Joe and Vanessa all kept quiet and Ken Stowe could go about his work without more worry.

Well – for the time being anyway.

Administrative arrangements for three days of talks with the Italian government were not encouraging:

> The insurance of baggage at the expense of HM Government is not permissible. Those travelling in the HS.125 are advised to check with their insurance companies whether they are covered for non-commercial flights. Only £25.00d in Sterling notes may be taken out of the country.

Subsistence. Detectives will provide their own funds. The embassy unable to cash personal cheques.

With an exchange rate of £1 = 2,275 Lira, a focus on decimal points was essential – as one of my colleagues found when he bought a crocodile handbag for his wife for £75. It was not an entire success, as he discovered when his credit card account was debited with £750 and he was forced to cancel the family holiday.

Following the Housden precedent, Joe Hazard was hoping to be included in the party as baggage master. However, to Private Office this seemed an extravagance and the RAF was persuaded to declare that his allocated seat was already taken. Rather than lose face with the mates he had already told, Joe showed commendable initiative by appearing on television news climbing the gangway of the prime minister's aircraft. As soon as the cameras switched off – and moments before the doors closed – he disembarked at the double and took a week's holiday with Else.

In Rome, word reached the detectives that all was not well between the prime minister and the British Embassy. It was alleged that he was making diplomatic gaffes and undermining a carefully nurtured accord with the Italian Foreign Office. He did not help things by insisting that two of his staff were admitted with him to a private meeting with the president. Apparently this breach of protocol was like taking your secretary to an Audience at Buckingham Palace.

During the morning of day three, Mr and Mrs Callaghan were driven to the Vatican and walked unscathed past the helmeted and piked Swiss Guard wearing polished breast plates, baggy trousers and sunglasses. As soon as they were stood down they lit cigarettes. No doubt they made the Pope feel safer.

While the Callaghans enjoyed a private audience with Pope Paul VI, I waited near the small window overlooking St Peter's Square – barely resisting the temptation to throw open the window and give the multitudes waiting below for a Sign from His Holiness a sign of my own. However, I was forestalled by a determined Monsignor, who pushed me with the half-dozen senior diplomats and Downing Street staff inside the private chamber, declaring, 'Do hurry along. I assure you His Holiness wants you all to go in.' When the obligatory photograph of the occasion arrived at Downing Street it showed that I was the only one inadequately dressed, because I was to go along for lunch in a public restaurant as soon as the prime minister had changed into something lighter. There was also a massive invoice for the Vatican's favours, which we split equally among us. But not without a grumble or two.

Back at the ambassador's residence – the Villa Wolkonsky, where the prime minister and party had been accommodated – there was a certain hiatus about the next move. The RAF HS.125 was near the limits of its range at Rome and they needed to plan the next leg. Perhaps No 10 firmly hoped for London and fortress Chequers. But prime ministerial obfuscation was such that it appeared likely that he and Mrs Callaghan were toying with the very last-minute idea of accepting an Italian government offer of hospitality over the coming weekend. A couple of days in Sicily was one offer, to the displeasure of the RAF for various technical reasons. Then, as we all stood on the steps of the villa prior to departure for the airport, Mrs Callaghan signalled approval of the Abruzzo Mountains inland retreat – or even Rome itself. Mr Callaghan sat on the fence and then huffily told the Italian and British officials who had to put it all into operation, 'Oh come on then. Let's go to Positano.' Can there be any doubt that while pretending to concede to *their* wishes, it was his own favoured choice from the outset?

As mayhem erupted among behind-the-scenes officials, who suddenly had to commandeer a hotel, relocate the guests already there, arrange transport and security, as well as communications, VIP protection and RAF re-positioning, Ken Stowe turned to me and said calmly, 'I think there may be something you want to tell me John? About that flight down at Shoreham?' The prime minister had leaked our secret and now I was in the dock. The principal private secretary listened to what I had to say, understood the points made and – with broad-shouldered disdain in formal red tape – forgot all about it too.

After half an hour of furious reorganisation we again waited on the steps to link up with the motorcade for a 150-mile drive to Positano. The ambassador's wife, who had ignored me for three days, demonstrated the diplomatic skill of Perfidious Albion by saying, 'I am so sorry not to have seen more of you, Mr Warwickshire. I do hope my staff have looked after you well during your stay here.'

As we finally set off, exhausted, pale-faced Garden Room girls hurried out with their typewriters and personal gear. Thanks to Italian charm and generosity, recovery in Positano was total. On day two, a modern naval cruiser appeared on the horizon to escort the prime minister's party to Capri in a comfortable launch, operated by unseamanlike vagabonds who stood around smoking. Roger Stott, MP and parliamentary private secretary to the prime minister, had once served in the mercantile marine and he and I decided on a plan of action in an emergency. I would take the bridge at pistol point, while he grabbed the wheel and assumed command until the cruiser drew alongside. It seemed a sound idea at the time but may have been influenced by the hospitality on offer.

On Sunday, the motorcade snaked back along the coast road toward Naples Airport, where the prefect of the city would bid a formal farewell to his country's guests. An efficient motorcycle escort marshalled the convoy and as they were a few minutes early made a short diversion. When he noticed what they were doing the prime minister exploded with rage. He brought the motorcade to a standstill and summoned the head of protocol. Having generously and efficiently organised the weekend and enjoyed a friendly relationship, he was completely taken aback by Mr Callaghan's change of demeanour and loud demands to know just what they all thought they were up to. By now, with a couple of minutes lost, it was academic anyway.

At the VIP lounge, the Naples VIPs were lined up and Mr Callaghan showed diplomatic skills by smiling and shaking hands, before disappearing promptly into the Gentlemen's.

But Private Office and British Embassy personnel were once again pale-faced.

⟹•◦•⟸

It would be a great mistake to imagine that the lives of Special Branch officers inside No 10 comprised simply of one huge round of sailing the blue seas, enjoying classic meals in the best hotels, or fox-trotting along red carpets. Although we certainly had to conduct ourselves at many levels and remain unobtrusive but alert, administration and planning were always focused on the final front-line activity: the protection of the prime minister. Everyday experiences were grim affairs more often than not. The appearance of the single word 'London' in the diary for Friday, 14 January 1977 heralded a day that was soon known in our office as Bloody Friday – or 'BF-Day'.

By this date, the prime minister and Private Office had come to a better understanding. Outside No 10, however, Mr Callaghan's last-minute changes of plan continued to be a challenge for the police service, for which we were the principal source of information and liaison. As the prime minister continued to benefit from the remarkable flexibility provided by police units – Special Branch and traffic patrols alike – and from their local knowledge, radio communications, driving expertise and initiative, it was a great problem for us that he never bothered to thank them.

The detectives each had a dozen or more forward diary entries to plan and, thanks to careless maladministration on my part, the Bloody Friday detail found its way into my tray. I was forced to spend time on it when police chiefs from the East End of London started to ask what was happening. The harassed private secretary with the main file showed me the contents. Not a single paper had come into Downing Street from any source. The Labour Party which, in those days, had a firm grip on London voters were believed to be responsible for Mr Callaghan's visit to oversee Greater London Council (GLC) and local authorities' regeneration plans for Newham and Tower Hamlets to the north, and Southwark and Greenwich south of the Thames. While City of London rentals and the cost of building land started to climb sky high, the East End of inner London was still full of holes and rubble from the Second World War Blitz. This day out may have had exciting prospects for Mr Callaghan but, unusually, Private Office washed its hands of the planning – except to provide the official car and driver.

As BF-Day minus five arrived and pressures grew, I put on a metaphoric hard hat and set out on foot to find out for myself just who was in charge of programming and organisation. The prime minister would spend the day in the proving ground of the Right-to-Work movement, comprising both the genuinely unemployed and well-placed militant troublemakers. We would need to work closely with five divisions of local police and the Port of London Authority Constabulary, who would all have to meld harmoniously on the day. Several hundred officers from more than a score of police stations would be involved, using different transport and radio frequencies. Their chiefs were still in the dark too and I would now have to start sorting it out.

First stop was Transport House in Smith Square. Reg Underhill (later Lord Underhill), director of Labour agents nationally, declared that it was all down to the London Labour Party and nothing to do with Transport House. Did I detect a touch of huffiness? The London Labour Party spokesperson then told me that it was nothing to do with them either – 'thanks to Greater London Council intransigence'. She said that I should try the ceremonials officer at GLC headquarters. He was grumpy about being excluded from an inner circle of organisers and declared a 'nothing doing' stance. I put him under pressure and he agreed to try to find out who was in charge – and to do so promptly! He rang later to say that it was all in the hands of the personal assistant to Sir Reg Goodwin, GLC Leader. He also told me we could get all we wanted from David Holt.

Now, David Holt was that young diplomat appointed by Mr Callaghan into Private Office from the Foreign and Commonwealth Office. If he had a political affiliation it accounted for a lot – although his competence had been well proven. However, David was away on holiday.

The temperature was rising in my office. Police chiefs – more used to working from precise and well-programmed visits by royalty – were getting irritated by political prevarication. They were increasingly anxious to draw up operation orders, work to a timetable to divert traffic, allocate police manpower at junctions and traffic lights, arrange escorts – both mobile and on foot – and to agree radio frequencies and relay handovers. Knowing that they might get the blame for log jams, they too were getting very cross with what they perceived as a vacillating sub-species – local government officials. It would have been hypocritical of me to pretend otherwise.

The first bombshell was dropped when I heard that Mr Callaghan had agreed to travel with VIPs in an executive coach. This implied that he would be separated from the official car and communications facilities. To be readily available for any emergency Joe Hazard would now have to follow with an empty car.

With no programme in sight on BF-Day minus three, I went down to the Royal Albert Dock to renew a long-standing acquaintance with Chief Superintendent Jim Tuplin, head of the Port of London police CID and – together with the militant Jack Dash, the port workers' leader – the acknowledged overlord of dockland. We combined what we knew and Jim set about outlining his own idea of the programme, calculating driving and walking distances and times between viewpoints, suitable parking and turning points for a motorcade and acceptable corrals for the press. Jim also established that the Port of London Authority chairman, Lord Aldington, and his personal assistant knew even less than we did. They too blamed GLC intransigence. Although we were supposed to be working to a programme instead of preparing one, I was now able to start collating and distributing a possible agenda. At no stage was the inner circle of organisers involved and GLC HQ was still intransigent.

However, on BF-Day minus one the GLC rang to say that the 'final version' was ready. At County Hall I met an unhappy, set-faced official coopted from the London Labour Party. In a disorganised file of papers he also found details of the executive coach hired for the day, the registration number, a seating plan and the driver's name. He was set-faced because he had been lumbered with the job at the very last minute, under pain of dismissal in the event of malfunction. He had been given no terms of reference or contact with the inner circle. A million telephone calls and numerous modifications later and a police operation order was prepared. Several hundred policemen polished their buttons ready for the big day.

Moments before lift off, Tom McCaffrey, the prime minister's press secretary, then confounded any system that might have been emerging by crumpling under pressure from Fleet Street and agreeing to let the press string along in their own coach. *He overlooked the need to tell anyone else!* A week earlier it might have been a good idea. The determined intention of the reporters to persuade the prime minister into ridiculous photo opportunities could have been controlled with passes and restricted areas. It was too late to warn the police and it had to be left to the Almighty to influence their marksman not to open fire on unidentified and unexpected interlopers. The convoy would now involve two coaches, several police and Special Branch lead and pursuit cars, and the No 10 limo.

On BF-Day the driver of the executive coach arrived in Downing Street early to work out how to do a ten-point turn. With auto-transmission, discreet curtaining, high-class furnishings and small round Parisian café-style tables, attractive hostesses and light snacks, it would provide some comfort during a long day.

Unfortunately, Mr Callaghan flatly refused to climb on board. Having noticed that it was a Mercedes, he declared that there was no way he would spend a day in London's East End in a foreign vehicle. He retreated into No 10 while the owners tried to lever the Mercedes logo from the body and wheel hubs; it proved impossible with the limited ironmongery available. A British coach was ordered as a replacement. The programme had slipped by an hour when an ancient AEC hove into view. With a lumpy diesel engine, old-fashioned crash gearbox, long clutch travel and short-legged driver, it finally ground out of Downing Street in a series of jolts and heaves. Conveyed in this ancient technology, it was impossible for passengers to keep coffee in cups as the driver experimented with the obsolete art of double-declutching.

It rained heavily all day. A cold wind ruined the ambience of dockland. Under these unpleasant conditions the prime minister, who normally refused to wear a hat, had been ill-advised to put on a fashionable mink fur hat given to him for attending Canada's winning World Ice Hockey match. Although many hundreds of photos were taken by scrambling pressmen that day, I cannot recall any appearing in the national newspapers, although originals must surely have been retained in archives for reproduction on very special occasions.

The whole party debussed at viewpoints and photographers crowded into deserted warehouses and bomb-damaged factories for demonstrations and photo-calls. VIPs got cold and wet listening to descriptions of 'the scheme' and climbed aboard again to steam dry. It was an ideal way to catch pneumonia. Policemen peered into the murk for the wrong coach. At one stage pressmen came to blows with security guards when they tried to follow the PM into a duty-free bonded store which – as the repository of casks of port steadily maturing to 'Vintage' status – was diligently protected by HM Customs on behalf of Her Majesty The Queen. At one stage, the GLC plan for coping with traffic congestion in central London was explained in a few seconds. It involved leaving all the roads as they were, marking trunk roads with lanes reserved for buses and letting all other vehicles remain in gridlock. The theory was that drivers would never return. It also seemed likely to guarantee a full stop to London's economic future.

The whole convoy finally came to a stop at County Hall during the evening rush hour. There were no fond farewells or promises of government support as Mr Callaghan gratefully transferred to the home comforts of his No 10 Rover. As Bloody Friday was a day of such unparalleled administrative incohesion, and factional dispute, Mr Callaghan must have become aware that the Labour Party had no chance of organising victory at the next election – irrespective of his government's merits.

Under the circumstances, the police service had done extraordinarily well and my colleague for the day, Peter Smither, assured me that the prime minister said, 'Thank you, John.' This was probably intended for all the policemen involved.

As I was the nearest it was strange – perhaps Freudian even – but I never heard those words myself.

FOURTEEN

'How's the old kettle looking … ?'
'Well. It's sort of black and round with a knob on top.'

Members of the drivers' room tea club, No 10 Downing Street

Step inside the black door of No 10 Downing Street into the entrance hall and turn right. The heavy door ahead opens into the drivers' room. In the 1970s it was also an iron curtain isolating 'up front' personnel – drivers, messengers, uniformed policemen off watch – from pen pushers. In spite of the egalitarian effort orchestrated from Private Office, a certain class distinction dictated that private secretaries, Garden Room girls, press officers and special advisers felt ill at ease and tended to keep clear of the space reserved for what, in other walks of life, might have been seen as 'below-stairs workers'.

It would have been a revelation to Downing Street believers to spend a few hours observing the drivers' different but very real world. Here, there were no worries about parliamentary majorities, party divisions or labour disputes, Cabinet reshuffles, opinion polls, budget forecasts or diplomatic incidents. Here, in this shabby, insular world, a good hand of cards, the promise of a few hours' overtime to improve the chance of getting enough cash together to buy a second-hand car to take the kids away for a week at Butlins holiday camp, or a decision to put the kettle on were of greater significance.

From their position as halfway between the two camps – or part members of each – the detectives were allowed in on an honorary basis.

It has already been pointed out how unsuitable the No 10 building was as the focal point of government. There is simply no accommodation within for visitors' support staff. It was for this reason that occasional temporary members had to be admitted to the drivers' room too. The worst case was the arrival of senior American diplomats such as Henry Kissinger. His note taker would also go up to see the prime minister and his press officers might be offered tea in the press office at No 10. The agent in charge would come into our tiny launch pad and try to look at home. But twenty or more State Department agents – reluctant to let their 'target' out of sight – would crowd through the front door after him. Then they either cluttered up the entrance lobby to the displeasure of the housekeeper Peter Taylor or, more usually, were directed into the drivers' room. There they would be obliged to stand around in embarrassed discomfort, muttering coded words such as 'OK. Ten-four' into the mini-mikes hidden up their sleeves.

Although politics and religion were fairly carefully avoided, isolation within the drivers' room normally gave the incumbents considerable confidence to display unusually earthy characteristics. The young, fresh-faced and flabby Peter, for example, might be standing looking at the public out of one of the two windows, boldly handling a large belly up and down in what he perceived to be a sexually inviting manner, and telling his colleagues to 'just come and look at all them bleedin' sheep out there'. Safe in the knowledge that, although he could see the visitors, he was safely out of their sight behind anti-blast mesh curtains.

'They're just waiting for a sign from you,' replied Jim. 'Why don't you pop out there and show them your loaves and fishes tricks again? Anyway, if they could see you they would just think you'd punctured your codpiece again.'

Perhaps Peter might be slumped in one of the battered armchairs, sharpening the lead in his pencil by leafing through a lascivious girlie magazine and mouthing an approving, 'mighty meaty matey!' Not all the lady messengers he drove about were happy to rifle through the glove pocket of his car and find pictures suitable for adult males only – but everyone had to admit he was a superb, fast, safe driver. I suppose this must have weighed heavily in his favour when he was appointed to No 10. To ensure that they were not subjected to scrutiny, the drivers protected one another with an unwritten code of confidentiality.

Peter was devoted to his wife and children, but whether Gladys was a happy participant in any of his intimate fantasies was never entirely clear. One evening, after losing money at cards, Jim encouraged him, 'With your luck the way it is, you should be in OK for a nice bit of crumpet tonight.'

'Well that's hopeful,' replied Peter. 'I'm getting really fed up with that lollypop lady down in Battersea. What I need is a young newboil buscombe [phon: young thing]. Anyway, I'm just being suppository.'

'What-what-what!' he muttered to himself as he sorted the cards of a new hand.

'Only three watts? That's not very bright Pete.' Bill told him.

A young policeman was invited to join in. 'I don't think I could stand all the wit,' he replied. 'Don't worry about it mate. None of it's funny anyway,' Bill assured him. 'Well. Shall I put the kettle on then?' asked the PC. 'Certainly. Go ahead if you think it suits you,' Ken advised.

In between hands, Bill started to talk about the posh cruise liner he and his missus were soon to join at Southampton. 'She's got cases full of evening wear and I don't know how I am going to manage it all. I'm just taking the usual two DJ outfits for the top occasions. I've told her I just don't care about the others. I'm still going to tuck the napkin into my collar during meals, no matter what the snooty ones think.'

'You'd better not drop off asleep then,' Ken told him, 'or else you might wake up with a short back-and-sides!'

Peter was a full member of the daily card school – usually five-card brag. The regulars were all skilful players and rarely took much money from one another. However, any passer-by was welcomed in and promptly relieved of a few quid in short order. Bill Housden, together with Peter, Ken and Jim, were the champion performers. Bill's additional extra was to abandon his seat in the school only at the very final millisecond before the departure of the Boss, just managing to draw the Rover into position with the engine running before the duty detective and the doorkeeper had a seizure. As already mentioned, Joe Hazard, when he arrived with Mr Callaghan, was not interested in gambling. Joe concentrated instead on often unwelcome descriptions of the new things he was buying for Else or the merits of caravan life down at Seasalter, or the splendid acceleration of his alloy-engined Triumph sports car. Amazingly, both Bill and Joe could tap dance rather well and the marble floor in the entrance hall might have been purpose-built for them as they hung around during long evenings.

Of the three regulars in the drivers' room, Ken was the longest serving. His vast experience was critical. He knew the best route to almost any likely venue, the best place to park securely and the chances of getting fed. The peaked caps abandoned during Harold Wilson's administration were not recalled for service under Mr Callaghan and the drab grey favoured by the Government Car Service ensured that drivers' appearances were more than likely to tend towards the scruffy. Although Joe and Jim managed to present at least a tidy appearance, the others habitually wore creased jackets without seeming to notice.

Ken was safe enough on the road, but was not the best driver. He even managed a couple of minor damage-only accidents. He was a hot shot at cryptic crosswords and this kept him close to the intellectuals he sometimes drove about. So did his ready Londoner's wit. As he and I drove past the Lewes cemetery during our first reconnaissance near Mr Callaghan's Sussex farmhouse, he pointed out that we were right in the dead centre of the town.

Ken was a heavy smoker and tried hard to cope with a nicotine-free brand that was on sale for a few months. To our dismay he even tried to give up. The problem was that he used cigarettes as a sort of rough calculator after Private Office requested a time-on-the-road forecast for a potential diary entry. His little black book, with records of previous journeys and times and distance, might record that an earlier positioning to Aberdeen, for example, had taken twenty-five fags. Divided by three this worked out at just over eight hours on the road. Ken did finally manage to break the habit completely after a few months in 1979. He had cleverly hidden the habit from Mr Callaghan but when Margaret Thatcher's chosen number one driver George Newell died suddenly from a heart attack, Private Office recommended Ken as his replacement. After decades, Ken became the official senior driver. Out went his tobacco habit in a hurry.

Jim was the smartest of the team. His army background shone through. A devoted family man, he was under some pressure from an attractive lady messenger with red hair and a strong Ulster accent, who fancied him, although it came to be known that she had a large brood of her own somewhere near Kings Cross. We did Jim a favour by keeping this to ourselves, because it would probably have caused the withdrawal of his security-vetted status. He was also the best driver overall. He was resourceful and we all hoped that when trouble came, we would have Jim at the wheel.

Although they had no co-ordinated driving training, and only one day in evasion tactics, all four were capable of driving fast – sometimes very fast – without provocation. Only once during nearly six years was I needed to intervene on their behalf with a provincial police chief after a minor motorway interception with traffic cops on the M4. The serious fact was that some prime ministers are easier to drive about than others. Mr Wilson was entirely content to leave it to his professionals. Mr Callaghan, on the other hand, rather fancied himself behind the wheel and tended to put Private Office in a difficult position by complaining to them instead of the driver. He liked to pass the buck for his incipient car sickness and once, when the Government Car Service experimented with new-model Rover limousines, he ordered a stop to the motorcade and moved himself into one of the older models in mid-journey. The new ones, with vastly improved equipment for us, were never seen at Downing Street again.

As George Newell weaved his way dramatically through Hyde Park Corner traffic, soon after Mrs Thatcher arrived, I enquired about the need for such urgent travel. That, apparently, was the way Mrs Thatcher preferred to move around. However, my own glances in the rear-view mirror tended to cast doubt on this assumption. Indeed, it was impossible for her to work with red boxes sliding from side to side as we cornered. As George had been with Mrs Thatcher for several years, he must have known what he was talking about, but I was grateful he was not at the wheel when stricken with heart failure. Had it not been for the determination of prime ministers to select their own man, it would have been opportune to introduce police drivers instead.

There was no rank structure within the Government Car Service. Seniority counted, but the top man in a team had no authority to give out orders. Moreover, we had no official authority over them either. As police drivers were fully trained in fast pursuit and evasion, it was my constant objective to have our own police team of drivers and bodyguards working jointly to the same discipline code, as well as being experts in communication. As it was, the Rover limos not only had the Home Office radio communication sets, through which police units could be contacted anywhere in the United Kingdom, a radio link with the AA and a radio telephone, but we also carried portable radios to keep in touch with one another and other sets to maintain contact with the local uniformed police headquarters at Cannon Row police station. Under pressure, the use of this jumble became an electronic act of contortion. At the same time it was vital to ensure that our judgement was respected by the No 10 drivers who knew they might one day be told to speed away or crash their car out of a hold up. However, our operational efficiency would have been immeasurably improved if the employment of a co-ordinated police and Special Branch unit had been agreed by the Home Office. Any hope of a police driver takeover at No 10 has never materialised. Unfortunately, the notion is apparently politically incorrect.

If it was indisputable that Government Car Service drivers were seriously underpaid, it was also a fact that they were not accorded adequate status. The uniform was undistinguished and its condition and appearance unsupervised. As a result, it was frequently the case that the Green Goddesses, the women in the Government Car Service, would wash and posh themselves up and brush dust from their cars, whereas too many of the men tended to slump around grumbling, smoking and getting unhealthy. It was high-class chauffeuring on the cheap. The good news was that all the drivers realised that alcohol was incompatible with the job. They also got some satisfaction from the admiration of outsiders impressed by the names they could drop. Admittedly, they rarely grumbled about the long hours demanded of them (and legally denied to lorry drivers, for example). Overtime was their only chance to earn some extra money – tips being on the prohibited list, and rarely offered anyway.

Anxious Bill Brown was on the 'phone to us two or three times a day as a diary entry developed for another prime ministerial constituency visit. Bill – the South Wales Constabulary liaison officer – was under intense pressure from his chief constable – who was unaware of life outside Cardiff and still concentrating on honours' aspirations. A couple of days before the event Private Office was still trying to amalgamate input from constituency sources, Labour Party HQ – and the prime minister himself.

Although Mr Callaghan had made concessions since the earlier Cardiff debacle, he was on this occasion still insisting on train travel outbound. To sharp-enders involved it became clear that the proposed schedule could not be made to work. A quart of commitments included the formality of opening a new rubbish tip; a constituents' surgery; a private working supper with Ron Hayward, Labour Party General Secretary; a black tie dinner with the Wales-Israel Friendship Society; some private appointments and a Saturday afternoon visit to Cardiff Arms Park to see Wales *v* Argentina playing rugby. Rugby was a game in which the prime minister had never expressed interest, but the occasion offered a welcome opportunity to improve his already substantial majority. The pint pot available was from midday on Friday until the end of the rugby match – after which it was away the lads along the M4 motorway to the blessed sanctuary of Chequers until Monday morning.

No 10 intended to protect its position at all costs. A senior private secretary was to oversee the operation on the ground. It turned out to be a one-off precedent. One Garden Room girl went ahead and Vanessa – the second now in the Garden Rooms and brand new to the job – travelled by train with the prime minister. Joe Hazard was a major player at the London end. His dual role was to collect the PM's heavy coat from the Kennington flat and load it with the Callaghans' luggage at No 10. He would then drive them to Paddington station in good time. Bill Brown's team would rendezvous at Cardiff railway station and British Rail would provide a porter. A local government car and driver would take the baggage to the flat and Vanessa would look after the official red boxes.

Unfortunately and unusually, Joe was very nearly late arriving at No 10 and had to rush around to collect the luggage in time to get away. Vanessa was dispatched to Paddington in advance to delay train departure if necessary. As Joe drove along the Mall, Mr Callaghan asked, 'Joe. Is my coat in the back with the bags?'

Joe's knuckles went white and he unaccountably accelerated. 'I couldn't find it, Prime Minister,' he replied.

A sudden back-seat hypertension surge was almost tangible and a third-degree interrogation started.

'Did you look where I told you?'

'Yes. And I couldn't see it.'

'Where *did* you look?'

'In the cupboard, like you said.'

'*Which* cupboard?'

'The cupboard in the bedroom.'

'But I told you the cupboard in the sitting room. Did you look in the sitting room cupboard on the right as you go in? I explained it all quite clearly!'

'I looked in the one on the right in the bedroom, Sir.'

'But I said the sitting room. Did you look in that one Joe?'

'I looked in the one on the left in the sitting room, Prime Minister.'

'But I said the one on the right. You know only too well Joe. The one with the photos on top.'

'Well. I had Mr Baxter with me!'

This was an unwise attempt by Joe to involve the caretaker of the Kennington block of flats.

'What's he got to do with it?' snapped Mr Callaghan.

'Well he was there and we couldn't find the coat.'

'Well. You wouldn't, would you, if you look in ALL THE WRONG CUPBOARDS!'

With a visible effort, the prime minister wound down after a final and very meaningful thrust. 'Anyway. Never mind Joe. I suppose you did your best.'

Ken and Jim left No 10 with their official cars well in advance of a wintry dawn over Westminster and motored to rendezvous with the rest of the motorcade. British Rail was only marginally late, but the prime minister, first into his car, created anticipated chaos by insisting on driving away as soon as he was aboard, leaving part of the police escort, Vanessa, the red boxes and his baggage. The prime minister had now added an extra call to his agenda.

Having briefly consulted Bud Brecon, a well turned out local Special Branch officer, we weaved away to a smart town-centre shop for men to buy a new overcoat. Mr Callaghan was not happy about it, but was now determined on do-it-yourself preparation for his winter afternoon at Cardiff Arms Park. It was rumoured that he usually frequented a second-hand shop for outsize men in Buckingham Palace Road, but I couldn't confirm or deny that.

After twenty minutes parked on double-yellow lines, the prime minister emerged in a whitish, unusually fashionable long trench coat, complaining grumpily that it had cost him £39. After a short wash and brush up, and with most of his entourage now assembled, he told his secretary Ruth Sharp to cancel the minor engagements. We all then set off for the rubbish tip.

His party arrived on time, a blessed relief for guests assembled on wet and windy Welsh marshes. Downwind of residential estates, the site was well chosen for the construction of modern mechanically driven machinery to sort rubbish and was no doubt light years ahead of its time. But it could not be described as a fun venue for local dignitaries, the press and television, or even the collected group of individuals who had been invited because of their rather esoteric interest in such matters. In between squalls, the prime minister pressed a button and machinery fired up first time – rolling and grinding, mashing, screeching, sorting and crushing automatically. Unfortunately, it is a concomitant of such arcane brilliance to create dense storms of possibly toxic and definitely smelly dust. Of course, this ascended briefly and then, gravity fed, settled on the prime minister's bare head and the shoulders of his new and hitherto pristine trench coat. It was not a scene of great joy at all until it was time to eat, when everyone trooped off to expensively prepared, heated and flapping marquees.

During lunch, my colleague Ian Bryan quietly whispered in my ear, 'I believe the Prime Minister's baggage was left on the train.' The private secretary, happy in the midst of the fish course, was the senior No 10 person present and found himself suddenly and unexpectedly thrust into a front-line position of executive responsibility. For a start, and we all agreed, it was wise not to tell Mr or Mrs Callaghan. Meanwhile, the Garden Room girls and some local police officers found a telephone – but no luggage with stationmasters at either Cardiff railway station or Swansea, where the service had terminated. The train was now heading back to London.

Mrs Callaghan then threw a spanner into the works by leaving early and returning to her flat to unpack and prepare for the formal affair in the evening. She had to be told about the missing cases. That meant no formal clothing, no make-up, no night things or toiletries. She too was in no doubt about not telling her husband. The private secretary spoke to his Treasury opposite number and was authorised to shop for all the Callaghans' needs at public expense. On the drive back to the flat he said to the prime minister, 'I have just spoken to No 10 Sir, and I need to discuss a couple of things with you.'

Mr Callaghan was suspicious. 'Oh yes?'

'There has been a run on Sterling in the Far East and the Treasury would appreciate your views.'

'Support it.'

'Well, thank you Prime Minister. I rather think that is what they were hoping to hear.'

After a pause. 'And …?'

'Your baggage was left on the train due to …'

'I KNEW IT! I COULD SEE THIS COMING. IN FUTURE I SHALL TAKE NAPOLEON'S ADVICE AND CARRY IT MYSELF!'

'Anyway, *we* have managed to recover it and your bags are now on their way back from Swansea,' put in Bud Brecon quickly.

The local SB officer had taken an initiative and got to an internal 'phone line directly into the Lost Property Office in Swansea. Yes, they had two pieces of luggage left from the London train and, yes, they answered the description. No, they didn't know they belonged to the prime minister (how could they, because in his rush Joe had forgotten to put official red Downing Street labels on them). No, of course they hadn't told the stationmaster. These things happened several times each day.

The cases arrived back on the 17.02 and were then rushed by police car to the flat. There was no time to uncrease the contents before the evening function, starting at 7.30 p.m. After a meal with Ron Hayward, Mr Callaghan was not hungry when he arrived at the evening dinner with the Welsh Friends of Israel. He was the only man in a lounge suit. The guests had been looking forward to a long meal and short speeches, but he pulled rank and insisted that speeches were made before the meal. Unfortunately, the Israeli ambassador's accent was hard to penetrate and his description of the complicated state of play in the Middle East lasted forty-five hungry minutes. The prime minister then spoke rather too hurriedly and left straight away.

It transpired that in the chaos caused by Mr Callaghan's precipitate departure during the morning disembarkation at Cardiff station, Vanessa carried the red boxes herself and instructed the porter, as normal, to hurry along with suitcases displaying red Downing Street labels. This did not include the Callaghans' private cases. After the worst day of her life, and convinced she would get the push, Vanessa retired to bed early with the vapours and aspirin. She was strongly supported by Private Office and lived in the Garden Rooms happily ever after.

On the drive to Chequers on Saturday I told the prime minister that the recovery of his cases was not a combined effort but the result of an initiative by the South Wales police – and Bud Brecon in particular.

'Thank you John. I rather thought that might be the case. Please see to it that a letter of appreciation is sent.'

The Private Office happily obliged and life in Downing Street under James Callaghan returned to turbulent normality for a while.

FIFTEEN

Our Satisfaction will be the Gratitude of the People.

The wording on a Calcutta memorial after a visit by Queen Mary

It is a long way down from six and a half miles up. Above I could see a moonless canopy of stars – ahead and below a seemingly endless matt black landscape. Seated in almost total silence on the flight deck of British Airways Boeing 747 'Speedbird 4321', Captain Reynolds maintained flight control, aided by readings from the dimly green-lit console. Still 100 miles from Kuwait Airport, he was in touch with air traffic control by radio. A deep Arab voice called up: 'Speedbird 4321. This is Kuwait Control. Good evening gentlemen. You are identified on radar. You are cleared to commence letdown to Flight Level 100. Call passing through. Please squawk 987 and report entering our Control Zone.'

'Do you hear that, John?' asked Captain Reynolds. 'Different from those cowboys in Cairo, eh? No muddle or confusion here. Kuwait controllers are trained in London, that's the difference.'

As the altimeter unwound, yellow dots appeared below, identifying clutches of wellhead gas flare-offs. In perfect night visibility, the circuit and final approach were conducted visually. The first officer had this landing. On the last lap Captain Reynolds calmly repeated readings from the radio altimeter: 'Fifty – Thirty – Twenty – Ten – Six – Four.' Then a pause and gentle touch down.

Kuwait was the second of four laps to get me to Dhaka (Dacca) in Bangladesh, where the prime minister would be starting a tour of the sub-continent in a week's time. I laid plans for a leapfrogging advance- and close-protection rota to include the two colleagues who would travel with Mr Callaghan in the VC10. A busy programme was already laid out.

Bernard Donoughue – who was too busy and preoccupied to keep a diary – wrote, 'This was the most exciting trip abroad I ever made.' During the next fifteen days my own life was changed forever, and the change started at the next stop, Kolkata (Calcutta). It was New Year's Day 1978.

I was not entirely prepared for the culture shock of everyday life in the sub-continent. Endemic corruption was not slow to appear. A sinisterly handsome, conspiratorially persuasive customs officer was hurt and bewildered by my refusal to collude in smuggling cigarettes and spirits. My Scotland Yard Warrant Card carried clout and saved me from a flogging or whatever mischief he was planning after non-co-operation. With an eight-hour wait for the onward feeder flight to Dhaka, I was tired and fatalistic about baggage theft and food poisoning. Fortunately neither became a problem, but a taxi tour of Kolkata was a different matter.

After booking into the airport hotel, I boarded an ancient side-valve Morris Oxford saloon-type of taxi – manufactured in India under licence and known there as the 'Ambassador'. Even India's prime minister travelled in one. Mine was unbelievably patched, dented and tattered – but still better than most. This one had curtains to provide privacy and shade from the intense sun. The turbaned driver was draped in dirty white linen and had worn sandals. He agreed to charge me only the meter reading plus 90 per cent. This included *baksheesh* for his helper, who took the front seat and waved a red flag from the window to warn that a VIP was aboard. The agreement was academic anyway. The meter jammed at 50 rupees.

The main road to the city was dusty, rutted and full of cows, rickshaws, carts, goats, chickens, people, lorries and assorted vehicles – and holes full of rainwater. In and around these, homeless refugees were washing themselves and their ragged clothing. Three million victims of conflict in Bangladesh had joined the 2 million or so permanently homeless living in the streets. Recent rains had provided much-needed water but destroyed their flimsy cardboard shelters. The contrast between areas developed during the days of British rule, with grand and elegant buildings and the squalor of beggars, lepers, the maimed, disabled and dead left in the streets, was shatteringly obscene. Alongside the squalor and filth, the hovels and smallpox-scarred faces were gorgeous palaces – now often museums.

Bustle and noisy activity went endlessly on around, alongside and over the weak, lying prone and immobile on the pavement hoping for help of any kind. Every time the Ambassador stopped, stumps of leper children's truncated arms thumped on the window for a coin or two. Scarred young faces – some deliberately maimed – pleaded at the window. Even my driver scattered a few almost worthless coins. Scavenging dogs snapped and snarled viciously. I assumed every one to be rabid. I never thought to bring a boy Scouts' stave to fend them off, as recommended by the late Lord Baden-Powell.

Within the city, scooters and bicycle rickshaws hurried about. The cyclists panted, sweated and strained – boldly challenging oncoming lorries and hooting cars until finally giving way at the very last minute, and barely a millisecond before imminent death – trying not to lose precious momentum.

In the markets, clamour and colour, heat and activity were almost overwhelming. Artists, artisans, gold and silversmiths, metal workers, carpet makers, tapestry and silk weavers all squatted in concentration and pounded and stitched producing exquisite, ornate, labour-intensive works for sale, with thousands of people around them. Everyone was intensely busy with the effort of survival.

This initial experience was not exceptional and came to be repeated time after time throughout the sub-continent. With caste problems, religious taboos, food distribution shortages, corruption and just too many children, there was admittedly little that Europeans could do and they sought self-justification. 'These people are used to it, you know. It's largely their own fault anyway,' I was told by self-satisfied, hard-faced European residents. 'They don't suffer the way we do! They are professional beggars from childhood. You will soon get used to it.'

They were wrong. I never did or ever could. But I did come to admire the work of do-gooders like Mother Teresa, not for an occasional success story but for managing to carry on at all in the face of such overwhelming failure.

By the time I boarded the sixty-seat feeder aircraft for Dhaka, which I shared with fifty-nine locals, one goat and several thousand chirping day-old chicks, I had abandoned the imperatives within which we live in the west. A bigger car, further promotion, more money in the bank – it was all pointless. Of course, I never managed any direct help to the world's poor. But I had learned important lessons of humility and respect; they could count on my sympathy and understanding from then on.

In 1978 the People's Republic of Bangladesh was struggling toward an Islamic form of democracy, and the largely Moslem population – once part of British Indian Bengal – had fought its way to independence from Pakistan in 1971, supported by the Indian Army. Bangladesh was humid, flat, appallingly poor and grossly overpopulated. If it is possible to imagine Kolkata plus 12,000 extra rickshaws, then that is Dhaka. Child beggars were more innovative too. Pushing forward to sell posies of flowers, one thrust a poster plea printed in clear English: 'NO MAMA! NO PAPA!'

Mr Callaghan's visit was seen as supportive and as such was warmly welcomed. The streets of Dhaka were prepared in advance. The usual refuse collection went satisfactorily along. It took two forms and cost the nation nothing. Anything that could be recycled was warmed, washed, filed, beaten, scraped, ground, sawn or hammered into shape and fitted somewhere as a spare part. Anything else was left to flocks of busy, healthy carrion crows. They were followed by flocks of chattering, colourful women with soft brushes who swept and giggled with relief at temporary release from domestic bondage. Finally, teams of men turned out with hammers, nails and boarding to shield VIP eyes from anything too squalid and erect instant archways. The prime minister's VC10 was due at 7.30 a.m. on day six and by then their work had been largely covered with great garlands of flowers.

Every state in British India had been lavishly endowed with red carpet and this was now in VIP use throughout the sub-continent. As the silver bird flew the circuit at Dhaka Airport exactly on time under a clear-blue sky, several hundred yards were unrolled, the guard of honour ordered to stand in some sort of line and missing music for the British National Anthem distributed to a seriously unpolished military band. There was just time for a few cacophonous practice blasts before the prime minister and Mrs Callaghan smiled down the gangway, fresh enough after a comfortable sleep in their suite. About twenty pale, drawn and tired support staff followed them. After a full day's work in Downing Street, a very long journey indeed (broken for official talks and handshakes in Moscow) and some imprudence once aboard, they now faced a sixteen-hour programme as VIP guests of honour.

To my surprise, buildings and procession security matched promises made by the minister of the interior and commissioner of police. However, close, personal protection was covered exclusively by three members of our Scotland Yard Special Branch team. With advance planning trips as well, we were understaffed from the start. However, Scotland Yard, who thought we were on a 'swan', had refused backup.

Women were now not allowed out and the streets were lined only with cheering, flag-waving men and children. First stop was Bangabhaban Palace, the official guesthouse, a glorious old mosque-like building with towers and minarets, shaded courtyards and fountains, ochre walls and mirrored ceilings. The palace was securely patrolled by foot police and ceremonially turbaned lancers on horseback. Peter Smither – who was scheduled to stay there with the prime minister's inner circle – was allocated the 'Little Pink Room'. He had some difficulty in living it down.

Officials in the No 10 party set up the communications and administrative network and hurried to deal with a backlog of messages. By the time they had watched interminable cultural displays and dances during a dinner of welcome that night, one distinguished civil servant finally and irrevocably dropped his head onto the table and fell asleep. Another – a diplomat – tumbled right off his chair and could not be roused from slumber on the carpet. Their careers were not impaired. Both became mandarins in due course, with appropriate knighthoods. But it was the last time any trip was organised around non-stop activity lasting little short of fifty hours. Mr Callaghan, admittedly with better rest opportunities, had paced himself well.

From the next day the prime minister was engaged in relaxed visits and inspections and talks. It had not been overlooked that he had a farming interest back home. As one of the advance planning team, I had been driven with a first secretary from the high commission and Bangladeshi officials, to Karnapara, said to be typical farming community. It was a desperately poor, small, smelly pimple set just above monsoon high-water mark, and now in dry season isolation overlooking a landscape of unlimited paddy fields. A huddle of fragile huts on stilts sheltered a small, scantily clad community. Children and chickens scratched around together in the dirt. The shelter on the longest pontoon was the communal toilet.

Mrs Callaghan was excused for this one, and when the prime minister arrived in a great motorcycle-escorted motorcade a couple of days later, the village had received a mark one makeover. Steps had been shaped, paths laid and new mud walls laid out. Only male village elders were granted an audience. They were freshly scrubbed and partly dressed, at least. The pontoon leading to the village toilet – a single straw hut perched over dry paddy – was shut and camouflaged with palm leaves. A water well was being dug by traditional means. Specially imported young ladies – film extras perhaps – were weaving cloth or gracefully swaying back and forth on their knees, crushing spices with hand rollers. It was an idyllic scene and the prime minister played his part by insisting on farmers' chat with the elders.

He recommended modern fertilisers and farm equipment. He proposed various crop diversifications and explained the benefits of modern machinery, mulch and tilth. The elders listened patiently, but when he invited their point of view he met an embarrassing wall of silence. Eventually a small, rather dirty, terrified and almost naked little man was produced from the forbidden area, where he had been told to stay. Now he was introduced as the local expert. Communication was still one way only. This was not surprising. The villagers spoke only an obscure local Bengali dialect and not a word of English.

No one had thought to tell the prime minister.

On day three visit time, after watching labourers with oxen-drawn single furrow ploughs and irrigation-deploying hollowed-out tree trunks,

Mr Callaghan was entertained at a jute mill. The health and safety of the workers was not an issue here. His party then boarded an elegant, two-storey modern motor vessel, *The Pathfinder*. A cruise followed along local waterways – a major system of transportation. We were taken back a hundred years, or perhaps a thousand. This was the bottom line of Bangladeshi life. Broad waterways flowed steadily downstream and were used by hundreds of small, gracefully shaped boats. Dangerously overloaded and without engine power they depended upon clever use of the stream, quanting, sculling and, on lucky days with the wind in the right quarter, tattered square sails. With great overhangs the boats may have looked historic but were monstrously unstable. Up to half a dozen crew made their home under a flimsy central shelter. Having taken a load downstream – animals, leather goods, hay, timber – the boats had to get back again. With no close-hauled capability, it was now down to manpower alone. So out came the quant poles or oars. If no progress could be made, then a 100m line was secured to the masthead and the crew walked in the muddy shallows or, where there was one, along a towpath, pulling their home with a single coxswain aboard. The silhouettes were stunning and the labour for these poor, sweating men barbarically intensive.

Meanwhile, we enjoyed considerable comforts on board *The Pathfinder*.

Mr Callaghan still looked forward to another couple of days of Bangladeshi hospitality. Colin Colson moved out to advance the prime minister's next stop in Chittagong with the navy. I flew back to Kolkata and on to Delhi in India for the following tour. Peter Smither remained in sole charge of the prime minister's protection, marshalling Bangladeshi police and army units from his control centre in The Little Pink Room.

Independence was granted to India in 1947. Until then this great country had been the jewel in the crown of the Empire. British administrators and officials enjoyed an unprecedented quality of life and affluence and the glories of Empire were flagrantly displayed with great buildings, glorious uniforms, unlimited servants and grand public spectacle.

Thirty years later, much of the grandeur was still evident in Delhi. New Delhi included Sir Edwin Lutyens' great Viceroy's House, the Rashtrapati Bhavan, sited prominently at the head of the Grand Mall. It was all on a greater scale than anything London could offer. Mr Callaghan's visit was considered a great honour by the Indian government and arrangements were commensurately grand.

First impressions were not helpful. The British high commissioner was incapacitated with typhoid. However, protection dispositions at the airport were encouraging. Security passes were thoroughly scrutinised and, although they hated it, media personnel were firmly confined on a tractor-driven open trailer called *The Queen Mary*. After greetings at the airport by senior ministers, a splendid guard of honour and a real military band performed well – and acres of red carpet were unrolled. It was in the Rashtrapati Bhavan – the official residence of the president of India – that the Callaghan delegation was accommodated in very considerable style.

We were now VVIPs – Very, *Very* Important People. James Callaghan was addressed variously as, 'Your Honourable', 'Your Excellency' and even 'King Sahib'. Those of us used to more modest things had to balance unlimited numbers of bearers, servants and soldiers and gardens, space and fountains, with our various responsibilities to a frenetic official programme. Back in the palace, peace and quiet efficiency was guaranteed by written directions to the staff. The public health officer, for example, was instructed to ensure that the guest wing was in a good state of cleanliness, that the personnel detailed for work there were in neat and clean uniform, with appropriate footwear, and that the wing was – 'sprayed with good, effective and scented liquid insecticide'.

Begging in the vicinity of the Mall was of a high order too. A flutter of poor, pleading women surrounded our car at traffic lights, claiming that one of them was about to give birth and could she be taken to a suitable hospital. This was firmly refused by the first secretary. He was probably right to do so in this case because when we drove past again three hours later they were still trying.

The prime minister and Mrs Callaghan handled all their commitments with dignity and patience. He paced himself carefully. Mr Desai, the prime minister of India, held an official dinner for his guests of honour. Mr and Mrs Callaghan remembered this unique occasion well. For different reasons, so did I.

During the afternoon of the great day Miss Peggy Metcalfe, head of the conference and protocol section of Foreign and Commonwealth Office – with whom I was frequently in the advance team – looked up from a busy desk and said, 'By the way, John. A place has been reserved for you at tonight's dinner.'

'There will be a couple of problems, I'm afraid,' I protested. 'First of all Prime Minister Desai attributes his healthy old age to the daily consumption of a glass of his own urine and I would hate to cause a diplomatic incident if he invited me to join him. And anyway, I haven't brought a dinner jacket.'

'Leave that to me,' she commanded.

Later in the day my three duty bearers unpacked a black-tie outfit borrowed from a first secretary at the high commission. A dress rehearsal seemed wise. Unfortunately the first secretary was about 3in shorter in the leg than me. I practised a leg-shortening crouch. Still showing an indecent 2in of sock, I moved to the starched white shirt and black bow tie. Familiar only with the modern, completely ready to strap-on version, I was dismayed to find this loaned one needed tying. If you don't know how to do it, don't try. Thirty minutes nearer the deadline for the grand procession, and with the starched shirt no longer pristine, I gave up. My private bearers shook their heads, probably laughing themselves silly. The Private Office was hard at work and full. I worked up the scale of officials. Surely the Garden Room girls came from the right stratum of society? Not for this job. How about the duty clerk? No luck here either. Surely such a skill would have been mandatory for Oxbridge honours' graduates? Not with the private secretary, however. As lift-off time grew near, Ken Stowe, the principal private secretary himself, wandered in – already dressed in penguin suit.

'Look here, Ken. You didn't get where you are today without being able to …' In the nick of time he tucked and tugged and it was done. Now dishevelled and still short of trouser leg, I fell in behind the prime minister, among diplomats, high officials, ministers, VVIP guests and gorgeous ladies – all impeccably turned out for the grand procession. It was quite a show. Under a warm starlit sky, we followed along, winding through gardens, under gentle lights, decorated hallways and passages, making inane small talk to impress the lancers on horseback and soldiers at the Present Arms lining the route. I pretended I preferred my socks to show.

On arrival in that gloriously appointed dining room I broke away to check the seating plan and prepare conversational gambits for those on either side. My name was not on the list. According to written instruction No. 9, I should have, at approximately 20.10 hours, '[…] been conducted to the Banqueting Hall to stand with other guests behind their chairs according to the Seating Plan, after which the Distinguished Guests and Prime Minister will be conducted to their seats. All other guests will then take their seats.'

Instead, I slunk away, back through all the horsemen and soldiers and admirers, looking as though I had never expected to be on the guest list. Someone had vetoed me over the heads of the FCO. Peggy Metcalfe didn't know who. If he had recovered, could it have been the high commissioner? More likely, it was Mr Callaghan, I concluded. Perhaps he thought I had insinuated myself into his party in the Vatican? If so he greatly misjudged and underestimated me.

But it was a wonderful example of the complexities of personal protection. On the one hand to undertake the task firmly and efficiently, and on the other to try to find a level acceptable to all senior and sometimes envious vested interests involved.

Colin Colson was getting tired and grumbled about having to get up early. I began to wish I had booked breakfast for myself on the Agra Express, one of the world's great train journeys, to advance the prime minister's sortie to the historic Red Fort and elegant Taj Mahal. Meanwhile, I set off by car for Old Delhi.

Mr Callaghan would visit the famous Ivory Market there. I was now accustomed to the colour, noise and all-star action of an Asian market place, but here were extra ingredients. Special qualities of skill, patience and concentration by hundreds of men crouching, cutting, filing and sawing ended up with delicate, ornate ingenious works of art for sale. Ivory was an astonishing medium. One set of table and chairs was reported to have taken a generation to complete. Even given that a generation in India was not all that long, it was clearly no exaggeration. In the adjacent second-hand market place around a shapely mosque, hundreds of other workers using fires bashed, bent and filed old tin cans into something useful. A discarded cola tin might finish up as a bicycle spoke, for example. Nothing that could be recycled was wasted. Teams of tradesmen squatted around fires sorting out the scrap and selling the end products. Everyone talked at the same time; it must have been pointless chatter because no one seemed to be listening. Fascinating though it was, I persuaded Indian security and protocol officials that Mr Callaghan's visit – partly on foot – would have to be limited to areas in which we could be assured of maintaining control.

Out there in Agra, where travelling members of the delegation arrived by VC10, the great Red Fort was inspected. Interestingly, an ancient assembly hall was named after my favourite Indian restaurant in London, the Diwan I Am. The next stop was the exquisite Taj Mahal. Colin had arranged for the public to be excluded and fortunately briefed himself thoroughly on the history of this memorial. The prime minister's official guide was a learned Indian professor with unrivalled knowledge of this exquisite monument and – with a strong accent and hurried speech – largely indecipherable with overexcitement in English. The marble walls were inlaid with real silver, he was trying to explain. Colin – in more measured words – felt the frequent need to interrupt. They often talked at the same time. The prime minister was patient but getting irritable.

Peter Smither whispered in my ear, 'If that prof fellow doesn't soon shut up I think Colin is going to inlay him with lead!'

Before lunch, the party re-emplaned – a word favoured by Indian officials – and helicoptered to the Palace of Fatehpur Sikri. Before independence, this was a hunting lodge reserved for the ruling elite. Sepia photographs showed (mainly European) men with moustaches, sun helmets and stern faces lined up before indecently large heaps of dead wildlife. The reserve was now flooded with shallow water and animal and bird wildlife was protected by law.

Transport was by a six-person punt. One sweating punter balanced on the stern with a long pole was perspiring in response to the manager's order to increase speed. Even at a quarter of a mile per hour, this was easier said than done. Extra protection was under Colin's control, seated in the bow section of a flying squad back-up gun punt. Meanwhile, Peter added food tasting to his security responsibilities in the palace itself. Although he missed the wildlife tour, he was not grumbling.

Back on home ground in the Rashtrapati Bhavan, Bernard Donoughue told me he was trying to keep fit for a football match on the day we were due back in London. This was an important game for the House of Commons against a German parliamentary team – a sort of replay of the World Cup final. Although I did not have the right gear, we agreed that it might be cool enough for jogging together at six o'clock the next morning. When I called at his room he was still fast asleep and suffering a classic hangover. He doggedly slipped into a tracksuit.

We went down to the basement of the palace, past surprised Gurkha guards struggling to the Present Arms, down the gravel drive, through the great iron gates and down the Mall. Generally speaking, Indians find it too hot to jog. Jogging down the Mall from the Rashtrapati Bhavan was unprecedented. Perhaps we were eligible for the *Guinness Book of Records*?

Through a dense mist, we passed the empty plinth, which had housed a statue of King George V until Independence Day in 1947. Delhi authorities were not rushing to make a hurried replacement. Then we heard bagpipes – a ghostly reminder for me of early-morning wake-up calls at Balmoral Castle. Into sight, at their favoured rapid march pace, strode the Gurkha drum major and his bagpipe and drum band. A smart 'eyes left' for two strange VVIPs and off they sped to the palace. We tried to overtake them on the way back but they were too fast for us.

It was the final great moment for me in India. I was now emplaned for the last leg of the prime minister's tour – Pakistan. Once settled on board, I read the English language copy of the *Hindustani Times*. Their Special Reporter had been at the Taj Mahal:

Agra. January 8.

'Will you hurry up? My bottom is getting cold,' he told the enthusiastic band of photographers.

'How many times have I told you, dear, that marble slabs are cold?' She looked at the rose in his buttonhole. He tried to hold her hand …

'I am at a loss for words,' said the British Prime Minister when questioned about his impressions of the Taj Mahal. Mrs Callaghan popped another cashew into her mouth. The security officers sidled close to suspicious looking journalists, their hidden guns rubbing against …

Although this reporter was less critical than most – everything was still reduced to the most trivial level.

⟹▸•◂⟸

The Fokker Friendship aircraft made a 'praise be to Allah' landing at Islamabad Airport. Pakistan was no more politically stable in 1977 than it is thirty years later. Democracy was abandoned and martial law declared. The army appointed General Muhammad Zia-ul-Haq as president and chief martial law administrator. The country was suspended from the Commonwealth and the British high commission became an embassy. For the advance, I was the guest of the head of chancery.

We agreed that – with the city situated in Himalayan foothills – it was climatically well-chosen. Islamabad was also the most incredibly boring place to be. Over private drinks we fantasised over the benefits of expense allowances in other, more hedonistic Asian countries. It was no substitute for the real thing.

Although the arrival ceremony at Rawalpindi passed with military precision, bands and red carpets as usual, it was the president's teeth that stole the show. They must have ranked in the top ten of the world's celebrity pearlies. By this time I had moved from the quiet comfort provided by my host and into a sort of Little Pink Room in the official guesthouse. This was a wonderfully atmospheric, single-storey fortress, adorned with minarets, mirrors, carpets and towers – but still boring. Although almost every comfort and convenience was on offer, alcohol was not. It was something of an honour to be there at all.

A short three-day programme was organised. Mr and Mrs Callaghan handled it brilliantly – unlike their No 10 staff, who were becoming progressively exhausted with a flood of office work and administration.

One of the few highlights was a trip by helicopter to Tarbela Dam, a giant earth-filled public work 70 miles from anywhere funded by the World Bank, with financial backup from the British exchequer. By this time the only blot on my horizon was a slightly built, tasselled and extremely bumptious army lieutenant appointed as ADC to the British delegation. It was his great moment and he and our team were soon in regular conflict over priorities. At the Tarbela helipad he led an escort of military motorcyclists – with solid frame, noisy single-cylinder Royal Enfield solos – from a commanding position standing erect in a leading jeep. It was intended that the dam would be inspected by the general and Mr Callaghan – and officials riding in eleven other enormous limousines – from the top level.

As we followed along it became evident that Mr Callaghan – hard though he was trying – was becoming increasingly testy over the noisy motorcyclists alongside and ahead. Consequently, conversation with the president dragged to a halt. On the way back Mr Callaghan asked if he could see the dam from the bottom and wasn't that a suitable side road downhill? The president barely had time to show his teeth and smile before I directed the driver to make a sharp turn to the left. We then led the cars down a dusty track, while the jeep, the unaware ADC and twenty motorcyclists continued on to the helipad. There, to his great consternation, the ADC discovered he had lost a president, a prime minister and a dozen vehicles loaded with VIPs.

It was a glorious moment when he finally caught up again. Hopefully his career was in tatters.

On the final day the prime minister commuted to Lahore by VC10 to watch a Pakistani-England one-day cricket match at the Gaddafi Stadium. After tea, he left just as the crowd rioted on to the pitch. An unpleasant scene unfolded when one of England's leading batsmen, now a distinguished commentator, complained too loudly about the absence of beer and was grossly offensive to the handsome wife of a distinguished Pakistani diplomat.

It was time to say farewell to the sub-continent and at the airport General Zia warmly shook my hand and said, 'Don't mention it.' As I hadn't already, I decided not to now. I wonder what it was?

⎯⎯⎯⋗•⋖⎯⎯⎯

The RAF VC10 landed in Egypt for refuelling and the prime minister enjoyed several hours of relaxed talks with President Anwar Sadat at his official guesthouse overlooking the Aswan Dam. Meanwhile, the Downing Street team beavered along to catch up with paperwork inherited from talks in Pakistan. Even on the final lap back home they were unable to stand down. The Aswan talks had generated another load of administration. They finally fell from the aircraft, frail, pale and exhausted, after arrival back in the United Kingdom. Although they never seemed to grumble they had seen virtually nothing of India.

Back in the press office at No 10 it had not gone unnoticed that while television pictures of Downing Street staff were rare, the special advisers seemed to have been on something of a swan. The following unsigned memo was circulated round the office:

The King of the Camera Angle Award – India 1978

The judges have now come to a decision on the 1978 India trip 'King of the Camera Angle Award'. They have awarded the prize to Bernard Donoughue for exceptional and persistent on-camera appearances throughout the trip, including some spectacular close ups and obliterations of the Prime Minister.

Donoughue showed the advantages of exceptional speed and fitness, coupled with a willingness to be ruthless in the final five yards.

Runner up was Mr T.D. McCaffrey [press secretary], now in the veteran stage but still showing an amazing talent for backing shyly into the limelight.

A disappointing third was the original hot favourite, Mr Roger Stott MP [parliamentary private secretary]. Stott had clearly over trained for the competition and the 112 injections to counteract all diseases known to man (and sacred cows) taken prior to the trip gave rise to some speculation that he had been nobbled.

Mr K. Stowe [principal private secretary], never one for a real rough and tumble, eased his way through the competition without ever exerting himself, while B. Cartledge [private secretary] never quite overcame the weight disadvantage of 17 Red Boxes.

Experts were left to speculate after Donoughue's comfortable victory whether he would have had such an easy ride if the formidable Sir John Hunt [cabinet secretary] had not been left at the starting gate.

Having arrived back in London in the nick of time, Bernard Donoughue also managed to score the winning goal for the Commons versus the German parliamentary delegation. It was a happy end to the trip for him.

However, our hosts did less well. President Zia of Bangladesh was soon voted out of office. The Indian prime minister gave up the fight against old age and went up in ceremonial flames. General Zia-ul-Haq of Pakistan and President Anwar Sadat of Egypt were assassinated.

Among our team, Peter Smither suffered a life-threatening illness from chicken eaten in the best Mumbai (Bombay) hotel. His life was probably saved by the last-minute intervention of the Hospital for Tropical Diseases in London.

The experience of the poor and suffering in the sub-continent had a profound effect on my outlook and I decided to change the direction of my life and retire as soon as possible.

But it would take another year before I could do so.

SIXTEEN

Prime Ministerial visits to distant lands were notable for his concerns for travelling companions, including journalists [...]

Callaghan – *A Life*, Kenneth O. Morgan

The telephone rang at home just before Christmas 1976. It was midnight. Although a call from No 10 was not unusual, it *was* unusual to find Ken Stowe, the prime minister's principal private secretary, on the line. His approach was tactful but sounded urgent. The government was flat out to prevent the total collapse of Sterling. Police help was needed.

A top-level delegation from the International Monetary Fund (IMF) would arrive at Heathrow between six and seven in the morning – bringing with them a multi-billion rescue package to counterbalance a potentially catastrophic world-wide run-on Sterling. It was a last-ditch safety net against imminent state bankruptcy. The Cabinet would be in early session, standing by to discuss the draconian conditions presented by the IMF. A decision had to be made and announced before the US currency markets opened. If the IMF package was refused, the government would certainly fall – and the 'pound-in-our-pockets' would become worthless. The IMF offer was dependent upon the acceptance of a package of increased taxes and reductions in public spending. A disaster *could* happen even then and if the decision was too late GB Incorporated would be on the dole. The latest deadline for an announcement was 10 a.m. I reached for my loose change.

I was left in no doubt that agreement by this deadline was essential, not just for the government but for Britain as a front-line country. Could I arrange police assistance, even at this late hour, to meet the bankers at Heathrow and ensure they were steered round the inevitable rush-hour traffic jam along the M4 motorway into London? Although clearly outside the commissioner's remit – and mine – I said I would do what I could. It was time to throw away the rule book and forget about precedents and undemocratic use of police resources. After all, the Conservative Opposition was hardly likely to complain, and the request had come from a top civil servant. But could the Traffic Branch see it that way too?

The traffic division of the Metropolitan Police had closed down and gone home at 11 p.m. In those days it was not back on line again until after 7 a.m. Overnight the senior controller's desk had a single lowly uniform inspector who did not readily see the implications. Yes, this was a one-off request, never to be repeated. No, his commander would not like it. Yes, it would be a good idea to telephone him NOW. No, he would not be happy about being woken in the middle of the night. Yes, I would be personally responsible. There was a considerable chasm between our normal duties and neither the inspector nor the commander was immediately receptive to interference from Special Branch. Deploying a combination of firmness and charm worthy of a top diplomat, I talked of responsibilities to the nation and the commissioner, and the advantages for a possible pay rise for police against the certainty of a cut.

I explained unambiguously that two Downing Street limousines would be at the international terminal of Heathrow Airport before dawn to collect five or six US civilians. The Government Car Service drivers would be expecting help. With no authority to do so, I implied that this request to Traffic Branch was not originating just from some lowly Downing Street pen-pusher but was backed by the prime minister's personal authority. Until then they thought it might be a spoof by one of the lads in the office.

I went into No 10 very early. Ken Godbeer and Joe Beatty had already left. As they approached Heathrow they saw inbound traffic build and queue as usual. After picking up their passengers on time, they joined the M4 motorway traffic – now log-jammed into London – with Home Office sets switched on, listening to police traffic channels.

With no hope of getting back to Downing Street in time to meet the deadline agenda, Ken told me later he heard a radio call for 'Metpol 701', then the call sign for the number one car. Having overheard Special Branch at work for many years, he acknowledged 'affirmative' and gave his location in the approved manner. The Scotland Yard controller – with brain now definitely in overdrive – instructed the two drivers to switch on dipped headlamps and position into the nearside lane. With the decision for limited co-operation made, Traffic Branch swung smoothly into action. Ken soon saw a speeding single police traffic car with headlights on, blue light flashing and bell ringing, headed out of town on the opposite carriageway. Through rear view mirrors he saw it take the next exit slipway, cross the motorway bridge, join the inflow and move steadily along the inside on the hard shoulder.

The two black Rovers were picked out and waved to follow along. From then it was comparatively simple teamwork for two professional drivers to tail the police car, exit the motorway and weave in convoy – gonging their way into Downing Street with just a couple of minutes to spare. With a rush, the bankers were introduced to the waiting Cabinet, doors closed and urgent discussions started. With final agreement, arrangements were completed for a stand-by financial safety net. After the release of an official announcement to the media, we all lived more or less happily ever after.

A British crisis was narrowly avoided thanks to two Government Car Service drivers and a pair of uniformed traffic cops in a jam-butty.

A self-important duty officer at the Yard then rang to demand a written explanation. As this was a very silly request, I wrote a very silly report. With a smile of experienced understanding, my branch happily pushed it upwards, where it was never heard of again. We have already seen that policemen usually consider politicians and civil servants as pragmatically irrelevant. But although the uniformed branch could never understand my own balancing act – a hard, low blow to the wallet with the idea of a pay cut and the pension plan terminated – together with a few words of sickening flattery about the gratitude of No 10 and the prime minister himself proved more than adequate.

⟫•◦•⟪

In the 1970s the governance of Britain demanded reaction to one crisis after another. I suppose it always had and always will. Within No 10 it sometimes became hard to distinguish between real disasters and those which were just shallow political panics.

But when I saw the name of Sir John Hunt, the formidable Cabinet secretary, on the travel list for Guadeloupe it was clear that he was not just a makeweight. Sir John was rarely involved in prime ministerial jollies. When the name of his deputy Sir Clive Rose turned up too, there could be no doubt about it. Something serious was up.

I was in the advance guard of the UKDEL to Guadeloupe. It had always been the policy of Whitehall for officials to travel long distances by British Airways and in those days when the national airline still worked along kick-and-rush guidelines, passenger satisfaction was never a priority. First or club class was reserved only for ministers and very senior officials. That must have been an improvement over the sardine-tin class to which the majority of us were consigned.

I had learned the hard way that BA followed certain assured travel guidelines with routes to the Caribbean. The aircraft was always late leaving and the passenger cabin invariably overfilled. The food was a bi-product from an oil terminal. If more people could be stuffed on board for the diversion airport than the scheduled destination, there was really no intention of heading anywhere else. Not that anyone was told until beyond the watershed in mid-Atlantic. This – and it was calculated in the office – enabled BA to send just one full or overfull jumbo jet instead of two partly filled. The totally unconvincing flight deck diversionary announcement in mid-Atlantic, from say Barbados to Antigua, came at about the time when the captain challenged the tropical storms where wing-flexing tests-to-destruction were apparently mandatory. What the office smarties never realised was that the regularity with which this deception took place created a substantial reservoir of travellers so infuriated they tried never to travel with BA again. EVER!

I was once welcomed as a regular customer at the Antiguan Hotel, provided for diverted BA passengers free of charge. From experience I kept a small case under the seat so that I could obviate the need to travel onward in a dirty shirt and with unwashed teeth.

With perhaps 70 per cent of the passengers happily disembarked at this diversion airport, 30 per cent were left waiting for onward flights to wherever they thought they were going in the first place. The second official sleight of hand then took place over the counter at Antigua. The angry 30 per cent were studiously ignored by the information desk staff, on the grounds that they were employees of LIAT (Leeward Islands Air Transport, a BA subsidiary) and had nothing to do with BA. On one occasion when I was persuaded to join an irate, blond young Austrian drug smuggler posing as a film director – with a travel bag full of well-used US dollars – a LIAT aircraft arrived as we were telexing for a private flight. Many of these passengers were also enraged at an unscheduled and unexplained diversion. The same counter staff – having successfully fended-off the BA refugees – were now busily preoccupied with the consumption of leftover plasticised food from our jumbo jet. Between mouthfuls they now denied any responsibility for LIAT on the grounds that 'we work for British Airways'.

For travel to Guadeloupe, therefore, it was a pleasure to commute to Paris on New Year's Day 1979 and there join the French team, who were hosting a four-nation conference. As this was organised by the French, we Brits no longer travelled steerage; the captain avoided the terror of tropical storms and the Air France Boeing 747 arrived at the right airport at the right time. Moreover, food on board proved conclusively that airborne nosh did not have to be camouflaged, soggy recycled cardboard. For instance: *pour commencer – Saumon de Loire glacé de la Parisienne, sauce au cresson* … and so on.

It was also useful to have informal meetings with security counterparts before we got down to serious business at Guadeloupe. Something of a feud existed with the Americans since the US Secret Service rampaged around in Rambouillet. At a 1976 summit at San Juan, Puerto Rico, the American host nation showed how they thought security checks should really be done. Admittedly they did well – following the French example – by confining the leaders within a double ring of security at a golf course resort on the coast and allowing free movement within for the leaders and top officials. This could be either on foot or bicycle or by 3mph golf buggy. A golf buggy was the choice of adventurous grand prix aspirants such as our British Chancellor of the Exchequer Denis Healey, who tried wheely skids in pursuit of other delegates.

On Guadeloupe, the French were determined to ratchet up security efficiency to yet another level. During the outbound airborne trip we were able to settle many of the outstanding issues for the British delegation and sit smugly on the sidelines once formal meetings started and friction developed with the US Secret Service.

The hosts established an early tactical advantage when their chairman decided that any discussion would be in French. The US Secret Service, initially wrong-footed with just one French linguist in their large party, mounted a successful counterattack by ignoring collective decisions and bringing with them all they needed anyway – arms, bottles of presidential blood, helicopters, armoured limousines and radio communications. In this way they were able to remain fairly independent of French resources. They kept another provocative ace up their sleeves too.

The chosen hotel was the Hamak. Individual bungalows overlooked the sea and in these the heads of state and their wives were accommodated in luxury. The brochure helped to paint the best picture: 'The Hamak is a New Resort – a State of Mind – a Total Vacation.' Simon Winchester for the British press, starved of real copy, confirmed for his readers shivering at home in the winter of discontent the presence of 'bronzed, topless Frenchwomen surf-boarding past the Callaghans' bungalow'. Unfortunately for the prime minister, security patrols at sea, under the watchful eye of Royal Navy frigate HMS *Scylla*, put a stop to any of that well before his arrival.

Until almost the last moment, it seemed the French were just not going to be ready in time. Although there was a safe inner lagoon, it began to look as though French honour would suffer from the absence of a sea beach from which to swim. However in the early morning of start day minus one I was woken by a threatening rumble of heavy traffic. Twenty or more giant ballast lorries, several cranes, bulldozers and transporters with three-dozen horizontal palm trees growled on to the rocky foreshore. An instant beach of eye-watering silver sand was spread. Holes were bulldozed, palm trees slotted in, rollers deployed and *voila!* – an instant beach was in place. The show was not over. Before breakfast a second squad hove into view with topsoil and plants and water cans. Before you could say 'Inspector Clouseau', each bungalow boasted a mature flower garden. Shaded from the sun, too, it looked as though it had been there for decades. Gallic flair won the day.

The Hamak bungalow complex was adjacent to the main hotel and this was all secured from other high-class beach resorts – including those with topless French women, no doubt – by a double ring of guards and lookout posts. Guadeloupe had full provincial standing and some security personnel were French gendarmerie. With HMS *Scylla* patrolling offshore, movement within land boundaries of the complex could be full and free from both terrorists and holidaymakers.

The understanding upon which the French advance guard had worked was for none of the usual daily press briefings – only a single press conference at the end. But at the very last minute the Americans played their next ace. Having unexpectedly given in to their press corps, who had threatened a boycott, US representatives announced that two aircraft full with journalists, photographers and television crews were on their way. Accommodation had to be found in a hurry on an island already crowded with winter sun lovers. It was made clear that US media men would not be happy to huddle round barbecues on the beach.

I joined a team which tried to commandeer luxury accommodation at the internationally famous Club Mediterranee. The resident director there – with the inducement of generous funding – finally agreed to vacate enough rooms to accommodate the US incomers. He intended to persuade enough of his clients to accept generous compensation and be relocated into inferior rooms elsewhere. Smiling at a job well done, we moved back to the Hamak – to discover that the director's *Direction* in Paris had firmly vetoed this plan. There was no way they were prepared to face civil claims by a hundred or more clients already on their way. Leverage was then applied to another hotel nearby and finally enough rooms were taken over.

French president Giscard d'Estaing was host and responsible for the honour of the Republic, Jimmy Carter for the United States had a stunning golf outfit and the most political clout, Chancellor Helmut Schmidt took snuff and was a much-admired politician for West Germany, James Callaghan meanwhile showed his independence by sticking to his heavy London winter suit. Confronted with tropical sunshine, he did remove his tie and got out those pre-war tennis shoes again.

Talks between the big four were held in total isolation. Although the French president was the host, the initiative for this conference had come from Jimmy Carter and the US administration. Carter was about to hold further talks with the

Soviet Union on strategic arms limitation (SALT II) and needed to co-ordinate the American defence position with his western allies. It was largely because his negotiating position had to remain entirely secret in advance of his SALT talks that at Guadeloupe the press were not given the expected daily briefings.

The press, however, were at a loose end with no daily copy, and the British contingent set about creating something out of nothing to account for their expense claims. It was bad news for the prime minister because he took the brunt of their displeasure.

In his autobiography, Mr Callaghan concedes that the timing of the conference was unfortunate. His policies were just starting to have a real effect on the state of the British nation's future chances and, in particular, he charts the real progress made – off-the-record – between workers and employers.

All this went over the heads of British readers and viewers. As they queued in the cold and rain for transport to get back home, they were easily persuaded that Guadeloupe was a swan and a good chance for the prime minister to get away from it all. They were regaled with cynical anti-conference propaganda. The *Daily Mail* labelled the event as 'The Summit of Absurdity' and published a provocative photograph captioned: 'A Place in the Sun for the Callaghans, the Schmidts, the Giscards and the Carters.' They had a point. It was bad timing to take wives for a jolly. They would have contributed nothing to strategic discussion.

The *Mail* aimed low blows at political weak points. For example, '[…] the whole solemn pretence about the gravity and importance of summit conferences started to slip' and '[…] the growing cult of summitry, far from being an aid to good international relations, is a menace'. Simon Winchester 'in Guadeloupe', reported on '£100 a day luxury for the Callaghans' and claimed that tourists were angry at being moved out of their chalets to make way for the big four conference.

It was not all bad for the Special Branch team, however. Winchester did have good news from an otherwise irate Belgian tourist: 'Unlike the American Secret Service, the British have been quiet and polite. The others are quite unspeakable.'

Whether speakable or unspeakable the security officers of four nations crouched, camouflaged in the shrubbery surrounding the open-air dance area and the top-level talkers. Dressed in tropical lightweights, we shadowed our principals as they broke for lunch. President Jimmy Carter pretended to be just another Joe and set off for a swim in the lagoon. Secret Service secret agents spoke up their sleeves to a control room – then doughnutted around him in close protective formation. Four US Navy frogmen flip-flopped alongside and plunged in with him. With not one member of the public in sight it was difficult for them all to appear with 'just another Joe'. Mr Callaghan was not prepared for the water but, seizing the opportunity to show another prowess, headed for the boat harbour and launched himself into a sailing dinghy before anyone else could interfere and sailed away across the lagoon. Temporarily left standing, our French liaison comrade and the on-duty Special Branch bodyguard commandeered a pedalo and set off in hot pursuit with a flurry of spume. Fortunately, as leg muscles tired, a security launch sped to the scene and took over with Gallic flourish.

Without an official programme *les épouses* were underemployed in style. Mrs Callaghan's sun hat brought derisory comments in the British press. The hosts, fearing boredom, prepared a barbecue and steel band for an outdoor party. As dusk fell, well-organised teams sped into action, as we close protection officers set up watch posts in surrounding undergrowth. Barbecues were lit and the band tuned up. With discreet candle-lamp lighting, the lucky eight took over the steaks and shellfish laid out ready for the duty chef to start work. This was Jimmy Carter. The band clanged away and couples paired up to dance in democratic harmony.

The French hosts now came into their own rather magnificently. With a gentle, balmy warm breeze blowing, a sailing catamaran – the winner of a recent transatlantic ocean race from La Rochelle to Martinique – stole quietly into position and anchored just offshore. While honoured guests chewed barbecued chicken drumsticks, danced and enjoyed delicious French Caribbean cool drinks, the sailboat was floodlit. The crew hoisted and let fly a large, red, shapely balloon spinnaker, leaving the sheets trailing onto the foredeck. A bare-chested, handsome, magnificently tanned athlete appeared from the saloon below, dressed only in elegant, tight-fitting white ducks. Silhouetted against the black tropical night, he shinned up the mast, grabbed those dangling sheets and swung stylishly into a ten-minute display sequence of airborne acrobatics. It was a winner. The ladies were bowled over and even their rather outmanoeuvred husbands gave a grudging round of applause. Security personnel of four nations, camouflaged in the instant flower garden, were tempted to join in too.

Fortunately, the media men and women corralled out of sight were unaware of all these shenanigans. They had to remain satisfied with a joint communiqué on the final day and interviews with the leaders, if they were lucky. Still, without a lot to write home about, they must have returned fearing that their editors would think they too had been on some sort of a winter holiday at considerable expense.

Some of the British Fleet Street contingent joined the prime minister's VC10 for the return journey to Heathrow, via a short jolly in Barbados. Also in the stern section were a number of Royal Military Police who had ensured the safety of the prime minister's papers and secretariat. Something of a reunion party developed by mid-Atlantic. An instant sobering process took place in the VIP lounge at Heathrow on 10 January 1979 when Her Majesty's Customs and Excise Waterguard officers discovered they had mistakenly assumed that their temporary attachment to a government delegation authorised them to stuff suitcases full of duty-free spirits and cigarettes. The Waterguard didn't see the funny side of it and I was called away to adjudicate. If I remember correctly, the treasury were substantial beneficiaries.

As a result, I missed some of the press conference given by Mr Callaghan against the advice of his press secretary Tom McCaffrey.

During final approach, news was received that the media had assembled and were demanding an interview. With the prime minister looking tanned and rested after a mid-Atlantic catnap and knowing that journalists were looking for the kill, Tom had wisely recommended avoiding confrontation. Mr Callaghan decided otherwise. It was now that he was paraphrased in *The Sun* newspaper, with the unfortunate phrase, 'Crisis! What Crisis?' He always denied that he said these words, seen as provoking the British public during a very definite winter of discontent at home.

Although I cannot possibly comment on this incident, the evidence of a national crisis became clear enough. Moreover, at the reception held at the Guildhall after Lady Thatcher's funeral in 2013, I was lucky enough to meet up with my colleague Ray Parker, who *was* at the press conference and well remembers every incident. He was adamant that, yes, James Callaghan definitely did say, 'Crisis! What Crisis?'

I am also reassured, unequivocally and on the highest authority, that with the maintenance of law and order at stake, Sir John Hunt and Sir Clive Rose had travelled to Guadeloupe explicitly to offer procedural and constitutional advice if a State of Emergency had been unavoidable in Great Britain while the prime minister was abroad.

So yes. It was a crisis alright.

SEVENTEEN

Where there is discord, may we bring harmony. Where there is error, may we bring truth. Where there is doubt, may we bring faith. And where there is despair may we bring hope.

St Francis's prayer

arch 1978 was a critical month for prime minister watchers within Downing Street but outside the inner circle. Their conclusion was that a General Election was imminent and the date favoured was 25 May 1978.

This was not mere guesswork but a conclusion reached from an amalgam of evidence and a few insider hints. It was remarked upon that the prime minister's official diary contained unusually few commitments for May. Travel out of town and abroad was noticeably limited and subject to cancellation. New committees appeared on the agenda – campaign committee and liaison committee were two. In town things looked quiet too, and surely it was significant that – while question marks were appended – Mr Callaghan was planning to see Harold Wilson's old antagonists at Transport House, headed by Labour Party General Secretary Ron Hayward.

Finally, it was noted that a joint Cabinet–National Executive Committee meeting was provisionally scheduled. One interpretation was that this signalled an essential pre-election end to the hostility between Downing Street and Transport House. A left wing committed to a siege economy was already out of step with any move toward what eventually became 'New' Labour.

Talk in the back seat of the official car seemed unusually guarded. Issues were referred to obliquely and when decoded hardly required a three-month course at the Detective Training School at Hendon to work out. The regular drivers came to similar conclusions about an impending election after a rumour bubbled noisomely to the surface that Private Office was being pressed to set up early official travel to Washington, where Peter Jay was the British ambassador. His wife – now Lady Jay – was the Callaghans' daughter Margaret, and contact with her and the grandchildren was important to both Mr and Mrs Callaghan. Cynics pointed out that a *private* visit at Easter would have been expensive, especially for a man notably careful with cash. The rumour was ratcheted up that a Concorde flight was under consideration – at public expense. In the event, travel to Washington was by a British Airways' 747 commercial flight on Wednesday, 22 March. Previously well-camouflaged crypto-Conservatives on the lower deck displayed small but bold signs of an impending winter of discontent; Jim Callaghan had not made himself universally popular at front-door level and the results were beginning to show through. The perception was that Labour could not possibly win this time.

What was not generally known was that Tom McNally *had* already put together provisional arrangements for a General Election campaign. On 10 March 1978 the prime minister, with a small group of political advisers, agreed his outline planning.

During a car journey from Chequers, the pace perceptibly stepped up for me. Mr Callaghan introduced a gentle third degree.

'I understand you were here at the last election, John? How was it organised? What role did Marcia Williams play? How did Mr Wilson travel? Did he come back to London each night?'

And finally, 'I hear you are thinking of retiring? I would be happy if you considered staying on until the election. You are one of the few here with previous experience.'

If he was trailing a red herring to see if I should be added to his leakers' list, I was ahead of him. Our unit followed the advice from a famous First World War poster:

> A wise old owl sat on an oak,
> The more he saw the less he spoke,
> The less he spoke the more he heard
> We should imitate that old bird!

Of course, the SB team could never have kept on top of our task had we not absorbed all that was happening, analysed the evidence and prepared for any operational eventuality. But political leaks to the media were firmly vetoed. Did Mr Callaghan's invitation to stay on board infer an assumption that Special

Branch terms of reference would permit *political* support? If so, the guidelines under which we worked – broadly only to ensure his physical security – clearly precluded police action which could be described outside the strictly official and necessary.

In fact, in spite of massive media speculation about the date of the General Election, leaks at Cabinet level and from Whitehall sources, it is doubtful if lickspittle reporters got the slightest clue from the staff inside No 10. Indeed, they were lucky not to do so. The final choice to go to the country was the gift of the incumbent prime minister and he and his party advisers had to live with the result. In this case the spring 1979 election, held after the disastrous winter of discontent, was catastrophic for the Labour Party, who found themselves excluded from office for some eighteen years. The assumption today is that Mr Callaghan missed the boat by avoiding the issue in 1978 and his reputation still carries the can in some quarters. The record now shows that he was keeping his options open on 20 March 1978, when he met David Steel (now Lord Steel), the Liberal Party leader, to discuss where the interests of both parties might meld harmoniously.

In the event, personnel in No 10 who had bet on May 1978 lost their deposits. It is doubtful that the prime minister was attempting deliberately to mislead me or to lay false trails for the No 10 staff – although I am not naive enough to think that he was incapable of such calculated deception.

There is ample evidence now to show that he had little choice for the delay. For instance, in the second volume of his *Downing Street Diary – With James Callaghan in No 10*, when he was head of the prime minister's Policy Unit, Bernard Donoughue summarises – almost in passing – just why an election in 1978 was never possible. On the positive side of the equation were Mr Callaghan's improving ratings in opinion polls, his domination of Mrs Thatcher and the Conservative Party in the House of Commons, the ever-increasing progress of the Cabinet under his chairmanship and encouragement from some of his ministers. The problem was with the old British disease, the economy, which was still in such a disastrous state that the chances of a 1978 election win were zero. Donoughue's diary for a date as early as Thursday, 23 September 1976 included:

> our reserves are down to £4 billion – and the deficit this year and next will absorb that. Sterling is at an all-time low. Inflation is no longer falling. The incomes policy is lacking. We have record interest rates to protect Sterling and finance the PSBR. Our import content is rising all the time. There is no prospect of unemployment falling.

Although this is not the point made in the diary, it is clear enough now that, with all these battles still far from won, a decision to go to the country in 1978 would have spelled certain disaster. Instead, a delay for a further year might signal enough green shoots of recovery in time to win his party's re-election. Mr Callaghan was not to know that in 1979 his chances would be even slimmer. The red herrings identified in Downing Street in the spring of 1978 may have led to the future condemnation of Mr Callaghan as a ditherer who missed the boat, whereas in reality it seems safe to claim now that he was doing his best to make an objective judgement – with very few aces up his sleeve.

The rest of the story is not in any doubt. Whether or not the British economy would have shown those critical signs of recovery, the combination of extreme left-wing penetration tolerated within the ranks of the Labour Party and the fierce antagonism of the trade union leaders upon whose support the prime minister had counted led to the infamous winter of discontent of 1978–79. Perhaps those unfortunate, unfeeling words, 'Crisis! What crisis?' attributed to the prime minister on his return – tanned and healthy from the summit in Guadeloupe – fuelled enough voters' antagonism finally to push the Labour Party into political oblivion.

An unspoken alliance of media barons, trade unions and the Trotskyite Militant Tendency within the Labour Party contributed to a political and economic revolution in Great Britain. The media may have gained some satisfaction but the Militant Tendency, hoping for a siege economy and full-scale government socialisation, sowed the seeds of their own eventual destruction. In the end, the Labour Party moved firmly away from the left and into the moderate centre of mainstream politics, gaining too much public support for the Tendency to be able to battle against.

Neil Kinnock started the change. Collars and ties were now worn at the annual conference, overweight, fly-away hair and flushed, unkempt appearance was no longer the fashion for lady members and Tony Blair and New Labour eventually consolidated a commanding role in Parliament.

⟹•◦•⟸

After losing a vote of confidence in the House of Commons by one vote, any further gamesmanship about the date became irrelevant and a General Election was called for 3 May 1979. As Mr Callaghan's official programme largely ground to a standstill, he placed himself at the disposal of the Labour Party – and much of the Downing Street infrastructure went on a three-day week. However, road transport and security remained with No 10.

Using the Harold Wilson blueprint that prime ministerial visits to marginal constituencies were critical, Mr Callaghan let Transport House staff organise his comprehensive speaking programme. His life, and ours, became a scramble of cars, trains and aircraft; of speeches, handshakes and meetings; of rush, crush, anxiety and danger; hotel rooms, quick changes of crumpled clothing; press briefings and photo opportunities; elbows, bruises, pushing, shoving and trodden toes; of fatigue, irregular meals and shortage of shirts and sleep. Just how anyone can aspire to political power and be motivated to sacrifice a quantifiable slice of civilised life is beyond me – particularly as the schedule is orchestrated to meld with media deadlines rather than any identifiable bio-rhythms. Without newspaper and television backing, though, the campaign is dead in the water.

Excited photographers, reporters and television crews can be particularly vile, jostling for advantage in the hope of a scoop, a memorable slip of the tongue or skid on a banana skin. They will go to any length to make a fool of their target by persuading him to wear a stupid hat or cuddle a photogenic child. Their bottom-sucking blandishments have no boundaries of decency or consideration for the meek and mild who are hoping to inherit the earth with their vote. They create a Twickenham scrum at any opportunity. One trio of cameraman, sound recordist and director – unwisely hired by a local Labour Party agent in a north-country town – linked arms and charged into a supermarket ahead of the prime minister.

They scattered shoppers merely out to find the best 'buy one, get one free' offer of the day, trampling on the elderly and disabled without concern and leaving a litter of the disgruntled and mildly injured to promise they would never vote Labour again. As the last thing that entered the reporters' minds was to complain about brutal policing, our team assisted by local officers were able to implement satisfactory countermeasures, warmed by the knowledge that we were definitely acting in the public interest.

At the outset, Mr Callaghan built up a reserve of brownie points, following a fine line by securing photo opportunities while maintaining prime ministerial dignity. Catnaps and snacks kept him going and, even when he must have fancied to throw himself off a cliff, the constant repetition of 'well, there we are then!' to everyone and no one, kept his features relaxed for photo images.

He was magnificent when crowds were pressing dangerously and occasionally threateningly. But for just how long would this Happy Jim image last? Behind the scenes, some of his family and staff were targeted with the occasional rumble of thunder. Even the faithful Mrs Callaghan was not exempt. For the moment, his much-needed Special Branch 'lads' were sheltered from the impending storm. Our No 10 team stayed close to him at all costs and one officer – often me – would back away into the crowd as he picked his way through. Keeping eye contact, his alert concerns were communicated directly and countermeasures taken. With invaluable help from local officers, we were able to pre-empt any of the overexciteds from getting too much out of hand.

———⇒►-◦-◄⇐———

At a General Election, the political party in power had certain built-in advantages. For example, the leader could nominate the date. Leading lights of the governing party have another asset – an entitlement to police services commensurate with the security risk assessment. Chief constables are appointed objectively rather than for political sympathies and, broadly speaking, their officers should not be instructed to provide direct assistance to a politician on any grounds other than national security and public safety.

In normal times this assistance can be low profile, but the 1970s were far from normal. What is now labelled almost indiscriminately as terrorism was proliferating in much of the western world. Here in the United Kingdom it was the IRA that constituted immediate danger, unaware it seemed, of the hatred they were generating among the majority of average, and often not otherwise unsympathetic members of the British public. With their role as intelligence gatherers, Special Branch had become aware of the presence on the mainland of at least two Active Service Units (ASUs) of the Provisional IRA, scouting for an opportunity to assassinate a leading politician during the election campaign.

On the reasonable assumption that Mr Callaghan was top of the hit list, our team at No 10 was doubled and we orchestrated a policy of counter-propaganda. This took the form of greater visibility and a harder approach to media men. We needed them to start complaining that, while probing for scoops and jockeying for action images, they were being prevented from doing their democratic duty by Special Branch heavies. Unusually, we needed them to publicise the increased security surrounding the prime minister, and they faithfully helped out. We also generated a few carefully contrived leaks to more responsible journalists and they, too, unwittingly did their bit.

After the election the branch found that the ASU scouts had changed their target from Mr Callaghan to Roy Mason, Secretary of State for Northern Ireland. His close protection team had deployed their own defensive stratagem.

A collateral advantage for Mr Callaghan and his team of organisers and advisers, also unwittingly, was that an increased security threat demanded an increased response from chief constables. As most of the prime minister's forty-three speaking engagements were out of London, and covered by constabularies rather than the Metropolitan Police, we had to lean on them without disclosing the source of Scotland Yard's information.

They reacted conscientiously; the result was improved planning, carefully checked timing, increased numbers of escorts, and men on the ground at every vulnerable point. Crowd control was well handled, with closely supervised policeman power. Armed Special Branch units were provided locally to check and guard Mr Callaghan's hotel rooms. British Rail police tooled themselves up too. All this allowed the staff at Transport House to fix up a prime ministerial speaking agenda far in excess of that available to the Conservatives – where police resources based on threat assessment could proportionately be scaled down. In the prime minister's case co-ordination fell upon the No 10 SB team. This could have left us open to allegations of assisting a political party. The final buck stopped with me and – keeping one eye carefully on my entrenching tool – I tried to ensure that we remained just the right side of our unwritten rules.

The prime minister had some knowledge of the risks he was facing. His programme – including mandatory walkabouts – was dangerously well publicised in advance, for the information of enemies as well as friends. Transport House, now with smooth backup both from Private Office, when they were involved, and by an unexpectedly co-operative national police network, automatically helped to step up Mr Callaghan's programme. Normally, Transport House was far from being a well-oiled machine.

However, toward the end of the campaign the polls were discouraging for Mr Callaghan. He was tiring and his fuse was getting noticeably short. Even the faithful Audrey Callaghan, usually exempt from his broadsides, was about to get some flak. During his meetings, either in public or private, at least one of the prime minister's SB team remained in eye contact with him. His indication that it was time to go was clearly signalled. The motorcade could then be called into position and police services stood-to in good time. In turn, this enhanced the capacity for close co-operation, with the excellent uniformed traffic cars and motorcyclists upon which we were dependent leading the way in unfamiliar territory and keeping the motorcade rolling smoothly. Hold ups represented possible danger.

Mrs Callaghan, more used to Labour Party *laissez faire*, was sometimes engaged in profound debate at one end of the room when she should have been on the starting blocks near the door. Waiting for her to realise that her husband had already embarked in the motorcade meant losing valuable seconds and vulnerability as a static target. Mr Callaghan's rule number one was broken. The driver could not be told to get on with it at once. In the end Mrs Callaghan got a severe rocket: 'If the detectives know when I want to get going there is no reason for you still to be in there talking!'

From then Mrs Callaghan was seen to break into a trot on a couple of occasions.

Mr Derek Gladwyn (later Lord Gladwyn), Southern Region secretary of the General Municipal Workers Union, was appointed to liaise with Transport House, and as Mr Callaghan's personal Mr Fix-It. Unaccustomed perhaps to his new authority, he strayed into a minefield by shouting and pointing excessively. A number of the benefits that the prime minister had come to appreciate from his staff instantly disappeared. Derek soon got the message and eventually won the approval of the Political Office, the Policy Unit and Labour Party appointees in the press office in No 10 after his heated declaration that Transport House was the most inefficient organisation he had ever encountered. This confirmed the experience of the core participants within Downing Street who had been forced to tolerate the problem for years.

Near the halfway point of the campaign, Mr Callaghan was driven one morning to Portsmouth, accompanied by Mr Gladwyn in the back seat of the number one limo. Derek had by then learned when it was wise to keep quiet – which was now more often than not – but could not ignore the bad news indicated by opinion polls. The Callaghan personal rating was well ahead of that of Mrs Thatcher but, although there were intermittent signs that the gap was closing, the persistent Tory lead overall averaged about five percentage points. The signs were that the race was already lost. It was not something likely to elevate Mr Callaghan's spirits and so, in probable combination with increasing pressure on his bladder, stormy weather was in the offing.

The programme had gone amazingly well so far. Complex and often rapidly changing operations had generally run smoothly. Nevertheless, today I was his nearest target.

With just one other limo in convoy – with my SB colleague Peter Smither and a couple of No 10 staff – Joe Hazard headed down the M3 motorway at a brisk speed. Without a police escort, speed limits were neither his main priority, nor mine. Scotland Yard had a particularly good relationship with the Hampshire Special Branch, with whom a successful joint operation was conducted in 1973 to detect and convict the IRA killer Noel Jenkinson, who had blown up the Parachute Regiment barracks in Aldershot. Today, Hampshire Special Branch would carry out advance planning and rendezvous (RV) with us at the southern end of the Winchester bypass. Together with local traffic cops, we would then shoot off to Portsmouth.

We drew steadily ahead of schedule and, concerned that we might be in advance of their team at the RV, I signalled Joe for a lower speed. Well done, Joe. Unfortunately as we rounded Winchester, he was forced to a standstill, then a slow crawl in a longish queue of slow-moving vehicles. As we trickled along, now in touch by radio with the RV team, a glance in my rearview mirror indicated that the black clouds of a thunderstorm were brewing. Sensing that something more important than a mere general election was preoccupying his boss, Derek kept quiet. Joe looked troubled. I was updating probabilities on the radio. The news was improving, when lightning struck. It was my turn to take shelter.

In an aggressive voice and with a black look, Mr Callaghan declared uncompromisingly that it had been foolish to slow down. Everybody knew about the daily delay on the Winchester bypass and now we would be late. He rumbled on. The bladder factor had struck, it seemed. I had seen its effect before. However, he wasn't the only one who was tired and not especially tolerant. Every single previous sortie for which I had some responsibility had gone well – often due as much to local police resourcefulness as to our own experience and planning. I was also on a short fuse and blessed with invaluable outsider status. My career was neither dependent upon prime ministerial patronage, nor his success at an election. Having got us into this mess it would have been more sensible to let me sort it out.

I turned and told him directly that I didn't make many mistakes and was expecting to iron this one out as soon as I could get on with it. At the same time I prepared my bottom line riposte: 'If you don't like what I have contributed, you will have another SB team by the morning.'

An unhappy silence followed. Mr Callaghan might not always be right but was never wrong.

Thanks to some splendid co-operation with the waiting Hampshire team, a joint motorcade smoothly reformed on the run and we sped to Portsmouth, arriving a mere five minutes adrift. Having been somewhere like this before, I was not surprised to see Mr Callaghan slip easily into the Happy Jim mode as he shook hands with party members lined up to greet him – and then take the earliest opportunity to disappear for a brisk wash and brush-up. I warned Peter Smither to prepare for change – but already Mr Callaghan's concerns were focused elsewhere.

⋙•0•⋘

The Tories won the election by a workable margin. Mr Callaghan had already considered a deal with the Liberals if Labour won the most seats but not enough for a majority. This was no longer an option. It was bad luck for a Labour prime minister who had done so much to rescue his party from humiliation and the waste bin of Opposition into which they were consigned.

The *Daily Mirror* prepared to name the guilty men. Trade Union leaders had fomented the winter of discontent which had drawn such obloquy upon the Labour government – notably Alan Fisher of the National Union of Public Employees and Moss Evans of the Transport and General Workers Union.

Bernard Donoughue also added the 'appalling National Union of Teachers', who came out on strike during the very week of the General Election.

Even greater treachery was inferred from Harold Wilson's comment to the *Daily Mail* that his wife Mary might vote for Mrs Thatcher. It was the sort of statement that might well have diverted a critical percentage of Labour voters.

Crushed between the left and right of his party, and with even his own constituency management committee deeply penetrated by the Trotskyite Militant Tendency, Mr Callaghan had been on a hiding from the start. The question remains – would he have been able to pull the country back onto its feet if he had been a benevolent dictator as he once hoped?

Bernard Donoughue and other commentators summarised the credit due to James Callaghan as prime minister and politician – and the only man to hold the four great offices of government. After 1979 he acquired an international reputation as a statesman in demand among the international great and good. This was not unusual. It must be something of a surprise for former prime ministers to find themselves lauded as lecturers, respected commentators and sometimes wise international negotiators, after suffering the effects of almost inevitable public humiliation while in Downing Street.

My own perspective was less academic, more pragmatic and based on virtually day-by-day, man-to-man contact over a period of two years. In my opinion he was a consummate actor; a control freak capable of personality changes appropriate to circumstances. In short order he could appear to be humble, confident, interested, sulky or resentful. Self-interest was involved. He was often overtly affectionate to his wife and I came to regard his attitude to her with suspicion. He was rarely humorous and when he chuckled it was time to take care. A chuckle could indicate that he was knowingly economical with the truth or it could be threatening. As a professional protection officer it was difficult to trust him. If he decided on a consultation mode, the best he could manage if he disagreed with a third party was to draw a line under the conversation and move on without comment. There was, however, little evidence that he changed his mind or modified his own opinion. Consultation seemed to be little more than a calculated process to produce a desired image.

The real weak link and the time when he was at his most honest was when he lost his temper. During one Labour Party Conference at Blackpool, Robin Day (the late Sir Robin) – the television interviewer and another bully – strayed from the agenda agreed with the prime minister's press secretary in advance. Here was a classic trial of strength between two heaving water buffaloes. After the Callaghan chuckle and some frosty politeness, the interview was peremptorily abandoned. Back in the car with the press secretary, Tom McCaffrey, Mr Callaghan was virtually out of control. Tom was loudly warned that he need not think his job was secure just because he had been personally chosen, or presume that he was indispensable or could do just what he liked.

Back in the hotel Mr Callaghan had to pass through a lounge crowded with party delegates. He was unable to display the necessary Happy Jim image until Ian Bryan, his protection officer, bought him a newspaper and advised him to sit down and read it calmly. Unbelievably, his advice was followed.

He was brave, personally scrupulous with his health and strength, and virtually teetotal. He ran the government more efficiently than his predecessor had ever done. The conclusion that he was let down by a Cabinet short of talent was probably true. He certainly lost the battle within No 10 to show political primacy over his civil servants and took them fully into his inner circle. I am not aware that he ever admitted failure.

I recall him as a man who governed by opinion poll rather than conviction. A politician who, as a supreme manipulator, persuaded some of his biographers to mistake a well-honed image for real aptitude.

Roy Jenkins said of him, 'Jim is like a pretty girl at a dance. She seems desirable and you approach her. And then you find she has bad breath.'

<hr>

Moving one prime minister out of Downing Street to make way for another had once been something of an abrasive business. When Sir Alec Douglas-Home gave way to Harold Wilson in 1964, his official car was apparently withdrawn at Buckingham Palace, leaving him to walk home alone. Fortunately, he was still in good shape and enjoyed a stroll before lunch, but officials realised that this was unnecessarily undignified and things were gradually improved. The Leader of the Opposition could now retain an official car on grounds of security and this guaranteed James Callaghan a lift home after being handed his P45 by the queen. Ken Stowe and Private Office orchestrated the whole affair in concert with both political parties and the palace.

This is how it went.

Within No 10, the political staff packed their bags while Garden Room girls shredded papers. Private secretaries scanned Cabinet Office briefs about the incoming administration and Ken Stowe took charge of planning car allocation and timings at the palace. After saying farewell to members of the Downing Street staff in the garden, the prime minister had a help-yourself lunch with the private secretaries and his closest political advisers. He finally left through the front door for the last time, on schedule for a short farewell audience with the queen at 2.25 p.m.

Joe had already packed the Callaghans' travel bags in the back of the official Rover. Mr Callaghan acknowledged the crowds, stepped into the limo and was driven away – followed after a discreet interval of time and distance by a second Downing Street Rover that waited in the forecourt of Buckingham Palace. After Mr Callaghan had left with Joe, I waited in the anteroom until Mrs Thatcher arrived in Conservative Party Central Office transport. She was not yet entitled to a Downing Street official car, with its special radio and anti-terrorist gadgetry.

As her courtesies with the queen went ahead, Mrs Thatcher's car left the palace inner courtyard and was replaced by the waiting Downing Street limo number two – which I boarded with her as she left for No 10. With radio contact soon established, uniformed officers at Downing Street were alert for her arrival and disembarkation into cheering crowds. Senior officers from A Division seized the chance for a historic photo opportunity, leaving their men to clear her route along Downing Street toward the front door.

Looking cheerfully exuberant in spite of extreme fatigue, the new prime minister then made mistake number one by assuming that the paparazzi and reporters were really on her side. I remembered Arthur Smith's words: 'All they really want is for the PM to be assassinated while they get their exclusives!'

It was time to remain alert! For five minutes or so she walked and talked to the throng and then settled to recite her chosen prayer from St Francis of Assisi. Perhaps it made good material for the moment – identifying her, as it seemed to do, with a warm, feminine tenderness – a new implant into an otherwise male-dominated, cold Whitehall world.

Her later image as the Iron Lady could hardly have differed more. When their time finally came, the media men and women, like elephants, never forgot the contrast with her very first day.

EIGHTEEN

There is now work to be done.

Margaret Thatcher on 4 May 1979 as she entered No 10 for
the first time as prime minister

Harold Wilson, it will be recalled, said very much the same thing in
1974. As the front door closed behind her, Mrs Thatcher was greeted
by several dozen ladies handclapping vigorously. I was appalled at this
display of party favour, but later persuaded myself that the applause was for her as
the first *woman* prime minister and not as a Tory.

It was time to weigh up the changes brought about under a new and totally
different administration. St Francis was recorded as 'one of the most popular
Saints of the Middle Ages with a love of nature and all living things; who enjoyed
a simple life of poverty; and survived shipwreck to continue preaching'. With
no sign on the agenda of poverty, a love of nature or the sea, it soon became
clear that these were areas where St Francis and Mrs Thatcher parted company.
Indeed, later that afternoon she attended a celebratory cocktail party in the
state rooms on the first floor. Butlers served champagne and their red jackets
added unusual distinction to the gathering. Mrs Thatcher, always immaculately
groomed and expensively dressed, showed none of Mother Teresa's dedication
to close proximity to poverty. May 1979 saw the end of the dandruff days in
Downing Street.

For several days, No 10 was in quiet turmoil. Mrs Thatcher had promised
the press corps outside that her first work would be to form a Cabinet. After a
wash and brush-up she started the necessarily complex negotiations – in spite
of fatigue and a succession of long briefings from Private Office. This kept her

indoors for several days. The front door was busy as men and women arrived, hopeful of senior appointments and new responsibilities. Not all were smiling as they left.

Mrs Thatcher was an unknown new broom. This called for compromise and change among the Tory hierarchy. Traditionally the party was – directly or indirectly – controlled by the old school, the grandees, the Eton and Oxbridge group, landowners and aristocrats. Ted Heath must have represented a shock to their system, but was seen as an expedient buffer to the white-hot technological Labour revolution promised by Harold Wilson. Recent Labour administrations had suffered the disadvantage of almost unworkably small parliamentary majorities. Now the grandees were confronted with a new challenge to their traditional hold on the party – a woman prime minister who was the daughter of a family grocer. Moreover, with an overall majority of forty-three in the House of Commons and powerful backing from constituency parties, she could count upon lower middle class support. Some of the old guard were no longer automatic contenders for top jobs.

Mrs Thatcher would be followed by John Major – with a justifiably strong claim to an understanding of the word 'poverty' – and other leaders without far-back accents. It took some thirty years for a certain class of person to anticipate a return to more traditional Tory style. Meanwhile, Mrs Thatcher's overwhelming support from Conservative grass roots hardly wavered during her good days and bad.

Private Office took an early chance to rotate some of their ground-floor staff, but the safe-handed Ken Stowe was retained as principal private secretary until replaced later by Clive Whitmore (now Sir Clive) from the Ministry of Defence. Things continued smoothly in the subterranean Garden Rooms and in the first floor offices of Church and Honours, where they had jobs for life. Smiling fresh faces appeared elsewhere, notably in the press office – where the now infamous Bernard Ingham (later Sir Bernard) was phased in after five weeks – and the Political Office. Most of the new wave then are elder statesmen now. A few made the transition via a spell in Her Majesty's custody.

Scotland Yard also changed the Special Branch team at No 10. Once they were assured of my intention to retire as soon as the new administration was running smoothly, a replacement chief inspector, Ray Parker, was confirmed as my number two, and Sergeant Barry Strevens and Detective Constable Robert Kingston were brought in. They were wise choices, having been responsible for Mrs Thatcher's personal close protection as Leader of the Opposition. She thought highly of them and they were devoted to her – rather more personally than I wished. They took responsibility for her constituency visits and surgeries at Finchley, where she had been elected with a substantial majority.

Some modification in their techniques was called for. In early days I saw Bob Kingston approached by one of the young Tory ladies at work in the Political Office. She was carrying a basket of flowers to put in the boot of the number one limo to be taken along later to the Thatchers' Chelsea home, but felt too shy to do so in front of the crowds waiting outside. Bob politely offered to take them out for her – before I could stop him. I laid down a firm guideline when he came back into the office. Never again! The royal protection officers were regularly targeted by photographers and their picture libraries were filled with shots of plain-clothes policemen carrying cakes or flowers or umbrellas or other domestic paraphernalia – clear impediments to their freedom to react immediately to any attack on their principal. This might be OK at the Royal Mews but not for Special Branch at No 10. We could never allow ourselves to be included in the 'something of a joke' album. Barry and Bob turned out to be first class at their job – physical when needed, positive, alert, diplomatic and popular.

Denis Thatcher, the prime minister's husband, was much in evidence on day one both outside and inside No 10. However, he was quickly marginalised as official duties took over. He was a cigarette smoker and she was not. Moreover, Mrs Thatcher did not approve and he was obliged to lurk furtively around with a fag cupped out of sight in his hand. He was capable of other politically incorrect behaviour it seemed, notably undiplomatic references to race and colour. Behind the scenes some corrective mechanisms were put in place, but he was outspoken and assumed that all his listeners took the same point of view. I saw very little of their daughter Carol during the rest of the time I was in Downing Street. She was apparently conducting her own young life.

Her twin brother Mark was a different matter, however. He often found his way into a pressman's camera angle but, unlike the former press secretary Tom McCaffrey, never did so shyly. Indeed, Mark courted publicity. On the first day of his mother's administration he came into my office and took a seat without being asked, and then demanded personal protection now that he was specially vulnerable at the right hand of his mother, in spite of 'being well known as something of a hero'! This was not at all how I saw it and both Scotland Yard and the Home Office thought the same. However, Mark kept at it and in the end, as terrorism escalated, they finally gave in and he proudly displayed his self-importance with a team of close protection officers of his own.

The Thatchers made early noises about living in their Chelsea residence and relaxing at their country address at Scotney Castle in Kent, courtesy of the National Trust. This retreat was particularly important to Denis, as it was where he kept his beloved Rolls-Royce. He had to give up the politically incorrect indulgence of driving around in style and I cannot recall Mrs Thatcher ever being seen in it after winning the election. The fact was – such was her devotion to duty and formidable work ethic – that as the ceaseless stream of red boxes arrived she soon saw the merits of using the flat above No 10 on a day-by-day basis and Chequers for weekends, conferences and entertaining.

The really big change for me was the annual party conference. This was then held on alternate years at either Blackpool, where the four-star Imperial Hotel was the base, or at the Grand Hotel in Brighton. It was more than ten years since I had attended these annual variety performances when I was protecting John Davies, then Secretary of State for Trade and Industry, after his London flat was bombed by the Angry Brigade. The public were swamped with television broadcasts during these conferences and there were signs that some people treated them as important. In fact, they were an opportunity for party supporters to meet and drink and dance until the early hours. The serious sessions were a chance for the inexperienced young, or those with more extreme opinions, to sound off and feel self-important. Superficially important propositions might be voted through but, where these eventually clashed with more profound party policy, later events or government initiatives, they were usually quietly dropped later.

After five years of Labour beer drinking, open-necked shirts and shrill, extreme left-wingers, I was brought up short by black-tie functions and the Valeta. Drinking was now champagne or gin and tonic, and riotous rather than hearty. The Imperial had some difficulty in displaying four-star qualities but, of course, it was the Grand that finally came to world attention when the IRA blew it up late one night in 1984. My successor told me it was a very near thing for the Thatchers and how magnificently Margaret Thatcher recovered her poise, dealing consummately with the press and recovering well enough to perform splendidly in time for that day's session.

Some of the prime minister's decisions made within Downing Street soon affected the detectives. Among them was her wish to dispose of the elderly Rovers and authorise their replacement with Daimler Jaguars, modifications for which were at an advanced stage. This authority was never forthcoming with Labour. The Treasury were always looking for economies and it was not hard for Messrs Wilson and Callaghan to persuade themselves that it was a politically unwise indulgence to spend so much money on a fleet of new limousines when the British economy was depressed and wage rises under severe restraint. While these arguments still applied, Mrs Thatcher read the tea leaves differently. Her opinion was that it was undignified for a prime minister to be driven around in an outdated and nearly decrepit vehicle, and a bad image for her country. I had to agree and was even more delighted to hear that the existing fleet of RAF Special Flights was to be replaced too – except for the acceptable HS.125

executive jets. I was not around long enough to see them all phased in, but I have no doubt her decision was right.

Government Car Service driver George Newell – having been with Mrs Thatcher in Opposition – was brought into the first slot in the drivers' room. He was smartly turned out and wore his cap. He drove too fast in town, claiming to be conforming to her preference. Unlike Joe Hazard he was not adorned in gold trinkets. Within a year George passed away and was replaced – no doubt on Private Office recommendation – by Ken Godbeer, who had never before held the number one slot but whose vast experience qualified him in every respect.

It cannot have gone unnoticed that work with Mrs Thatcher called for revised planning. Although I had taken on toilet patrol for Harold Wilson during post-conference debriefs in Jamaica, the female factor now made such close support impossible. It might seem obvious enough that we would have to co-opt a lady officer into the team. Unfortunately this was too much for the brains at the top and neither Scotland Yard nor the Home Office could come to terms with this. We were left 'to manage somehow'. Temporary help was sometimes available from Special Branch in London and when away was unfailingly provided by local police forces. This meant, of course, that new faces had to be introduced on every occasion. Special Branch women detectives fitted well but, not surprisingly, Mrs Thatcher was sometimes bewildered with changes of women personnel as she moved from one constabulary to another. Nevertheless, thanks to personal initiatives and well-chosen assistance, the scheme was made to work and Mrs Thatcher – who did not favour unscheduled en route stops for all-day bacon and egg breakfast butties at motorway service stations – was greatly helpful. She and her secretariat kept to scheduled programmes and she was as well organised as her appearance. As a result, it was possible to phase in a woman officer on the occasions that were personal and private to her, but not prohibited to the IRA, who did not have to concern themselves with fine points.

This typified her approach to protection. She was on duty and so were we. She accepted our recommendations knowing that, in spite of politically inspired preferences, the bottom line was that we were likely to know more about her safe keeping than she. Harold Wilson had accepted his protection team similarly. We were necessary. He trusted us and the wisdom of Scotland Yard. Our difficulties with him were caused by frequent periods of urgency bordering upon panic. Consequently, planning ahead was often a problem. With Mr Callaghan there was more order, but he was intensely authoritative and resistant to Special Branch. We were not politically correct and – for a time at least – mistrusted. He was meddlesome and always thought he knew our job better than we did.

Mrs Thatcher, however, simply regarded us as one part of her composite team. In spite of the fact that she was arguably a more tempting target for desperate men and women with a cause, she did make our lives easier and our ability to maintain high professional standards more achievable.

<hr/>

British Airways' shuttle to Glasgow and Loganair feeder brought me down to earth on the tiny western Scotland airport on the Isle of Islay. It was to advance one of Margaret Thatcher's first out-of-town trips at the invitation of (the late) Lord Margadale of Islay and owner of thirty-eight whisky distilleries there. Formerly Conservative Member of Parliament for Salisbury – and owner of much of Wiltshire – a former Master of Foxhounds and a doyen of the Conservative Party, he had been among the first to identify Margaret Thatcher as a future leader of the party. He was still one of her most stalwart supporters and, it was rumoured, now hoped to arrange a reduction in alcohol tax.

Baron Margadale ran a grand, shabby-genteel mansion on Islay. I was hosted by his factor David Boyd – son of the designer of *Sceptre*, the first post-war British America's Cup challenger – and he and his wife provided a fund of local knowledge, a raft of common sense and kind hospitality. During one reconnaissance on the windswept, almost treeless and frequently deserted island, David took gentle avoiding action in the Land Rover at the only accident black spot to avoid a lone pedestrian wandering unsteadily in the middle of the road, miles from anywhere.

'That's Tam – the finest gamekeeper in the isles,' David told me. 'He's totally reliable for weeks but then lost to the world for two or three days each month – thanks to our fine malt whisky.'

I came to understand his point during the following couple of days.

Baron Margadale was very deaf and finding it difficult to work out what all the fuss was about for a private visit by a prime minister. The world and the occasional threat of nuclear war had passed unnoticed on Islay. I had been preceded by the Cabinet Office teams of radio and electronics technicians. They had commandeered the top floor and installed complex bleeping and flashing electronics with dishes and aerials poking out of the eaves. A small office had been taken over for the Garden Room girls. Worst of all, the technicians would not now allow him to climb up into the rooms to see what they were doing.

His Lordship wondered what the purpose of it all was and complained disparagingly that all this seemed very modern. He wondered whether the entire disturbance was necessary? I explained that the prime minister's communication network had to be in place no matter where she was. 'What is the longest she could be out of touch?' he asked peevishly. He had planned several outward-bound-type walks, Arctic Circle picnics and hearty boat trips for her. 'I understand that four minutes is the most she would have for really vital decisions,' I explained, to arguably the only man in the United Kingdom who did not already know. I never felt reassured that he had mastered the complexities of his hearing aid.

The name of the family was Morrison. They ran a cold house with a green Wellington boot ambience. If you did not take to the malt whisky there was no central heating. I explain all this because it was into this raw environment that the newly elected prime minister was introduced a couple of days later. It was soon evident that she was not a person to enjoy an outdoor life. She was not readily accustomed to green wellies and showed no signs of changing. Boat trips around Scottish isles call for steady stomachs and are not conducive to carefully groomed hair.

I never did find out what influence, if any, she brought to bear on Treasury planning for alcohol tax but I was able to report without qualification that it was not the type of weekend that was ever likely to appear in her diary again. During the summer, she was persuaded to travel to Glyndebourne in Sussex, for a picnic outdoors and an evening performance of Beethoven's *Fidelio*. It was a grand evening and a stunning performance. But in respect of these cultures, Mrs Thatcher was not dissimilar to Messrs Wilson and Callaghan. The only conclusion was that to stay at the top of the political tree there was simply no time to waste on almost anything else.

Margaret Thatcher had other commitments to those who had helped in her election – one way or another. It took the form of a 'thank you' visit at a function held by the construction and property development company Taylor Woodrow. For the new prime minister it proved to be indoctrination into the perils of her real new world. She appeared to handle it calmly.

The agreement was to visit a project-opening event in a London suburb, a private function for a limited number of guests. As they were all personally invited by the board of management, Taylor Woodrow created a useful form of built-in vetting. As a precaution, I checked that they had also notified the local uniformed police, who put a number of men outside. In a rush of events, we were satisfied with the arrangements. All this was routine, but made no difference to the outcome. On arrival Mrs Thatcher was met and escorted round the project site by directors and board members. Internal security was tight and the programme was all very smooth. Nevertheless, Barry Strevens and I kept within close range. It was fortunate that we did so.

At one stage before lunch, when she was about to make a speech, Mrs Thatcher stood with the directors before the invited guests. It was all highly organised. Suddenly, unexpectedly, a tall young man thrust his way through and confronted the prime minister directly face-to-face, aggressively shouting his particular political thing, pointing threateningly for a second until my arm snapped his neck back and Barry and I wrestled him to the ground. Barry hammer-locked his arm and led him away and handed him over to uniformed officers outside. I remained on the spot in case there was another conspirator among the guests. It turned out that he was a left of left student with a history of agit-prop, who had talked his way past Taylor Woodrow security officers at the gate, posing as a newspaper reporter. I expect that after his student days he became a respected journalist himself, or took a steady, pensionable job-for-life in the Inland Revenue or the BBC – or some charitable organisation – and lived in a suburban semi-detached house with his wife, two children and a mortgage.

In other countries he would have been shot dead.

Our reaction sounds simple enough now, and would certainly have been effective, although possibly a fraction of a second too late, had he been an armed aggressor intent on her injury. Indeed, when we saw the video a few days later – subsequently used for training purposes within Special Branch – it became clear that in spite of our alert presence he had a microsecond's advantage over our reaction.

This incident highlighted one of the great problems for protection officers – how to remain close enough to the target and adequately equipped for any eventuality, in a low key, informal ambiance where 'heavies' were frowned upon or where diplomatic protocol was paramount. The Taylor Woodrow incident could have been just some public relations prank. If so, it could have been catastrophic because a protection team must always react proportionately to the worst-case possibilities as they look at the instant of activation. They have to do so in the full knowledge that if it goes wrong they are likely to be left carrying the can at any board of enquiry.

On a different scale, if we look at the annual Armistice Service in Whitehall, for instance, it must be clear that it is not possible for a protection team to walk *directly* with the queen or the prime minister as they lay wreaths at the foot of the Cenotaph. Moreover, that ceremony is traditionally an assembly point for the mildly manic – an occasion where even potty Lords of the Land can guarantee worldwide publicity on television by making a scene. The result is that the police authority has to take countermeasures which are disproportionately well over the top for a solemn occasion. In turn, this could result in someone getting shot from an armed rooftop lookout. That someone might not necessarily be a potential assassin.

At about the same time I grew dissatisfied with security at Common Market press conferences in Brussels. The Private Office passed my concerns upwards. The result from the commission security was a whitewash I regret to say, but

I never doubted that the best opportunity for a sophisticated attacker was by posing as a journalist.

Before the end of her first year in office, Margaret Thatcher was confronted with a more intimidating experience altogether. To keep these things in context, it will be recognised that she was a woman without any 'front-line' experience at all. She had probably been faced with nothing more violent than student meetings or disagreements at Tory Party committees. Northern Ireland was different. There was a war on in 1979 and she was suddenly projected into the middle of it by agreeing to visit the troops directly after the IRA had wreaked horrible revenge on the Parachute Regiment on 27 August for its part in the catastrophic Bloody Sunday massacre. At Warrenpoint, near Newry, they blew up an army lorry, killing eighteen paratroopers and wounding more. The army was outraged and Mrs Thatcher − blameworthy only as a British politician − found herself in the forefront of their anger. It was a grim day with grim weather.

Wearing a camouflaged flak jacket and unglamorous headgear, she was shuttled around in armoured vehicles and helicopters. The Northern Ireland Office, army high command and the Royal Ulster Constabulary arranged a tough schedule. It was bleak and windy. Apart from one visit to a shopping centre in Belfast, this was not a photo opportunity for the press at all. Mrs Thatcher visited Musgrave Park Hospital, to talk to wounded soldiers, and then Crossmaglen, to see the most heavily fortified but still prominently damaged police station in the province. During a hard day she was subjected to a calculated exercise by the army. She saw bandit country in missile-evading helicopter swoops, and was conducted to the high command's underground HQ bunker. Once inside, she was given a horrendous presentation of dead and horribly injured soldiers found at Warrenpoint. She remained dignified and properly concerned throughout, but it was an experience that very few politicians were ever likely to have to face. For women, the possibility was even less.

It was later reported that the army took the opportunity to highlight the everyday danger that soldiers faced, and the restrictions placed upon the defensive counter-action available to them by political rather than operational embargoes. They made the point that while troops were faced with a dedicated, armed and increasingly efficient civilian army, their ability to fire back was restricted while politically inspired restrictions tied one hand behind their backs. She was invited to authorise amendments. If these strictures were loosened, preferably in agreement with the government of the Irish Republic, it could give the army a fighting chance of making real progress in their campaign against terrorism at a time when political progress seemed to be dead in the water. However, according to her autobiography, in initial approaches to Jack Lynch, Taoiseach of the Irish

Republic, during attendance at Lord Mountbatten's funeral service shortly afterwards, he responded discouragingly that her ideas would be 'studied'.

This day was a briefing in practice – rather than from dossiers – of just where the buck stopped. No doubt it was one of many which helped to prepare her for the Falklands confrontation a few years later during which – if I understand it correctly – she won the affection of the armed forces for her firm resolution during many crises.

This was all part of a sequence of events which eventually identified her as the Iron Lady of British politics.

NINETEEN

The New Otani is a completely modern structure. Earthquake proof, fireproof, and soundproof.

Claims listed under 'Accommodations' in the brochure of the
prime minister's Tokyo hotel

The merits of her host country were not understated by the official New Otani Hotel public relations blurb: 'Japan – Land of Varied Charm – a land of scenic wonder, long praised as ideal vacationland in the Pacific. A land of contrast and harmony, unparalleled scenery, gay city life, refined stage arts, unique works of tiny and applied arts, colourful festivals and varied sports.'

This attractive scenario came as a surprise to Britons who remembered the Second World War and who now tried to picture the 'varied sports'. Nevertheless, times had certainly changed by the time Margaret Thatcher flew to Tokyo in June 1979 for a 'Big Eight' summit – by which time it was more politically correct to forgive and forget.

I got there well in advance, courtesy of British Airways – who else? The pilot took off from Heathrow and headed off the wrong way – across the North Atlantic, the eternal, glistening icecap of Greenland and the forests and lakes of Canada. Obviously lost but too proud to ask me where he had gone wrong, he then let down into Anchorage, Alaska, to refuel – or so the cabin crew assured us. In reality he was looking for a policeman to tell him the way. A fresh captain boarded and somehow found his way down the long leg to Nerita Airport outside Tokyo.

The control tower there had recently been taken over by notorious Japanese terrorists, the Red Brigade. They took exception to the whole new airport and selected the control tower as an ideal forum from which to broadcast threats and grievances to the world. Fortunately they had now taken the day off. I was driven along what was laughingly called a freeway, to sleep for a solid twelve hours in the New Otani and recover from a nasty attack of jet lag. I was happily unaware that the Red Brigade had recently booked in too.

I woke at 6 p.m. local time to hotel life, Tokyo style. The computer-automated wake-up telephone call came with early morning electronic bird song and a woman sounding like the infamous Japanese Second World War propaganda broadcaster *Tokyo Rose*. She ordered me to 'rise and shine and have a good day'. No options were on offer. Bird song preceded me in the bathroom, the elevator and the dining room. Mirrors were hung at midget level. The hall porter could not have been more helpful, telling me that further enquiries could be answered at desks in either 'the robby' or 'the rounge'.

With neither fouled pavements to negotiate nor incipient death from rabid Rottweilers, the good news came with a stroll at dusk when I discovered dogs were banned in Tokyo.

<hr />

With brain refurbished I settled to work in the British Embassy, together with teams from the Cabinet Office and the conference section of the Foreign and Commonwealth Office. An early introduction to the Japanese police liaison officer was not encouraging. His name sounded suspiciously like Fukada (phonetic). He was grim, uncommunicative, often unavailable, and unresponsive to bad news. Rather than worry about Mrs Thatcher, his prime task was to put all things Japanese in the best light. We did not become close friends and, in spite of his efforts in public relations, I concluded that Tokyo was schizoid. It was – at the same time – beautiful in parts and ugly with plagiarised foreign vulgarities; it possessed excessive humility mingled with self-assured arrogance; it had a dreadful concern to save face but, admittedly, often with patriotic motives; it had pretty girls with very strange legs and stylised politeness contrasting with insensitive attitudes toward women. These contrasts were polarised one night as we were driven past a multi-storey, floodlit golf range with dozens of men concentrating on their swing. According to the embassy chauffeur only a handful would ever get to see an actual golf course.

Security was not in any sense subtle or discreet. Instead of small teams of well-trained specialist men and women and systematic pre-emptive measures, our hosts relied upon overwhelming numbers. Some 30,000 troops and policemen were littered around the streets, smoking and trying to look important. There were many things against this technique, especially as these inadequately briefed, low-grade functionaries were disciplined by a structured, largely invisible hierarchy.

This meant that each front-line man followed orders slavishly, with no scope for personal initiative. With this low and over-armed level being disallowed from making any decisions of their own, they were virtually useless. Every problem had to be referred upward, often by several levels and preferably on paper in triplicate.

The Japanese authorities intended to security-sanitise the area surrounding the conference centre. Rather quaintly, they started by temporarily suppressing television porn channels. Physical security of the hotel seemed to be adequate enough and the lower floors of this multi-storey edifice were cleared of clientele. For the duration of the conference all unofficial guests were excluded and a system of passes with photographs installed. A corridor was purpose built from the vehicle set-down point into the hotel and on to the elevator system.

However, this was a country where anti-government hostility often boiled over into outright terrorism. The bad boys held most of the aces – particularly any element of surprise. It was clearly inadequate for the security authorities to depend upon a response predicated on quantity rather than quality and at the British Embassy our own close protection was listed as a top priority.

All this was bound to create hostility with the Fukada team. There was absolutely no way that he placed efficiency before face-saving. He avoided controversial issues altogether – including arrangements for me to meet his superiors.

At the embassy, liaison with the Japanese police was notoriously difficult. The first secretary delegated to smooth my security preparations had recently returned from a successful China watch-tour of duty in Beijing, where he had been injured during a notable display of bravery while the embassy was controversially under siege. In Tokyo he had gradually developed some useful contacts at police HQ and with the Ministry of the Interior, and was not anxious to compromise his long-term standing there with short-term demands for better close security now.

As I was getting out of my depth I asked for backing from Miss Nancy Deeves, a formidable, sturdy tugboat of a lady leading the FCO conference section team. Without hesitation she was on the telephone to the ambassador, explaining that Scotland Yard was not getting the backing she expected from the embassy and that the prime minister might be recommended to cancel her visit unless remedial action was taken very soon. After a commendably brief delay, the telephone in her office started to ring. Invitations to attend security conferences and meet the previously well-hidden heads of departments soon got my wagon back on the trail. Fukada was successfully sidelined for a time. He took revenge by addressing me as 'Mr Wallicoll'.

Much of Tokyo was really ugly and in those days roads were constantly traffic-jammed. Irritatingly, one journey with Fukada in an unmarked police car was brought to yet another standstill on an inner-city dual carriageway, while the oncoming lane alongside ran out of traffic. This was because of the approach of a student demonstration, covered by uniformed police. Fukada never intended me to see it and now – speechless with embarrassment – he ran out of English altogether.

An intimidating silence preceded the demonstrators. So did a grey armoured wagon full of reserve police units armed with staves and light machine pistols. And then a grey armoured mobile water cannon. And a grey armoured control centre with the boss-man in charge, standing in a sort of crow's nest at the top of a steel tower. And a solid phalanx of marching policemen. Each policeman was 5ft 3in tall, wore blue overalls and a crash helmet with visor, knee and elbow protective pads, and a cosh held at the ready.

After a 10yd space came the demonstrators. Each was 5ft 3in tall, dressed in anarchist red shirt and black trousers and wearing a crash helmet with perspex visor and knee and elbow pads. They were completely surrounded by double ranks of uniformed police leaning inward to contain them like sardines. The protesters marched a sullen, threatening four paces in step. Then they paused, raised their right arms and shouted a single chant in unison. The backup was further phalanxes and vehicles with police. I could get no details from our liaison officer other than the fact that the demonstration was *not* expected to be violent.

Clearly, student demonstrators in London had much to learn.

⎯⎯⎯➤◦◄⎯⎯⎯

Mrs Thatcher walked down the steps from the VC10 looking cool, groomed and elegant. Her Private Office staff followed in crumpled lightweight suits, carrying piles of official red boxes. As usual, without the private facilities arranged on board for a prime minister – and on-call in suits and neckties at all times – it was impossible to appear as immaculately as tailors' dummies in the window of a West End department store. We were all left shaken by the motorcade into town, led by small men on large motorcycles, who seemed to be practising for international cross-country championships. Personnel from the embassy explained helpfully that only the city's kamikaze noodle salesmen – delivering heated canisters of lunchtime delicacies in heated containers, gimballed on the backs of teledraulically sprung motorised bicycles – could have got into town faster.

Mrs Thatcher was welcomed by management at the New Otani Hotel and ushered through the narrow, purpose-built corridor toward the lift. She was too busy to notice the security plain-clothed policemen at 2yd intervals, posted close to the walls. In large crowds it was routine for every other officer to face outward. In this narrow and otherwise entirely empty passageway, those ordered to face outward were committed to nothing more useful than the very close inspection of sheets of hardboard. Orders were always orders in Japan and no one was innovative enough to countermand the ludicrously absurd instruction now.

In her spotless room, Mrs Thatcher noted every aspect of management attention to detail. In the room adjoining, now in use as her Private Office, the edges of a portable notice board were wrapped in sterilised silver paper, to prevent official fingers becoming contaminated with dust. In contravention of basic security precautions, plant pots were tastefully spaced in the ground-floor corridor, unnoticed by the thirty policemen permanently posted there. After a few short words with Fukada there was an immediate scuffle of activity to take them away.

The US president was sensibly accommodated in his embassy. With the bottom floors of the New Otani cleared of clientele in advance, the heads of other delegations occupied upper floors and admired the view.

Heavy rain failed to catch the various authorities unprepared. Purpose-built transparent waterproof covers were produced and fitted neatly over portable radios and motorcycle policemen. Detectives were issued with tiny umbrellas to clamp onto their hand-held torches.

Our first hint that important things were not what they seemed came from media men, smiling at our discomfort as they recounted what should have been coming our way from the now frequently absent Fukada. Or, preferably prevented altogether with commonsense measures.

During the evening of day two, the Red Brigade parked a car on the main trans-city freeway. This created a massive rush-hour log jam even before it exploded. Mayhem was the outcome. Riot police HQ was soon another target. The front of the building was devastated after a petrol tanker was left outside and roasted with lighted gas cylinders until it exploded, with numerous deaths and injuries. Just before delegates left, all telephone communication with the control tower at Nerita Airport was cut off. Such a failure at the nerve centre was potentially catastrophic, of course.

Finally, a firebomb had been hidden in a room on the eighteenth floor of the New Otani by the last member of the Red Brigade to book in – and safely out – before the conference. Fortunately, only the detonator exploded while we were there. Otherwise the fireproof nature of the New Otani would have been very actively tested. Had the device been assembled with high explosive, the boasted earthquake-free construction might also have come under scrutiny, and we might all have been victims of something approaching an early 9/11 or Grand Hotel, Brighton, disaster.

The US Secret Service and other visiting delegations were equally outraged, as their own Japanese liaison officers had failed to mention these tourist attractions to them either.

The conference was held in the distinguished Akasaka Palace. In the autobiography of her Downing Street years written years later, Margaret Thatcher recalled with diplomatic understatement, 'for all their hospitality it would be difficult to claim too much for the quality of Japan's chairmanship'. It is fair to say, in spite of remarkable economic and industrial achievements, that none of the British delegation came away overawed by their experience in Tokyo.

Life at 30,000ft seemed pleasantly tranquil as the prime minister headed for Canberra on the way home. While there she played 'Greensleeves' on the electronic keyboard of a purpose-built bell tower in the middle of a lake. I am pleased to report that this was the most exciting event in an otherwise incredibly uneventful city, with almost nowhere to eat out and little to rave about. After the anxieties created in Tokyo by Japanese failures to orchestrate security or chair the conference with distinction, a little tedium in Australia was nothing less than sheer bliss.

<hr />

Rather furtively the prime minister's principal private secretary drew a chain and a bunch of keys from his pocket. Keeping his back to me, he unlocked a substantial door that, during nearly six years inside No 10, I had not been shown previously. He was escorting me from the headquarters of *arriviste* government – No 10 Downing Street – through a secret entrance and into the focal point of Britain's permanent establishment next door – the Cabinet Office.

The Cabinet Office was the clearing house of government at an official rather than political level. Here was the real seat of long-term British power. Everything was more than usually secret. Although the Mandarins who were at home there understood politics, parliamentary democracy and public relations – and were masters of every aspect of arcane short termism such as spin – they were elevated above it all, maintaining a supervisory watch over the deployment of powers temporarily vested by the electorate upon their chosen representatives in the Palace of Westminster. The staff in the Cabinet Office – all carefully selected and with above-average talents – were under the overlordship of the Cabinet secretary and head of the home civil service, the only non-political figure always present at the prime minister's Cabinet meetings.

With a foot in both camps, the Cabinet secretary in 1979 was the formidable Sir John Hunt (later Lord Hunt).

We arrived in Sir John's impressive office to join the directors of the Security Service (MI5) and the Secret Intelligence Service (MI6), permanent secretaries from the Ministry of Defence and FCO, and two senior officers from Scotland Yard's Special Branch. This small high-level meeting was assembled under

Sir John's chairmanship to discuss security arrangements at the forthcoming Commonwealth Heads of Government Conference planned to convene during the first week of August in Lusaka, the capital of Zambia. Her Majesty The Queen was scheduled to attend. She and the prime minister were particularly vulnerable, and controversial problems around their security had to be resolved. Discussion ranged round a police report written after an on-the-spot survey by a commander, Special Branch.

In addition to the usual problems, the top subject on the conference agenda was Rhodesia. It was intended to discuss a solution to conclude the future of the white residents' rebellious Unilateral Declaration of Independence in 1965. This had dominated the peace and prosperity of the region for more than a decade. In the face of worldwide condemnation it was no longer possible to allow the retention of absolute power by a white minority. With military intervention firmly ruled out, it was now decision time for the Commonwealth, whose heads of state had to find some way to impose democracy without violence upon the Rhodesian regime. Britain, with responsibility for the original colonial rule, was particularly in the firing line. Mrs Thatcher was faced with her first major diplomatic challenge at international level. Her problem was the clear imperative to find a pathway to justice for the black indigenous majority while reconciling Britain's close blood ties – and an awareness of the disproportionately large contribution to the Allied cause by Rhodesia during the Second World War.

The task was immense and controversial. Not only was almost all world opinion against Prime Minister Smith's illegal regime, but so was Mrs Thatcher's own Foreign and Commonwealth Office, led by Secretary of State Lord Carrington, who by now regarded the Smith regime as unsupportable. In addition, many British businessmen with interests in Rhodesia could also see no alternative but an immediate agreement to establish basic democracy in the form of a 'one man, one vote' resolution.

This political and diplomatic conundrum was compounded by continuing armed conflict in the region. Front-line states bordering Rhodesia included Zambia itself. Depending upon an individual's point of view, these states were either safe havens for freedom fighters, or dangerous snake pits hosting bands of heavily armed, ill-disciplined, communist-trained guerrillas. Rhodesian defence forces had taken effective countermeasures, and carried out reprisal raids for incursions and atrocities inside their borders. Their mobile commando force, the famed Selous Scouts – of mainly white officers and well-trained black soldiers – had recently succeeded in advancing unopposed to the outskirts of the Zambian capital Lusaka to destroy the home of one of their 'revolutionary' expatriates, the Matabele leader, Josh Nkomo. Using lorry and helicopter transport they had then exfiltrated with negligible casualties.

Against this violent and unstable background, the immediate problem for Sir John Hunt and his advisers was to calculate the odds of violent action at the conference. In particular, they had to decide whether the normal level of personal security for HM The Queen and Prime Minister Thatcher was adequate and, if not, how to rebalance those odds.

The Scotland Yard survey had concluded that the Zambian police were loyal to the constitution and Prime Minister Kenneth Kaunda. The local security forces also showed residual signs of the training received from British colonial police officers before independence. On balance they were judged capable of maintaining public order and of defending the custom-built conference building – and the fifty or more residences set-aside for Commonwealth leaders. The officers were also satisfied with assurances made by freedom fighters' commanders that their men would remain in jungle camps throughout the conference. The report boldly expressed confidence that fears of Kalashnikov-toting, undisciplined freedom fighters roaming the streets of Lusaka were unfounded.

Arrangements had already been made for a second RAF VC10 to be on permanent standby at Nairobi, Kenya – ready to evacuate the queen and other British VIPs. As a further precaution a number of armed SAS soldiers equipped with the latest satellite radio communications equipment were positioned inside the British High Commission in Lusaka, ready to deal with last-ditch emergencies. A Royal Military Police detachment was also detailed for the physical protection of premises and secret papers. On this understanding the meeting appeared to agree that a few extra Special Branch personal protection officers would be adequate for my team and the royals' policemen headed by Commander Mike Trestrail, the queen's personal officer. He was not represented at the meeting and, although very much in the sharp-end myself, as a mere detective superintendent I was not at that stage called upon for an opinion.

However, as the others left, Sir John asked me to stay behind. It appeared that he and his Cabinet Office secret service advisers were less than satisfied with opinions that all would be peaceful and calm in Lusaka. It is probable that he already had the benefit of inside information. He and I discussed the decision. His point of view and mine were not dissimilar. It appeared that the Scotland Yard brief had not taken into account the ability – perhaps the intention even – of the Rhodesians to mount a daring and potentially devastating operation across their border with Zambia and right into the heart of Lusaka. With this scenario it was far from impossible that the leaders of the Commonwealth could even be taken hostage.

Sir John was a man of decisive action. Within fifteen minutes, I later learned, he had telephoned the Home Office and given orders that the commissioner of police was to be instructed to prepare a team of forty adequately armed and trained Special Branch detectives, headed by a commander, to be flown to Lusaka in advance of the queen and her prime minister. Although the Rhodesians did not in the end decide to mount an invasive military operation – and by-and-large the freedom fighters did remain encamped in the jungle – this decision turned out to be invaluable.

———⟫·0·⟪———

As the prime minister's RAF VC10 left London, a report came through that all was quiet and orderly in Zambia. By the time the captain started a night letdown to Lusaka Airport I was in contact with our advancing officer, Chief Inspector Ray Parker, on our new personal radios. As part of a hierarchical, disciplined service he was technically part of the forty-strong back-up team headed by a commander. Waiting with them on the tarmac, Ray's authority was far from absolute. He reported, 'The airport is in a state of chaos. Hundreds of reporters have been given freedom to roam about. Nobody knows who is who. There is nothing I can do to control it.'

A British prime minister's arrival might not always have been perfectly orchestrated, but this was unprecedented. Ray was comparatively new to the No 10 team, but was familiar enough with required techniques and acceptable practices to forestall this mass takeover, had he been in charge on the ground. If there was a system of personal identification passes it had clearly broken down. For obvious reasons, access to the apron of any major airport was sacrosanct and usually well supervised both by local customs officers and air traffic control. This was automatically of great benefit to security planners but must somehow have been obviated now. It was doubly unfortunate that conference planning was in the hands of the Commonwealth Secretariat, leaving our usual last-ditch support from the FCO conference and visits section under Peggy Metcalfe, with only comparatively minor travel and accommodation co-ordination. Some higher authority must have allowed – perhaps encouraged? – this disorderly melee. Had the Americans been there – which, of course, they were not – the US Secret Service would have promptly ordered Air Force One to return the president to Washington.

I passed the information to Private Office and assumed that the conditions she was about to meet were explained in a last-minute brief for Mrs Thatcher, who had no similar option. She looked startled and pale but remained composed as she appeared at the brightly floodlit door of the VC10. She descended into the melee. Fortunately, Ray had fought his way to the foot of the gangway and stood there reassuringly with those colleagues from the Special Branch advance team who were able to get there too. He had not exaggerated the scene. A multitude of unknowns were pushing close from all sides. There was no chance of a red-carpet reception and no sight of a military band. It was difficult to know who was there to greet her officially. An impromptu phalanx of our officers closed protectively round her. As it was impossible to pick out local officials, no one else was identifiable to guide her towards the VIP lounge.

Under these extraordinary circumstances the prime minister was just able to make determined progress through the shouting and flash bulbs. We all heaved and crashed into microphones, tripping and shoving our way. The last-minute appearance of local security personnel was helpful and finally the whole scrum arrived and entered sanctuary in the lounge. Mrs Thatcher looked remarkably dignified still. More importantly, she was unscathed, although it is difficult to recall many occasions when she was more at close-quarters risk. In her autobiography she claimed that she had not been told what to expect, but it is difficult to believe that Private Office would have been guilty of such a lapse and – as many years had passed when it was written – this must have been a lapse of memory.

In any event, to suggest that I was not on a short fuse would be a slanderous understatement. I was incandescent with rage. Every close-protection guideline had been broken. Nearly six years of effort to upgrade our standards and establish Scotland Yard's reputation had been sidelined. My own branch had to take much of the blame. It is unfortunate within the police service that sideways promotion often took newly promoted senior officers into areas of responsibility for which they had little or no expertise. This was just such an occasion, and although the commander present on the ground was hugely competent in other fields of counterterrorism, he had been unable to direct this arrival with the benefit of any useful previous experience. Thanks to wise counsel from Private Office, and immediate colleagues, I soon had to unwind and concentrate on the immediate task of recovering control. With poor overall direction on the ground, the Cabinet Office decision to send those forty extra Special Branch officers had so far produced a confusing balance sheet of assets and liabilities.

The problem of leadership on the ground became clearer many years later, however, when I learned that this chaotic arrival had been deliberately contrived by front-line African statesmen intent upon *non-violent* intimidation of the new lady prime minister. If so, it was dangerously foolish in every respect.

Fortunately, Mrs Thatcher turned her immediate displeasure upon the Commonwealth Secretariat, who had undiplomatically succumbed to persuasive foreign opportunism by obtaining Mercedes saloons for each delegation. Car buffs will be aware that – although these limousines were excellent in many respects – there was nothing remotely British about them.

Liaison with the Zambian police went well enough from then on and, with the freedom fighters absent somewhere and the Selous Scouts still checking weaponry in their Rhodesian barracks, the conference settled into some sort of routine. However, on the final scheduled day Rhodesia was top of the remaining agenda. Discussions dragged on all day and into the night. It appeared that every delegate except Mrs Thatcher was unanimous that majority rule was inevitable. At about 11 p.m., as the support staff waited for final agreement, the prime minister's husband Denis arrived and waited with us.

The meeting eventually broke up at around midnight. Mrs Thatcher emerged, clearly distressed, and I took it as read that she had finally been forced into majority acceptance and that an appropriate communiqué was now being worded by the Sherpas.* She got silently into the left-side, rear seat. Denis embarked in the middle and I took the right-hand place. Mrs Thatcher was silent – tearful even.

As the Mercedes was driven away after a dreadful day, she collected herself and noticed her husband for the first time.

'Hello Denis. I do hope you have had a good day?' Denis was, of course, the only male spouse at the conference. A one-man programme had been arranged for him alone.

'Well yes, I suppose I have. I managed some golf this morning. Then I was taken for an interesting trip up-country. We had a nice long lunch and then visited a copper mine. Splendid hospitality.'

And then – as a diplomatic afterthought – 'My only real regret is that I haven't had the chance to see more of you sweetie!'

After a pause, Mrs Thatcher leaned forward and looked across at me.

'Well, Superintendent. I don't know what you think but I don't feel we shall be able to find time for any of *that* today. Do you?'

---

* Margaret Thatcher's autobiography makes it clear that I was anticipating events. Apparently, a unanimous decision was still awaited and over the weekend the Australian prime minister, Malcolm Fraser, who like other impatient heads of delegation wanted the matter settled so he could get on his way home, announced a pre-emptive decision during a press conference to the Australian media. This forced the hands of other white delegates who, at a private ad hoc meeting held later during a barbecue at the Australian High Commission arrived at an agreement, and by declaring a *diktat* finally brought the conference to a close.

TWENTY

Move forward with the queue in orderly fashion. When next in line, come to a stop. Turn left. Take one pace forward and bow. The Queen will pin on the medal and may talk to you. It will be clear when she wants you to pass on. Take one pace backwards. Bow. Turn right and walk briskly away.

An extract from the brief for the Queen's Investiture at Buckingham Palace

Having agreed with Mr Callaghan's invitation to accept the offer of Membership of the Order of the British Empire, I was summoned to the Investiture in December 1979, during the final weeks of my service with the Metropolitan Police Special Branch.

After six years at No 10, and now with complete mastery of knife and fork protocol, I was resistant to advice from Scotland Yard that I was obliged to wear formal dress for the occasion. Better news was available from the staff in the Downing Street Honours Office. With a decent grey suit, and appropriate shirt and tie, it was – as usual – totally unnecessary to prance around in morning dress.

Even for the greatest sceptic, an Investiture is an impressive event. Royal Household staff of all ranks are trained to a standard of deferential politeness. No matter how false this may really be, it would be churlish to deny that their intentions are well meant and far more realistically performed than the fawning of an Italian waiter. Of course, honours' recipients are all vetted in advance and carefully identified on the day. From then on, it all borders upon the matey. My briefing took place in gold-plated surroundings before I joined the queue – snaking to the rear and side of the seated guests – with a backdrop of tunes from popular West End musicals played by a heavenly Guards' orchestra somewhere up there in a minstrel's gallery.

In spite of all official antidotes to panic, the nervousness of many of those waiting in line to be greeted by the queen was palpable and embarrassing. In front of me, a well-known television star looked as though a seizure was imminent. His embarrassment took the form of highly visible runnels of facial perspiration. Had he been on camera his understudy would have been told to deputise.

After the pinning on and a few kind, well-wishing words for my future, I bowed out as instructed. At a counter outside the Investiture chamber, my medal – engraved optimistically 'For God and The Empire' – was unpinned and boxed up by a gentleman of the Royal Household dressed in the most extraordinary drag who, from within the depths of his ermine did his best to remember his 'one of the lads' script as he wished me good luck. I have wondered ever since if I should have settled for a barometer.

Margaret Thatcher created a precedent by agreeing to a Private Office proposition that I could have the state rooms on the first floor of No 10 Downing Street for a farewell party when I retired in December 1979. Perhaps it was some sort of acknowledgement that all the personalities for whose close protection I had been responsible during more than twenty-five years service in Special Branch – including three prime ministers – had survived the United Kingdom experience still alive and kicking. Once back in their home countries, not all of them lasted for long. I calculated that about eight had since died from unnatural causes.

Peter Taylor, the resident housekeeper, told me how to go about things. He had always been obstructive and it was my impression that we did not get along together. On this final lap I was surprised to discover that he was like it to nearly everyone else in No 10, too, and was equally at cross purposes with Private Office, the duty clerks, and the Garden Room girls. However, he was now at pains not to enter into disputes after a prime minister's instruction. He also did his best to be helpful and less unpleasant and, after it became clear to him that I was fully aware of rule one – namely that he could invoice me for all the costs – his advice and experience turned out to be valuable.

For instance, Peter agreed not to impose a limit on the number of guests invited. He also recommended against spending a lot of my money on drinks. His theory was that most guests would be more than happy to find themselves in Downing Street and would be too impressed to distinguish between Château-bottled and everyday plonk. He detailed the staff needed for the two-and-a-half-hour occasion and arranged for an array of snacks to be prepared and served.

It seemed the proper opportunity not only to assemble certain colleagues from Scotland Yard, all the permanent staff of No. 10 and a few political appointees, the press officers and some friends, but also back-room personnel; those responsible for the smooth running of a prime minister's administration. These included men and women such as the management and mechanics at the Government Car Service headquarters in Peckham, some policemen from the local station at Cannon Row, the telephone switchboard ladies up there under the roof tiles, and the cleaners who saw to it that each day's activities started decently.

Mrs Thatcher kindly turned up as well and I was greatly pleased to ensure that as many vital workers as possible were introduced to her. It all seemed to run along smoothly and May, the cockney cleaning lady who looked after our living quarters and started my day with strong tea, put the proposal that she would be available for certain favours after the close of proceedings. This was indeed a thoughtful and in some ways appropriate offer, but not one May's husband – or my wife – was likely to approve. Declined 'with thanks' was in order and, after a couple more glasses of plonk, accepted by the kindly May with no visible sign of a broken heart.

Indeed, as she toddled flush-faced from the front door with a fag in the corner of her mouth – waving acknowledgement to the crowd waiting outside as if she were the Queen Mother herself – May could hardly have looked happier.

Between them, Margaret and May summed up the whole Downing Street experience.

⟫◦⟪

After spending so much time in the presence of prime ministers I was not the most impartial of their judges. As a variety of idiosyncrasies became evident, perhaps I was influenced more by their not infrequent descents into ordinariness than by their great deeds on record in history books. Because Harold Wilson, James Callaghan and Margaret Thatcher all appeared to be well organised and self-assured on the television screen, the public was usually unaware just how tough life could be for them behind the scenes. Off-stage anxieties were sometimes the product of great and unforeseeable crises – and their own misjudgement at others. The fact is that a *really* confident prime minister – if there is such an animal – could select much of his own diarised agenda and workload, leaving the bulk of public appearances, statements and associated flak from the media and the House of Commons to the ministers appointed to head departments. This should have allowed the incumbent at No 10 to dodge the fallout and controversy which often followed front-line appearances. However, in modern times – whenever political advantage or populist appeal to voters appeared likely – all prime ministers found the temptation to appear on television screens impossible to resist.

The 'Dog Mauls Toddler' type of headline was a typical example. Beware the likely public and parliamentary swing from outrage against Pit Bull terriers on the mauled child's behalf to outrage about injustice from millions of cuddly pet owners. After watching from a safe haven on the sidelines, and without targeting any specific prime minister, I started to draw up a list of guidelines for any politician unwise enough to aspire to residence in the never-never land of Downing Street, and the even more unfortunate few who succeed:

Never seek to be appointed if you have a regional accent. It may be unfair, but do not ignore the precedents. Coolly calculate your chances if you are a Brummie, a Scouser, or have a Lancastrian or Devonian brogue. They are virtually nil. Do not sound too posh either. It is the accent that is anathema to the electorate it seems, irrespective of ability. It matters not where you come from. Bizarrely it is more a matter of *how* you speak. Harold Wilson just got away with his Yorkshire accent. William Hague did not. Strangely perhaps, it was alright to go ahead if you were from Scotland or Wales. Indeed, the figures show that you would have a better than average chance. Incidentally – and in spite of Margaret Thatcher's incumbency – it is not wise to be a woman either. Statistically there is much against it.

Never overlook the job description. A prime minister has to be on call for twenty–four hours of every day he or she is in office. Quiet, uninterrupted holidays with the family are impossible.

Never quote St Francis of Assisi on day one.

Never forget that the euphoria of that first glowing entry into No 10 as a new prime minister will inevitably be followed by a grimly unwelcome and possibly tearful final departure – sometimes sooner than later.

Never ignore the imperative to mistrust the media. Genuine friends and supporters will be rare and even they may be exploitive or careless with your confidences. When the honeymoon period is over, stand alert for a spontaneous conspiracy to devastate your character and that of your spouse; to devalue your record and to paint a dismal picture of you as grey and uninspirational.

Never forget that the media can be skilfully inventive in the absence of facts or useful insider information. What they consider to be evidence will not be sourced, and would rarely stand scrutiny in a court of law. Exploitation of bar-room scuttlebutt will be impossible for malevolent writers and editors to avoid.

Never forget that democratic government is a very sneaky process. Leaking to the media is endemic at all levels – from within trade unions, county and district councils, Whitehall and at press offices. You will never have sole access to the tactic of insider leaks or manage to retain control over lesser leakers. Remain phlegmatic when leaks occur.

Don't anticipate that perpetrators will be named and shamed even – or especially – after *wide-ranging enquiries*. A whitewash is a more probable outcome. The only possible advantage will be a delay to the publication of bad news. It is rash to expect serious support from a self-regulatory system of management. Leaks occasionally occur even from otherwise scrupulously straightforward senior civil servants. Their motives are unlikely to be politically inspired or for personal advantage. Their justification will be demands of conscience as seen from the moral high ground.

Never expect unconditional loyalty and avoid paranoia when treachery is discovered in inner circles. As a corollary it may become necessary from time to time to give even the best of friends their marching orders.

Never relinquish control of the party manifesto. Every word will be used in evidence against you, so make sure it is in line with your long-term wishes. Do not anticipate unqualified support from your own party. Back benchers will sometimes cause more trouble than the Opposition.

Never underestimate the need to work well with your senior civil servants. They will have access to precedents and sources of information previously unimagined. Whatever their personal political preferences, they will try to give impartial advice. If it is not, then their position will be very cleverly disguised. Scan every moment of the *Yes, Prime Minister* series. Viewers – including me – may have enjoyed the television series as a humorous sitcom, but it was in fact only just less than a documentary. A prime minister should look upon Jim Hacker as a model to be respected.

Never overlook the need for prime ministerial dignity. Historians may belatedly take a cool, calculated look at the merits of your government, but in the expectation of selling their wares the media will try to foment political hysteria. In the long term, however, the electorate is more likely to be influenced by a calm and honest demeanour. Above all, never get dragged into adolescent, yah-boo frivolities at Prime Minister's Questions in the House of Commons. Avoid intemperate verbal combat in debate. Remain calm.

Never forget the promise inevitably made to the electorate to govern by conviction. Worthy principles and integrity are more important than opinion polls. In a crisis, avoid knee-jerk responses. It is sometimes wise to admit mistakes and explain reasons for changes of mind. Be aware of a suspicious public – but do not necessarily grovel around with apologies. Such stratagems will rightly be seen as a last-ditch resort. Spin doctors may negotiate short-term advantage but will usually be counter-productive in the end. The modern tendency to believe that an apology will guarantee popular sympathy and understanding, and even circumvent a few months of suffering porridge and hard labour in Pentonvillle Prison, is a transparent and specious tactic. Men should usually wear a collar and tie. Jeans and open-necked shirts give an appearance of detachment from the vital job in hand – especially when weekending with US presidents at Camp David.

Never overlook the fact – in spite of all this rectitude – that you will still usually have something to hide. If the furtive secret is in any way vulnerable to exposure, do not think you can outwit the investigative interrogator on flagship BBC radio and television programmes. Tell your press secretary to decline the invitation with the greatest regret and leave immediately for a long-standing appointment in Washington. Or anywhere.

Never drive around in your Rolls-Royce or Porsche. Never sing solo in public. Never sing at all unless you know the words.

Never envy a US president. His troubles will be even greater than yours.

Never be involved in covert exploitation of your unique and powerful position to benefit yourself, your family and friends, your supporters or the political party you represent. Mistresses invariably become a problem. If you cannot act openly don't do so at all. It may be a great bore but if you find a dubious offer irresistible – DON'T GET CAUGHT.

Although he will be incorruptible, remember that your close protection officer will get to know one way or another.

BIBLIOGRAPHY

Callaghan, J., *Time and Chance* (London: Collins, 1987).

Crossman, R., *The Diaries of a Cabinet Minister* (London: Hamish Hamilton, 1975).

Donoughue, B., *Downing Street Diary – With Harold Wilson in No. 10* (London: Jonathan Cape, 2005).

Donoughue, B., *Downing Street Diary – With James Callaghan in No. 10* (London: Jonathan Cape, 2008).

Dorril, S. and Ramsay R., *Smear! Wilson and the Secret State* (London: Grafton, 1992).

Evans, E.J., *Thatcher and Thatcherism* (London: Routledge, 1997).

Haines, J., *The Politics of Power* (London: Jonathan Cape, 1977).

Leich, D., *The Wilson Plot* (London: Heinemann, 1988).

Major, N., *Chequers – The Prime Minister's Country House and its History* (London: Harper Collins Publishers, 1996).

Morgan, K.O., *Callaghan – A Life* (Oxford: Oxford University Press, 1997).

Pimlott, B., *Harold Wilson* (London: Harper Collins Publishers, 1992).

Ring, J., *Erskine Childers – Author of Riddle of the Sands* (London: John Murray, 1996).

Thatcher, M., *Margaret Thatcher – The Downing Street Years* (London: Harper Collins Publishers, 1993).

Thatcher, M., *The Path to Power* (London: Harper Collins Publishers, 1995).

INDEX